Development of the

P-51

Long-Range Escort Fighter

MUSTANG

Development of the
P-51
Long-Range Escort Fighter
MUSTANG

Paul A. Ludwig

CLASSIC

An imprint of
Ian Allan Publishing

Dedicated to the memory of my father and mother

Pierce Kenneth Ludwig
who taught me discipline
and
Wanda Clara (Ashmun) Ludwig
who taught me the arts

First published 2003

ISBN 1-903223-14-8

Produced by Chevron Publishing Limited
Project Editor: Robert Forsyth
Cover and book design by Colin Woodman Design

Published by Classic Publications

an imprint of Ian Allan Publishing Ltd, Hersham, Surrey KT12 4RG

Printed by Ian Allan Printing Ltd, Hersham, Surrey KT12 4RG

Visit the Classic Publications website at www.classic-books.co.uk

Paul Ludwig grew up in Detroit, Michigan and has been interested in aeroplanes since he was a boy. "I had a small, metal toy Waco biplane," he recalls, "which I 'flew' hourly."

In 1941 his parents moved to a small farm in the suburb of Trenton, where the family could grow food and raise chickens for the dinner table. "We had an open acre which flight instructors and students flying out of nearby Grosse Isle Naval Air Station used as a practice emergency landing field. Colorfully painted Stearmans and other Navy trainer biplanes were maneuvered down to simulated engine-off approaches and landings and then would zoom upward at full power at the end of the practice maneuver. This happened daily a few yards from our house during the war. Nothing was more important in life to me than to witness these close-at-hand maneuvers. My mother dressed chickens for the skillet and neighbors, passers-by, and pilots would buy them. So I met some of the wartime Navy pilots and I was impressed. They were gods. I wanted to be a pilot."

"I discovered balsa kit model airplanes and spent hours carving, painting, and marking those fragile airplanes which my sisters dusted to destruction."

Following high school graduation and university, it was Paul's intention to join the US Navy flight training program which, at the time, specified a requirement of two years of college. Then came the Korean War and his eighteenth birthday and the reality of military draft: "I didn't want to be forced into the army and when I was twenty years old I applied for, and was accepted into the Navy flight training program."

"All went well until entering Advanced Training where an officer asked me for my preferences for fleet flying once I won my wings six months later, and I asked for single-engined prop or single-engined jet advanced training. Instead of giving me what I wanted, he stuck me into anti-submarine flight training. My class was one of the first to win our wings in the Grumman S2F. We missed training in war-weary TBF Avengers by just a few months. Near the end of my training, the Navy offered orders to graduating students to an unknown base for an unknown flying assignment, to fill out units needing men, after cuts at the end of the Korean War had reduced the size of the Navy. I jumped at the chance to get away from the S2F and perhaps fly the AD or one of the jets."

Ludwig won his wings and was ordered to Naval Air Ordnance Test Station Chincoteague, Virginia – now known as NASA Wallops Island. After flying co-pilot for many hours in the Lockheed P2V Neptune, his Commander allowed him to check out the AD Skyraider; he remembers: "I was absolutely thrilled. In those days the check-out was, to read the manual and get in and start her up and take off and fly wing on a trained pilot. Another senior officer took an interest in me, the most junior officer there and fresh out of knickers, and he got my boss to let him train me in the Douglas F3D twin-jet night fighter. I soloed the F3D and suddenly I was a jet pilot! For a kid of twenty-three, life had jumped me to the top of the heap. Mere months after feeling my career was to have been throttled by eventual assignment to an S2F squadron, I had checked out in the AD and a jet and I had my eye on the very hazardous F7U we had at NAOTS. There was no stopping me."

But NAOTS wanted fleet-experienced pilots and as Paul admits: "… I was not what they wanted!"

It was during a trip to the Pentagon whilst accompanying some senior officers, that his commanding officer persuaded the Fleet Detail Officer to find the young Ludwig a place in an active AD squadron at Miramar near San Diego. "I was delighted! After nine months at NAOTS doing very little except checking out solo in new types, I was ordered to VA-145. To have been stuck in late 1955 into S2Fs and a year later to be ordered to fly AD-6s in a fleet squadron was a complete turnabout. How lucky could I get? Very."

Within months Paul was a trained carrier pilot at sea on the USS *Hornet* heading for a WestPac cruise among some of the heroes of the Second World War who were now senior officers in his squadron. Following the cruise in 1957, he returned to San Diego to Cabaniss Field as an instructor in ADs. He instructed until early 1958 and was then released from active duty. He then joined Northwest Airlines and whilst based in Minneapolis, joined a Navy Reserve squadron and flew the AD-5. He flew airliners for Northwest for the next 36 years, spending the last eight as Captain of a Boeing 747 on the Tokyo run out of Seattle, Washington. He retired in 1994.

With Malcolm Laird, Paul Ludwig is co-author of the two-part *American Spitfire Camouflage and Markings* (1998).

During World War Two, American air power was spearheaded by the four-engined, heavy, long-range bomber. At the beginning of the war, Allied leaders decided to defeat Germany first. Of the three enemy countries – Germany, Italy, and Japan – to be opposed by Allied bombers, Germany's closeness to bases in England presented the earliest opportunity to deploy four-engined bombers. The English Channel was a natural barrier to German land warfare and because Germany's sea and air forces could not defeat the English defenses, the United Kingdom was ideally placed for the creation of many Allied air bases from which to launch an air offensive against the Reich and the occupied territories. American four-engined bombers began combat operations in mid-1942.

America – among the countries at war with the Axis powers – was as unprepared as the others. Early American bombing operations over Germany forced the European Theater of Operations (ETO) to become the proving ground for the United States Army Air Forces' (USAAF) development of up-to-date equipment and tactics. USAAF insistence upon visual, daylight, high-altitude bombing, in order to achieve what was believed to be pinpoint accuracy, initially was accompanied by two mistaken ideas: that the four-engined, unescorted bomber could defend itself, and that German fighter aircraft defenses formed a thin wall beyond which unescorted bombers could operate successfully. By early 1943, it was painfully apparent that USAAF bombers were being shot down in great numbers by German fighters. Many Air Corps officers held the euphoric belief that Germany would be bombed into submission, without need for a land invasion, by late 1943 or at least no later than 1944. That belief was not sustained. The awful destructiveness that *Luftwaffe* fighters applied to downing AAF bombers sent such mistaken beliefs into a turnaround. Losses of 120 bombers on two missions to Schweinfurt in August and October 1943, were to convince senior officers in Washington to return the P-38 to units in England. It was to be too little and too late. By late 1943, there was a desperate feeling of impending defeat in the European air war.

The only solution to protecting daylight bombers was to develop an escort fighter, but an unconscionable slowness in the 1930s to develop superior fighter aircraft forced bomber operations to continue unescorted until late 1943. Amid the disasters over Schweinfurt and Regensburg in August and October, there seemed to be no end in sight to the air war over North West Europe. Generals pressed on with their intention to send unescorted bombers over Germany no matter what the cost in aircraft and lives because attack was the only agreed-upon venture.

The USAAF was nearing defeat in the air. Something had to be done, and quickly.

In the fall seasons of 1984 and 1985, I was drawn to the National Archives to research the story of the P-51 because intuition told me the story was incomplete. In 1982, one famous and prolific author dismissed the findings of almost every other author who had said the USAAF disliked the Mustang. I had to know the truth. Original documents revealed the true story. Official records kept in the National Archives and used in this study were, at the time, maintained in Army Air Forces, Record Group 18. The Dewey Decimal System of classification was used and Section 452 was most instructive.

All authors – except the one – sensed that there had been a pattern of slow acceptance of the Mustang and said so. Those books, and the official, eight-volume history of the USAAF – otherwise known as "Craven and Cate" – have pointed the way to research in the archives.

The greatest event of the twentieth century if not of the millennium was World War Two. Books will be published well into this millennium to unearth why men invent new ways to kill each other.

This study is not intended to criticize any one man or a group of men. Any errors in interpreting the words of other men not now able to defend themselves are mine alone.

Paul Ludwig

During the late 1920s and throughout the 1930s, Air Corps official policy concentrated upon bomber development, while the parent organisation – the Army – failed to provide leadership in regard to fighter development. However, theoreticians in Air Corps uniform had agreed upon bomber development and neglected fighters. In 1926, America missed its chance to win possession of the famed Schneider Trophy in order to fund bomber technology, thereby reducing interest in fast fighters. In other countries – Britain especially – the technology inspired by the Schneider Trophy races was often transformed into advanced fighters. In America, it was not.

As long as the Air Corps and its re-named organization, the Army Air Forces (AAF) were subordinate to the Army, it was required to adhere to Army decisions and to develop aircraft which satisfied the Army. By 1936 Germany, Japan, Italy, Russia, and Britain had developed superior fighter aircraft types and the Army and its Air Corps finally were forced to play catch-up. Aircraft required approximately five years to proceed from concept to first flight and it was not until 1942 – three years after Hitler invaded Poland – that the AAF had two new fighters which were equal to the best in the world. There remained the contested decision of whether to define a specific mission for each type. While the Army preferred types built to perform specific missions, Air Corps officers planned for multi-mission types. The mission which ultimately seemed impossible to fulfill was that of the bomber escort.

As global conflict drew near toward the end of the 1930s and fast, high-altitude bombers emerged from the factories of several nations, the old US Air Corps "Pursuit" type fighter was to be changed dramatically. America needed an air defense system. New fighters needed high-altitude capability and engines and superchargers to get them there. The new fighter had to be fast enough to intercept bombers which, although slower than fighters, were expected to arrive overhead in America unannounced in an age when advance warning was rudimentary at best. This new type of fighter – the "interceptor" – did not require long range, but initially it did require greater firepower.

As will be shown, adequate engines and superchargers were to spell the difference between success and failure in developing suitable fighters. However, the new science of aerodynamics was just then being expanded and applied as the world went to war, and one of aerodynamics' first contributions to advancement in flight was in drag reduction. An aircraft would fly faster and farther not just because it had higher horsepower, but also because it flew more efficiently. Aerodynamics was first applied to bomber technology.

When, finally, aerodynamicists applied their skills to fighter design, one company in particular achieved all that was possible in fighter development in the piston-engine era. By December 1943, the great North American Aviation, Inc. (NAA) P-51B Mustang could fly as far as a B-17 or B-24 four-engined bomber! The Republic P-47D and Lockheed P-38H could not. The P-51 Mustang saved the USAAF daylight bombing campaign in the ETO from defeat, but it did not appear in combat until slightly more than a year before the war in Europe ended. Had it appeared later, the AAF bombing campaign in the ETO would already have been defeated.

General of the Army Air Forces, H.H. Arnold, said long after the war that the P-51 appeared "...over Germany at just the saving

Major General H.H. Arnold, Chief of the US Army Air Forces, stops for the photographer as he enters his transport which is appropriately marked with three stars.

moment, in the very nick of time."(1) He said the P-51 was a "miracle" and he "debated...how much of that story" he should tell. Arnold never told the story. The official history of the AAF said "...the story of the P-51 came close to representing the costliest mistake made by the AAF in World War Two."(2) In January or February 1942, Arnold decided the P-51 should be produced "...in spite of the Materiel Division's turning it down."

The near-mistake was not Materiel's alone. That Arnold said it appeared in the nick of time says nothing about what transpired during the two years from when it was authorized for American use to the point it escorted bombers. The AAF did not want the P-51 as an escort because it preferred the P-38 and P-47 as fighters and type-cast the P-51 as an Army ground support weapon. Slowness to appreciate the outstanding qualities of the P-51 was caused by wartime squabbles among officers. The story Arnold did not tell is one of dislike of the Mustang, distrust of the British, interest in developing American industry, delay in development of escorts, Army intervention, and the beginning of the jet age.

Along the way the Mustang acquired a reputation as a ground support, tactical weapon. When its burgeoning and superior capabilities began to dazzle everyone in 1943 it was seen as the answer to the Army's changing needs. Unfortunately it was soon neatly pigeonholed into becoming a tactical aircraft almost indispensable for the June 1944 invasion of France. It was to be employed as a low-altitude, fighter-bomber carrying cameras, guns, and bombs – not as an escort.

By December 1943 – the month it began service as an escort – almost all of the P-51Bs produced were consigned to the Ninth Air Force (9th AF), a huge tactical organization commanded by a British officer whose intention it was to reserve them for one big air battle on D-Day! More incongruous was the decision of the American Commanding General of the strategic Eighth Air Force, Lt. Gen. Ira Eaker, who gave them to the 9th AF! Eaker needed those bomber escorts desperately, but misunderstood their capabilities.

Eaker gave them away because he preferred the P-38 and P-47 for escort duties, even though – by that time – the P-38 was encountering serious mechanical problems and the P-47 had short range. Such was the pervasive, ground support reputation of the long-range, untroubled Mustang!

Clearly, the near-mistake of the entire war lay with several persons and departments.

This book would not have been possible without the generosity, encouragement and support received from so many kind individuals. First and foremost has been the steadfast praise, prepared lunches and limitless assistance with my endless computer problems given by my lovely wife JoAnne who has a full-time teaching job. Robert Forsyth of Chevron Publishing came to my rescue by providing me the opportunity to write this story after so many others had rejected "…one more P-51 book." Arthur Bentley and his wonderful wife, Sue, took me into their home on my trips to England when I researched Spitfires for my first two books, and we became friends. Arthur believed in my idea for this book and provided his world-class, outstanding, scale engineering drawings of the P-51. I must acknowledge the generous support and kindness of Mrs Pat Keen, author, who provided my name to Ventura Publishing of New Zealand. Pat's help resulted in Ventura publishing my first two books, Parts One and Two of *American Spitfire Camouflage and Markings*. Malcolm Laird, editor and owner of Ventura, generously offered me the job of writing those books which he co-authored and illustrated with color profiles. Walter Boyne has been my mentor and he brought me down to earth from my cloud of a thousand pages to what you, the reader, now hold in your hands. J. Leland Atwood of NAA introduced me to men and asked them to help. Foremost among these was Gene Kerrigan. My friend Jim Schubert assisted me with technical matters.

The story of the Packard Motor Company's production of the Merlin would have been lost, if not for David and Roberta (Bobbie) Mocabee. Bobbie is the daughter of the late C.H. Vincent and Bobbie and Dave provided me with one of the rare copies of Col. Jesse Vincent's report used herein.

Correspondence is often a researcher's only recourse to obtaining material – unless that researcher's pocketbook for travel expenses is deep. Those who kindly answered with professional or personal history or references to other sources include Irving Ashkenas, Morgan 'Mac' Blair (NAA), Eugene Clay (NAA), Stanley A. Cayce, Jan Churchill, H.A. Evans (NAA), Mrs. Margaret M. Hitchcock, Col. Cass Hough, Brig. Gen. Gustav Lundquist, M.W. Malsby (NAA), Charles S. McVeigh Jr., John P. 'Jack' Reeder (NASA), Richard L. Schleicher (NAA), Lt. Gen. Ralph Swofford, and Earl Theaker (NAA).

Many others invited me into their homes or offices or we met face-to-face on neutral ground, wrote letters and/or unearthed pertinent documents. Among them are Col. Donald J.M. Blakeslee, Gen. Mark Bradley, Bob Chilton, General Ira Eaker, George Gherkens (NAA), Edward Horkey (NAA), Col. Jack Jenkins, E.L. Miller (Eagle Squadron), Maj. Gen. Homer Sanders, Edgar Schmued (NAA), and Col. Hubert Zemke.

At the National Archives in Washington, DC, Wilbert 'Will' Mahoney and Miss Terry Hammett provided me with all that was needed to delve into dozens of boxes of documents within minutes as each day began. At the Washington National Records Center which, at the time was at Suitland, Maryland, Mr. George Chalou, Rick Wayman, Richard Boylan, Bill Lewis, and John Butler made research simple for me. Mrs. Vivian White and Robert J. Smith at the Air Force Museum and Wright-Patterson AFB were a great help. At the Detroit Public Library, James J. Bradley, Ron Grant and Peggy Peters guided me to material. Miss Francis at the Detroit Historical Museum helped. At the Library at Maxwell Air Force Base, Maj. Les Sliter, Pressley Bickerstaff, Mrs. Margaret Clairborn, Mrs. Lynn Gamma and Jim Kitchens made research fun. Several people at the NASM helped.

Without photographs, ten thousand words are insufficient. From personal collections or access to collections came photographs and occasional letters from Gerald Adams, the Air Force Museum, Mike Alba, Joseph Anders, Rudy Arnold (via E.T. Wooldridge), Dick Asbury, Ken Ashbaugh, Norm Avery, Letitia 'Char' Baldridge, Malcolm Bates, Tyrone Beason, Dana Bell, Leon Blanding, Peter Bowers, Mark E. Bradley, Gerald Brown, Robert J. Burgmeier III, the Canadian National Archives, Bob Chilton, Cloud 9 Photography, Jerry Cogal, Jack Cook, Eddie Creek, the Detroit Public Library, Harry Dewall, Fred Dickey Jr., Robert F. Dorr, Urban Drew, Bill du Fosse, William D. Dunwoody, Clyde East, Ronald Erickson, Jeff Ethell, Walt Fink, John Florence, Robert Forsyth, Lee Fray (EAA Museum), John M. Gray, Robert Hadley, Robert Hanes, Phillip Heacox, Art Heiden, Mrs. John Howard Sr., Ed Horkey, Jack Ilfrey, the Imperial War Museum, Tom Ivie, Jack Jenkins, Felix Kozaczka, J.A. Mandli, Stan Marsh, Russell E. Mayden, Joan McGinn, William McTavish, Robert E. Miles, E.L. 'Dusty' Miller, Dave and Bobbie Mocabee, James W. Morris, NACA/LMAL, NASM, National Archives, J.W. Noah, MSgt. Merle Olmsted, Charles Parker, George Peck (brother of), Bruno Peters, J.W. Phegley, Popperfoto, Robert H. Powell Jr., the RAF Museum, Larry Redmond, Frank B. Robinson, Rockwell Corporation (NAA), Thomas Russell, James J. Ryland, Mark A. Savage, the Seattle Museum of Flight, Selfridge ANG Military Air Museum, Walter Sempowicz, the Smithsonian Institution, S.L. Sox Jr., Trevor Stanley, Robert A. Stone, Dwayne Tabatt, Joe Thompson Jr., the US Air Force, the US Polo Association, June Warner, Hoyt Warren, E.T. Wooldridge (NASM), and Jesse O. Yaryan.

Still others gave permission for the use of privately-held reference material and these include Ms. Paula S. Smith of the Society of Experimental Test Pilots.

PAL
2002

The publishers wish to thank Jerry Scutts for his assistance during the editorial preparation of this book.

I am glad that someone has done the research telling the whole story of escort development. The P-51 Mustang was a little slow in coming to us in England, but I knew the first time I flew it that it was the plane to do the job.

I flew the Spitfire in the RCAF, the Eagle Squadron (RAF), and the USAAF. Flying "Spits" was about as good as it can get, but our job was to escort bombers and the "Spit" just didn't have the legs. When the P-47s arrived in late 1942, they were a great improvement but still not the full answer range-wise.

We first heard about the Mustang from men like Lt.Col. Tommy Hitchcock at the US Embassy in England and people in the RAF who had flown the first ones, but until Washington, DC got them to us, we did our job the best we could with our limitations. Naturally, the bomber crews would have liked escort for the entire mission – as we all would.

The P-38 was supposed to be the USAAF's best long-range fighter but our P-38 air groups were in North Africa and there were no P-38s in the European Theater of Operations before late 1943. Things began to change in late 1943 when we were told we had to gain air superiority over the *Luftwaffe* before an invasion took place. The German pilots would not tangle with us as often as we wanted, therefore making it difficult to destroy them. Then, in December, the 354th Fighter Group of the Ninth Air Force began operations with Mustangs and finally, in early 1944, the Eighth Air Force began receiving them. Fuel ceased to be a big problem. We had plenty of fuel to loiter around the bomber, chase the *Luftwaffe* or go to the deck and strafe at will. No area in the ETO was out of reach.

It was the beginning of the end.

Colonel Don Blakeslee
USAF Ret.

A1
P-51 /char/

Description:

Wings: Low-wing monoplane, sweptback leading edge, tapered trailing edge, nearly square tips, small dihedral.

Engines: Single liquid cooled.

Fuselage: Elongated and streamlined with long pointed nose, enclosed, flush type cockpit. Retractable landing gear and tail wheel.

Tail: Slightly sweptback stabilizer. Nearly straight elevator and tips. Medium high nearly square cut fin and rudder.

Specifications: Resembles in appearance Messerschmitt 109E. Span 37 feet Length 32 feet 3 inches - height 8 feet 8 inches. Weight empty 5,990 lbs. Gross weight 7,708 lbs. Allison V type liquid cooled engine 960 hp. Fuel capacity 170 gals.

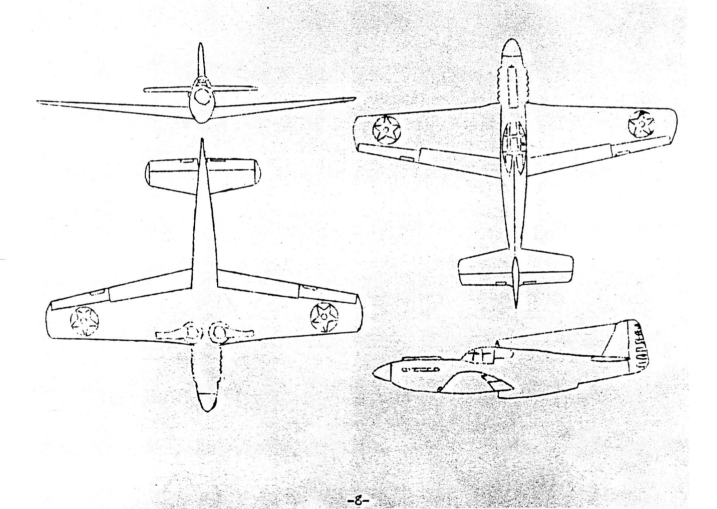

-8-

A document taken from an Air Corps intelligence briefing folder showing the North American Mustang 'Interceptor'. It is significant because it shows a set-back carburetor intake on top of the nose and an underside view showing landing gear that had no cover doors and possibly no wheel wells. No armament is shown. Though described here as an 'Interceptor', at the time this drawing was produced, the Air Corps criticized severely the Mustang's poor rate of climb.

Chapter 1

"The only defense against bombardment is the fighter…"

Toward Better Fighters

The successful struggle to develop good fighters in the mid-1940s had its very modest beginnings back in the 1920s in the US Air Service and Air Corps when development of fighter aircraft followed precedents set in World War One. During the 1930s, development of bombers and bombing theory hampered interest in fighters. War speeded the design of fighter aircraft. When all the problems were swept away in 1944, the world witnessed an amazing development. For the first and only time in history, a single-engine fighter aircraft could fly as far as a bomber. Correspondingly, the fighter escort became an absolute necessity.

Shortly after the Wright brothers first flew a heavier-than-air craft, men found ways to race and fight in aircraft. The Frenchman, Jacques Schneider, originated air races in 1913 with a trophy named after him, and with the exception of the interference of World War One, the races continued into the 1930s. Major countries sponsored entries and pilots for these international competitions. The US employed active-duty Army Air Service officers to fly military-sanctioned racing planes outfitted with pontoons and devoid of weapons. To keep the Schneider Cup outright, a country had to win three races in five years. America won in 1923 and 1925. Accidents plagued the US racers in 1926. In 1927, Congress withdrew support because the funds were earmarked for bomber development.[1] Quite a few influential Air Corps officers thought air racing and stunt flying had no bearing upon aircraft development. Air Corps fighter development suffered from the change.

Britain won three times and took permanent possession of the trophy in 1931, applying racing technology into its famous Supermarine Spitfire and Rolls Royce Merlin engine. The Air Corps was impressed by the in-line, liquid-cooled engines employed in the races and began an in-line development program around 1932. However, delay, poor engineering decisions and lack of funds for military spending slowed development drastically. Failure led to alternative engine projects.

America's foremost air officer in the Great War was Brigadier General William "Billy" Mitchell and in 1921 and 1923, he organized the demonstration of sinking captured, anchored, unmanned German battleships in American waters. Doubt had existed that a bomber could even damage such a well-armored vessel and in doing it, Mitchell advanced the theory of aerial bombardment and drew disciples of air power to his ideas. However, though he was court-martialed in 1925 for being rudely outspoken and derisive about lack of national attention to air power, his followers were so impressed by the future of the bomber that they established the Air Corps Tactical School (ACTS), created to teach officers about bomber theory.

The Air Corps Act of 1926

Before the Great Depression began, government created the Air Corps Act which gave the former Air Service the new name "Air Corps" and infused a greater percentage of Army funds than it had in the past to improve the air arm. Coming as it did in the year the US could have won the Schneider Trophy, the Act allowed Air Corps officers to choose to put more emphasis on bomber development, while government interest in racing plummeted. Fighter development took a downward turn.

No Interest in Fighters

Manufacturers designed new ideas into bombers and monoplane construction for the Air Corps bomber preceded that for fighters. The Keystone was the final biplane bomber and the Douglas Y1B-7 was the first of the monoplanes. Following this was the Fokker XB-8 of 1929 and the Boeing Y1B-9 of 1931, which, because it was faster than fighters of the time, is remembered as the point of departure from which less interest in fighters is measured. Following government disinterest in the Schneider racers, Air Corps theorists assumed that bombers would be self-defending and faster because they had more engines; "... for a number of years in the middle of the 1930s the Army was seriously considering the complete abolition of single-seat fighters."[2] The ACTS almost ceased instructing student officers about fighter theory. Single-seat aircraft offered to the Materiel Command by manufacturers or racing pilots for possible acceptance as fighters were slow, had a lot of drag and were underpowered. From the P-26 of 1932 to the P-35, no fighter design is memorable. In the mid-1930s officers responsible for developing fighters allowed a decrease in performance specifications. Fighter technology was at a standstill.

The Failed In-Line Engine Program

Aside from a reduction in the use of bracing wires and struts, monoplane design was followed by new creations such as retractable landing gear, enclosed cockpits and enclosed bomb loads. But the most promising advance conceived for bombers was to put in-line engines inside the wings to reduce drag. Big, barrel-shaped nacelles and the blunt, radial, air-cooled engines they enclosed – which hung ahead of the wings like barn doors – created drag. The small frontal area of Schneider race engines and the use of an internally mounted liquid-cooling system promised to reduce drag considerably in large, multi-engined bombers. Additional drag reduction could be gained by designing pusher-prop layouts for bombers. It was believed that if such things could be done, ranges and load-carrying capability of bombers would be improved dramatically. A 1930s bomber with a few hundred miles range was thought to be an amazing development. By 1940, the intercontinental bomber had become necessary.

The in-line engine development program created the radial-versus-in-line controversy. The attraction of the in-line's small frontal area had one drawback: the in-line required a heavy cooling jacket, a radiator, and lengthy, space-taking piping. Conversely, many experts believed that it was nearly impossible to air-cool more than one row of cylinders in a radial engine and going to twin-row radials was not tried before 1930. The promise of higher horsepower, and quick development of superior bombers led officers to opt for the new in-line engine program.

A host of advances were considered almost simultaneously in the hope that within ten years – to 1940 – new in-line engines would be available to power bombers and fighters. The fatter wings of bombers could accommodate a flat in-line engine whose cylinders were designed to be opposed directly across the crankshaft. Engines in single-engined fighters could be put in mid-fuselage or at the rear. A few bombers were quickly designed with in-line engines buried inside wings. After the Martin XB-16 was designed, the Martin XB-16 Final Design employed two pusher-props and four tractors. No pusher types flew in the 1930s or in combat during the war. The most successful buried-engine design was the post-war Convair B-36 Peacemaker powered by six pusher-prop R-4360 radial engines

The terrible economic depression began at about the same time as the in-line engine program in 1932. Initially trying to foster a new era in piston engine technology, the Air Corps pushed too many of its own ideas at once and officers thrust them upon an impoverished industry without appreciating the dire straits of the American economy. The in-line program was shepherded through the Depression by officers who made too many changes too quickly. Although America was at peace and cherished its neutrality, before long, trouble was brewing in far off China, Ethiopia and Spain. By 1937 the world was drifting toward global war once again, while the Air Corps sponsored a slow engine development program expected to achieve success no sooner than 1943. Common sense did not prevail in the prosecution of the program and the threat of war was countered by dreams of engines of almost unlimited horsepower.

In 1931, S.D. Heron at Wright Field experimented with the use of ethylene glycol when it was discovered that it provided the same cooling properties as water – and in less quantity. Officers capitalized on that idea by demanding that industry raise the temperature to 300 deg. F at which cooling began because it was thought that a massive reduction in the sizes and weights of the radiator and jacket was possible. Unfortunately, 300 degree cooling necessitated a larger oil cooler, and leakage of glycol into cylinders caused engine problems and slowed the faltering program.[3] Fingers of blame were pointed in all directions. An idea emerged

guaranteeing that the simplest way to increase the horsepower of an in-line was to double the number of cylinders along the line of the crankshaft, thereby doubling the power output. A 12-cylinder engine became a 24-cylinder engine at the wave of an official notification to proceed.

Of course the cooling system was the most vulnerable feature of an aircraft powered by an in-line, and the radial-versus-in-line controversy which was then initiated, continues to this day among veterans who flew P-47s and P-51s. Nevertheless, through the 1930s the program proceeded with far more urgency than was applied to radials. The following were the most promising in-lines, only one of which (the V-1710) became mass-produced:

Allison	V-1710 and V-3420
Chrysler	IV-2220
Continental	IV-1430 and H-2860
Ford	XV-1650 (not built)
Lycoming	O-1230, H-2470 and
	XR-7755 (not built)
Pratt & Whitney	X-1800 (the H-2600), XH-3130 and
	H-3730
Studebaker	H-9350 (not built)
Wright	H-2120, XH-4240 and the
	liquid-and-air-cooled R-2160

In their haste to achieve success, officers seemed not to care about the difficulties faced by industry. They put their faith in concepts, made too many changes and caused much grief among companies trying desperately to perform and survive – to make a profit. One report stated: "...*by the middle of 1939 the Air Corps Research Board had decided that the 1,000 hp engine was obsolete and that the primary needs in the liquid-cooled field were for: flat engines of 1,800 to 2,000 hp for submerged installation in bomber wings, multibank engines of 1,000 to 2,400 hp for nacelle installation in bombers and inverted vee engines of 1,500 to 1,800 hp for pursuit planes."* The Air Corps Research Board stated that the Air Corps "...*failed to realize the length of time required to develop a new engine*" and "...*was talking at this time of the need for bomber engines producing 4,000 to 5,000 hp, and complained that the manufacturers were not interested.*"[4]

The Air Corps, having wasted nearly ten fruitless years, was aware by 1938 of Germany's, Japan's and Italy's aggressive intentions and yet had no really powerful in-line engines of any worth as another world war was about to begin. During those ten years spent on the development of in-line engines, the theory of invincibility of the long-range bomber was simultaneously taught. There was one masterful, saving event achieved during that time, when the great

Boeing B-17 Flying Fortress four-engined bomber was built and flown in the mid-1930s. It was not powered by in-lines and its supremacy was quickly recognized. The decade of the 1930s was not without its successes in bomber development, but fighter development was at a standstill. The B-17 permitted ACTS instructors to teach students about the promising future of strategic air warfare.

The Air Corps Tactical School

Mitchell's disciples created the ACTS in 1929 and Maj. Harold Lee George led its instructors to teach that bomber technology would always be better than that of a fighter because a large, multi-engined aircraft could carry more destructive and defensive weapons. The long-range bomber was soon accepted by the parent Army as its coastal defense weapon, and was elevated in theory to be a new form of artillery – though airborne – supplementing ground-based cannon. The Army supported ACTS instructors. Air Corps officers knew the strategic, intercontinental capability of the bomber would, one day, make their mission independent of the Army's mission. The ACTS staff took their theory one step farther – since they were convinced about the impregnability of the B-17 – and decreed there was no need to develop an escort if a bomber could be armed well enough to defend itself.

Theory of Escort

The foremost authority on fighters in the Air Corps in 1931 was Major Carl Spaatz, who pronounced his name "spots". He had been a fighter pilot during the World War One with three aerial victories and was the natural choice to command the only Pursuit Group in the Air Service from 1921 to 1924. Spaatz, even then, a thin, rather unsmiling and impatient-looking man who brooked no interference, was asked to report on fighter escort and stated in 1931 that it was needed

Right to left: General H.H. Arnold, Brigadier General Donald Wilson, and Lieutenant General Millard Harmon. In 1940 Harmon advised Arnold on the theory of fighter escort.

for bomber missions flown below 15,000 ft while above 20,000 ft bombers did not need escort.[5]

Despite Spaatz' record as a fighter expert in the 1920s, he became the most adamant senior, wartime proponent of bomber superiority. Despite his demeanor, he was a very impressive officer and his career grew apace with Arnold's. He became the second-most powerful air officer in the AAF in World War Two. His opinions had the force of an edict. As a field officer and combat commander he had immense influence upon General Arnold back in Washington, DC. As time went on Spaatz had more to say about bombers not needing escort. In 1943 however, he reversed his ideas and advocated escort by 1944.

In January 1933 a Pursuit Board met at Wright Field to determine if a bomber should be capable of defending itself and if not, what an escort would be required to do. Officers on the Board, all of whom later became generals, were George Brett, Spaatz, Millard Harmon, Harold Lee George, Frank Hunter, and Claire Chennault. They reported that escorts should carry cannon that could be fired against air or ground targets – to satisfy the Army – and escorts would carry enough fuel to have the range only of a medium bomber (see Chapter Three). Discussion was raised as to whether or not an escort should carry bombs. The Board led the concept of the escort type into a downward spiral of multi-mission capability, complexity and weight escalation.

The Air Mail Scandal

The Air Corps Act had dismayed a number of Army generals because it seemed a considerable amount of money had been allocated to the air arm and comparatively less by percentage

Brigadier General Harold Lee George commanded the ACTS between 1934-1936 when instruction of fighter theory was at its lowest.

Lieutenant General George Brett — seen here with Lowell Thomas, a famous radio personality — preceded Echols as Commanding General of Materiel.

to the Army itself. By 1934, generals believed their Air Corps had been pampered compared to treatment of the Army, and they expected that by that year it should have become quite capable of looking after itself.

President Franklin Roosevelt cancelled contracts with commercial air mail airlines because of the high charges levied by these monopolies, and Maj. Gen. Benjamin Foulois, Chief of the Air Corps, proud of his men and planes, saw the cancellation as a chance to demonstrate the readiness of the Air Corps, and to carry the mail. However the terrible winter conditions of 1934 caused many crashes and pilot deaths, and instead of appearing capable, the Air Corps drew criticism to itself. Army generals and politicians joined hands to investigate the failure of the Air Corps and Foulois was relieved of his command in 1935. His assistant, Brig. Gen. Oscar Westover, was named Chief. The situation with the Air Corps' delivery of air mail revealed that the Army had not provided its Air Corps with sufficient funds to improve instrument flying, to create de-icing equipment, or to provide better safety equipment in aircraft.

The General Headquarters Air Force

Dismay over the findings of the investigation revealed that the Army had not managed its Air Corps well and politicians provided some of the first autonomy to an Air Corps seeking outright independence. Autonomy finally came when the

Army understood the bomber's potential and created an aerial striking force for its own use and not tied to coastal defense. The new force would have mobility and the Army gave it a form of self-determination, and named it the General Headquarters Air Force (GHQ AF). In the event of a war, the mobilization of troops took time and getting them to the scene of battle took longer, but the GHQ AF's three air wings could be flown anywhere in a hurry. The GHQ AF was mainly a bomber force. Its significance was changed during World War Two and gradually it became known as Bomber Command. Fighters played little part in the GHQ AF, which became the seed of the fully independent, United States Strategic Air Force.

The Fateful 1933 Exercise

Brig. Gen. Oscar Westover was an officer swayed by Army generals and politicians. As Assistant Chief of the Air Corps in 1933, he commanded a large military exercise and his own Chief of Staff, Col. H.H. Arnold, wrote the report which downgraded fighters: "*The modern trend of thought is that high speed and otherwise high performing bombardment aircraft, together with observation aviation of superior speed and range and communications characteristics, will suffice for the adequate defense of this country. During these exercises, observation aviation appeared woefully obsolete in performance, as did pursuit aviation in speed characteristics. Since new bombardment aircraft possesses speed above two hundred miles per hour, any intercepting or supporting aircraft must possess greater speed characteristics if they are to perform this mission. In the case of pursuit aviation, this increase in speed must be so great as to make it doubtful whether pursuit can be efficiently or safely operated either individually or in mass. No known agency can frustrate the accomplishment of a bombardment mission.*" [6]

Until Westover died in a plane crash in 1938, he and the government guided the Air Corps away from the development of superior fighter types.[7] Arnold, though Westover's assistant, changed his mind about fighters without telling Westover and after he became Chief in 1938, he originated in 1940 the most sweeping change to fighter development in Air Force history. However, the long period of disinterest in fighters which began in 1926 and lasted for over a decade, was to have a damaging effect upon the AAF's ability to escort bombers until late in 1943.

Claire Chennault

The biplane fighters employed in the 1933 exercise were commanded by Capt. (later Lt. Gen.) Claire Chennault, whose own report of the exercise written in 1933, *The Role of Defensive Pursuit*, angered Arnold who demanded to know who the upstart and disloyal officer was.[8] Chennault irritated Westover and Arnold by claiming in his report that, in fact, his pursuit aircraft – guided by Chennault's revolutionary new air defense system controlled by ground observers and radio communications – would have defeated Westover's bombers. Chennault claimed that Army umpires judging the exercise ruled unfairly against his pursuit aircraft. However, neither Westover nor Arnold took any notice of Chennault's invention of an air defense system.

Chennault had emerged from a number of bomber theorists to become the great prophet of the mission of fighter aircraft, but in an era of the teachings of bomber invincibility, he was ignored. After Spaatz switched to the camp of bomber supporters, the Air Corps had no real use for a fighter expert. Chennault's assignment in the 1933 exercise vaulted him into the unenviable, undesirable position of the token fighter expert. He taught at the ACTS to students who did not believe him. Yet there was more to this young officer than his willingness to speak openly. His report was the first to advocate the creation of an air defense system and he opposed the unproven issue of bomber invincibility. In doing so he drew Arnold's lasting displeasure.

Chennault was perhaps the only Pursuit Instructor at the ACTS. The ACTS had known about the writings of Italian Marshal Guilio Douhet who prophesied the brilliant and conquering future of the aerial bomber, derived from his personal experiences gained in combat in 1911. Translated into English by 1921, Douhet's theories were to transform military aviation around the world, and the ACTS found use for his teachings. After 1930, the ACTS taught the superiority of the bomber and allowed Chennault to teach about fighters only as a token gesture. He was in the difficult position of instructing officers who believed in bombers. Chennault's future in the Air Corps would have been secure, until his 1933 report questioned Douhet's uncompromising theories. Arnold read the report in which Chennault said Douhet advocated: "*...the concentration of all aeronautical effort*

Major General Oscar Westover commanded the Air Corps until his death in 1938.

toward the accumulation of an enormous number of bombardment airplanes. No nation has wholly abandoned pursuit yet but more and more attention is being paid to the development of the bomber." The only "*... effective defense against hostile bombardment is the fighter,*" but the Air Corps' fighter force was as small as those in "*...the same European nations who subscribe to the theory of the invincibility of bombardment masses.*" Fighters and "*...improved tactical methods involving the employment of special pursuit weapons have reversed bombardment's former great advantage.*" [9]

For Chennault to say, years before the B-17 was being mass-produced, that the bomber's advantage was passed, was to court ostracism, and he received it. Chennault had a leather-like face, a jutting jaw and squinting eyes and looked like an eagle eyeing prey. He suffered from bronchitis and deafness, but not meekness. Having stepped on toes he was asked to form an aerobatics flying team. Before he was "retired" in 1937 a Chinese General witnessed one of his team's demonstrations and, perhaps aware of Chennault's

In 1933, Captain Claire Chennault devised an air defence system and applied it during a military exercise, but his criticism of the doctrines of Guilio Douhet, the Italian air theorist, caused a decline in Chennault's career.

expertise and incipient availability, offered him a position in China to help organize flight training. After four years as head of instruction there and by the time Japan bombed Pearl Harbor, Chennault and others formed the famous "Flying Tigers", the American Volunteer Group which fought bravely against greater Japanese forces until 1942. Like General Douglas MacArthur, who was helping the Philippine government prepare for war, Chennault was recalled into service to take command of American forces in foreign countries in which they were currently residing.

The bomber was not invincible. Chennault knew it. A counter to every weapon can be devised, given the time in which to develop it. The counter to the bomber is the fighter. The bomber can be protected better by escorts than it can by its defensive armament, which can seldom be aimed at fast-flying enemy fighters. It is not an overstatement to say that Chennault would have developed an escort sooner than 1943 had he been given the job of developing it because the P-51 would have impressed him.

In retrospect it can be said that the long period of disinterest in fighters within the Air Corps also resulted in the loss of its finest fighter advocate. Chennault's air defense system was not implemented until 1940, and although credited to another officer, was run by a confusion of disparate notions even after America went to war in December 1941. The Air Corps had exiled the one expert in uniform who knew the bomber was not invincible, and said so.

"The Bomber Will Always Get Through"

Douhet and other advocates knew a long-range bomber could fly over and well beyond front lines and strike at an enemy's rear industrial base, reducing his ability to wage war. During the 1930s a number of theorists in several countries declared that the bomber would always "get through." The bomber soon attained status as the ultimate weapon of war. Many came to believe with near-mysticism in the coming age of air power. They dreamed of fleets of high-flying bombers so well armed that they would fend off an enemy's puny, disorganized, and outnumbered fighter forces. Publicists said bombers would be massed together over urban centers and their vast numbers would "darken the sky," destroying factories and troop centers with pinpoint accuracy. Propagandists said cowed leaders of terrorized citizens would "beg to surrender" under a rain of falling bombs. Artists were hired to paint scenes of an enemy's open sky dotted with Air Corps bombers raining an endless precipitation of bombs upon defenseless factories. Enemy fighters were depicted firing harmlessly from out of range of the bombers, or spinning and burning down to destruction. It was a fantasy, but not without its uniformed advocates.

In 1931 General MacArthur, Chief of Staff of the Army, and a Navy Admiral agreed that the Air Corps would accept the mission of coastal defense as far as 100 miles out to sea, thus freeing harbour-bound battleships for greater maneuver. There was no good coastal defense bomber at the time, and no proof that a bomber's crew could locate an enemy ship advancing across a broad ocean. Nevertheless MacArthur's agreement boosted beyond all expectation the strategic mission of the Air Corps. To acquire a suitable coastal defense bomber and to provide the Air Corps with new types of

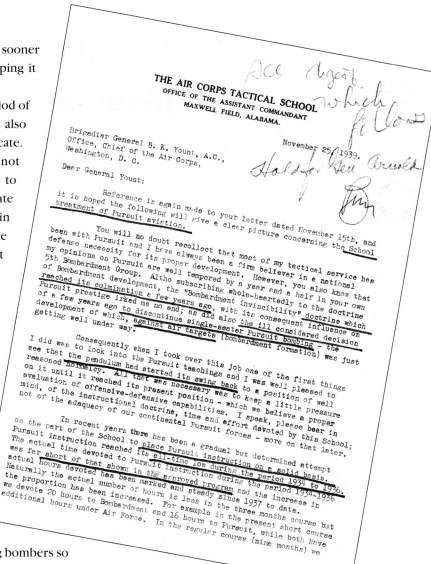

Colonel Millard F. Harmon's letter of November 25, 1939 to Brig.Gen. Barton Yount in which he put forward the case for pursuit aviation.

aircraft, MacArthur authorized four projects. Project A specified obtaining a bomber which could carry a 2,000 lb bomb 5,000 miles at 200 mph.[10]

In the competition for Project A, the aircraft manufacturers Martin, Douglas, and Boeing all designed and built entries. Martin and Douglas believed a twin-engined bomber was adequate and, respectively, built the A-22 Maryland/A-30 Baltimore and the B-18 Bolo. Boeing responded with the four-engined B-17 Flying Fortress.

The B-17 had twice the range of the B-18. Westover, seeking accommodation with Congress and the Army, ordered dozens of B-18s but allowed Boeing to produce only a handful of B-17s. The Maryland and the Baltimore were sold abroad. More B-18s could be purchased for the same amount of money it cost to buy a handful of B-17s. Either way, Westover mistakenly believed the Air Corps would have its first modern bombers. Air Corps students at the ACTS were more impressed by the strategic capability now possible, than they were by fulfilling the mission of coastal defense.

MacArthur's Project B was to provide a twin-engined attack bomber, Project C was to be the multi-seat fighter and Project D was to result in the intercontinental bomber. Project C will be discussed in detail later, but briefly, the multi-seat fighter was to be the first example of an escort fighter. In 1933 MacArthur and the Air Corps embarked upon defining by sets of characteristics, the basic aerial weapons that exist today.

It is apparent that several countries designed and built four-engined, long-range bombers intended for World War Two. However, only one country – America – began limited mass-production in the mid-1930s; and only one country – America – operated thousands of them in broad daylight, unescorted, over enemy territory (Great Britain produced thousands of four-engined bombers which later were used at night). The fact that other countries did not proceed intentionally from Douhet's theories to the actual mass production of four-engined bombers is a story more of emphasis upon *tactical* air war than it was of military unpreparedness. America's and Britain's four-engined bombers constituted one of the reasons why the Allies won the war. The two countries alone, employed fleets of four-engined "heavies" and used them on a near-daily, round-the-clock basis against Germany later in the war.

The First Escorts

Before Project C got under way in the late 1930s, some single-engined, multi-seat escorts *were* built. While debate ranged over a disputed need for escorts, the first examples took to the sky. The Berliner-Joyce P-16 of 1929 was the last two-seat biplane built in which the second crewman operated a rearward-aimed .30 caliber machine gun. Even then it was assumed that the escort would be required to defend against attackers coming only from behind bomber formations. The P-16 was also designated "PB-1" for Pursuit, Bi-place. It flew at 186 mph and had two .50 caliber fixed machine guns which could be fired through the arc of the moving propeller. Since the B-17 flew for the first time in 1935 and could reach a speed of 250 mph, the first escorts were obsolete before 1935. Following the P-16 was the Detroit-Lockheed YP-24 two-seater of 1931, the Consolidated Y1P-25 of 1932, and the Consolidated P-30, (also known as the PB-2), of 1934.

Development of two-seater escorts with rear-facing armament ceased for a while when Boeing's P-26, having a speed of 234 mph, arrived on the scene in 1932. Yet in aerial practice intercepts, the P-26 was ineffective in attack against a B-17. The bomber had monoplane, all-metal construction, retractable landing gear, an enclosed cockpit, and no bracing wires or struts. The P-26 was just the opposite, but it was a monoplane and colorful, and was purchased in quantity. The biplane era was at an end, although biplanes were operated in combat elsewhere briefly by other countries after 1940.

The issue of developing escort fighters seemed like a useless exercise in academics, because in 1935 no fighter could fly as far as a B-17. It was apparent both to those who believed in its invincibility and those who knew something about the true threat of enemy fighters, that bombers would be forced to operate unescorted to the most distant targets and into the teeth of enemy air defense. Even as late as 1941 and 1942, when Arnold was a Major General and Ira C. Eaker was a Colonel, the two officers co-authored two books which stated that bomber invincibility was open to question because "*…the greatest protection of the bomber – lies in tight formation.*" Fighters have "*…a distinct advantage over the bomber*" and could "*…pretty nearly bar the air to the bomber.*" [11]

An inability to conceive an adequate escort, married to the worrisome and feared belief that enemy fighters would yet devastate Air Corps bomber formations – if war was to be declared – forced Arnold to do the best with what was available. Many bomber losses were to be expected and crews' lives lost if there was no escort fighter available, but well prior to 1940, MacArthur's Project C had begun to draw much attention.

Fighter Armament Theory

The old interruptor gear of World War One allowed the mounting of machine guns around an engine and the interrupting of fire as a propeller blade traveled in front of a gun. As World War Two approached, so there was a desire to cease using the gear to upgrade weapons from the light firepower of the .30 caliber gun and to carry a heavier cannon aloft. The Army wanted cannon fire directed from the air onto enemy troop concentrations, their tanks and facilities and instructed its Air Corps to develop cannon-carrying aircraft. The all-metal construction of foreign aircraft made the .30 caliber gun obsolete. Toward the end of the 1930s, tests were sponsored for trying ever-larger weapons mounted in aircraft, culminating in the test-firing of a 75 mm artillery piece carried in the belly of a B-18. Choices in armament forced changes in the design of fighters whose structure had to be strong to carry the weight of larger and heavier guns and to withstand the recoil of fire. By 1940, the Air Corps believed larger fighters powered by the more powerful in-line engines under development could carry several cannon.

Better Air Corps Fighters

While the Air Corps revolutionized air power and astounded the world's observers in 1935 with its shiny, massive, four-engined B-17, it had neglected fighters. However, racing planes did not disappear from the scene in America after Congress cut off funds for the Schneider Trophy competition – quite the contrary. Aviation reached its golden age. Charles Lindbergh's famous 1927 crossing of the Atlantic inspired

Above: A 75 mm cannon protrudes from the modified belly of a B-18. A demand by the Army for carrying artillery pieces aloft to use against ground targets in the late-1930s, was accompanied by Air Corps plans to use the cannon against enemy bombers. The Curtiss XP-71 two-seat bomber destroyer was designed around the 75 mm cannon.

The Gee Bee racer of 1932 set the record at 296 mph and in 1935, Howard Hughes raised it to 352 mph in his H-1. The Air Corps was more interested in the B-17 and struggled to develop fighters while air racers held all the speed records. A few racers, such as Frank Hawks' and Howell Miller's '*Time Flies,*' were inspected at Wright Field, but most were made of wood and were declared unsuitable. In the case of the H-1, Hughes was asked to fly it to Wright Field but there was a mix-up and Capt. Oliver Echols felt he had been snubbed. The H-1 had wooden wings but it certainly made an impression upon design staffs, particularly with its radial engine, flush rivets, and metal skin sections with smooth joints. Eventually, military types would fly faster than racers. In 1937 Germany's Messerschmitt Bf 109 V-13 achieved 379 mph and in 1939 the Messerschmitt Me 209 V-1 flew at an astoundingly fast 469 mph. Hughes also flew his H-1 non-stop across America in 1937 in record time when no Air Corps fighter could cross the continent non-stop.

people in all walks of life to find excitement in aviation and air races drew thousands of people to events in the impoverished and lacklustre 1930s. By 1932, air racers upped world speed records and although America's Army commanded some output of industry, foreign military aircraft and American racers set all the world's speed records.

These achievements in speed and range rankled some Air Corps officers who were concerned less with civilian stunts than they were alarmed by superior fighter developments, particularly within German and British military air organizations. By 1936 the Supermarine Spitfire, the crate-like Hawker Hurricane, and the Bf 109 were solidly built weapons which no flimsily built racer could emulate.

Above: The Army and its Air Corps wanted to upgrade armament on fighters, and in 1939 tested a 75 mm cannon on the B-18 shown here. The cannon was designed into the XP-71 which was canceled, but the North American B-25G and H were produced with the cannon. After R-40C's entries were examined, the AAF decided to use .50 caliber machine guns in fighters. The fin-like protrusion visible above the B-18's fuselage in this photograph probably carried a camera.

During Westover's uninspired tenure, there was some urgency to make fighters as fast as foreign developments. The technology was available but not the engines or foresight. A competition was set for 1935 and was judged by Capt. Oliver P. Echols. It resulted in the Air Corps' first fast monoplanes. These were all-metal fighters having retractable landing gear, enclosed cockpits and more powerful engines. The Seversky and Curtiss companies offered the P-35 and P-36 respectively. The P-35 won the 1935 competition and 77 were ordered for production, the first arriving in 1937. Curtiss revised its P-36 and in 1937, 210 were ordered. The Air Corps had its first 300 mph fighters (not as fast as Hughes' H-1), yet a growing number of Air Corps officers wanted a 400 mph fighter. Westover's unsteady grip upon fighter policy was being loosened in the year before his death, when a competition to choose an interceptor was offered in 1937. From X-608 came the Lockheed XP-38. Foreign fighters were pushing American standards higher.

As a Major, Ben S. Kelsey held the post of Chief of Fighter Projects longer than any man in the history of the United States Army Air Force. He led the fight for drop tanks and twin-engined fighters, but it was his assertion that a fighter should not perform just one function that helped change the nature of fighter design. Yet as General Echols' officer in charge of fighters, Kelsey did not contest Echols' aversion to the Mustang. Kelsey's flight-test report of an XP-51 was brief to the point of damnation; instead he had praise for the P-40.

The other type of supercharger – the integral, engine-driven type – was less popular because lack of development had not produced improvements, and an integral required a portion of engine power to drive it. Worse for turbos, one corporation, General Electric, "…was the sole source for the entire industry." Few officers realized that they were putting all their eggs in one basket. Reliance upon one source of supply for turbos, coupled with lack of development of integrals, and married to the result of having only one type of in-line was to court disaster. The V-1710, as we shall see, had problems of its own which lasted throughout World War Two. Lack of low fuel consumption engines and reliable high-altitude superchargers were two factors which delayed the introduction of the escort fighter.

Ben S. Kelsey

The Chief of Fighter Projects at Wright Field was an officer at the cutting edge of fighter technology. Even during the lean years, when dreams of bombers were the only thoughts of those responsible for advancing air power in the Air Corps, there was Lt. (later Brig. Gen.) B.S. Kelsey,

V-1710 and Superchargers

The lengthy in-line engine development program bore one result. Begun as a private venture the Allison V-1710 was ordered without a supercharger by the Navy in 1933 for airship use. Development continued but the Navy withdrew support and the Army ordered another version of it in 1935, hoping it would attain 1,000 hp. The engine met expectations but broke down. It was re-designed, again and put out 1,000 hp before being flight-tested. Two authorities, Robert Schlaifer and S.D. Heron, said the 12-cylinder V-1710 "… *was specifically designed for glycol cooling and for use of a turbosupercharger; the possibility of using the turbosupercharger was, of course, one of the Army's chief reasons for supporting the development of liquid-cooled engines.*" [12]

Unwittingly, the Air Corps' total reliance upon turbo and liquid-cooled engines, to be mated in new aircraft, sent fighter development on a very narrow and nearly dead-end course.

The turbo appeared to offer the best solution to maintaining high horsepower at high altitude because it employed engine exhaust to drive a turbine mounted on a common shaft with a compressor which increased the density of the fuel-air mixture before it entered the manifold system.

responsible for evaluating fighters. As would be expected, Kelsey's superiors decided which fighters would be tested and/or produced and the Chief of Fighter Projects tested what Wright Field received from industry. A taciturn man who nevertheless held strong opinions, Kelsey put little to print which conveyed what he thought. After retirement he lectured, gave interviews, and wrote articles and one book. He said others held "… the erroneous conclusion that an aircraft could only be designed to do one job. It was so bad in the late 1920s and 1930s that there was an attempt to classify as different types, low, medium and high-altitude fighters when what was actually being demanded was a wider range of combat performance. Another error which came out of World War One, and still plagues us in more areas than fighters alone, was the penchant for picking a mission and then calling the aircraft by that name." [13]

Kelsey's concept of an airplane with a wider range of performance was the multi-mission fighter. MacArthur's Project C resulted in the Bell XFM-1 Airacuda which will be discussed shortly. In the 1930s and 1940s, engines were not powerful enough to load up a fighter with every conceivable

Lieutenant Ben Kelsey was at the controls of this XFM-1 seen here over Wright Field on 21 October 1937, probably during its delivery flight.

item of equipment to permit it to perform dissimilar missions equally well.

To counteract the incoming enemy bomber (which never appeared over America) the Air Corps – from the end of the 1930s to late 1944 – strived unceasingly throughout the war for the finest interceptor. Yet Kelsey hated the term, saying "...the term 'interceptor' was coined in the development areas to permit development of true combat types with adequate armament and excluding baggage compartments for golf bags." He wanted fighters to have "...overloads and alternate loads (that would) become not only feasible but attractive." [14]

Kelsey wanted a fighter that could do everything. That was impossible. At a much later date, when he was quoted giving the above statements, he was looking back at his stewardship in helping develop the Air Corps' first, modern fighter, the Lockheed P-38 Lightning, which far outclassed the hopeless Bell XFM-1. Kelsey basked in praise for having been allowed to share in developing the P-38, which came as close to being a multi-purpose fighter as was possible in 1939. In 1937, the multi-mission fighter was a thing of the future. Lack of good engines forced restrictions upon fighter design and the relatively low horsepower of the V-1710 forced two alternatives. Kelsey said designers could "...produce the lightest possible machine with restrictive loads" and the Bell P-39 Airacobra was "...the small solution," or designers could design a twin-engined fighter which allowed overloads and multi-mission capability. That was the P-38. The choice of two engines was "...born from the necessity to counteract a deficiency in engine development." [15]

Kelsey's tour as Chief of Fighter Projects spanned the decade of greatest change in fighter development – up to mid-1943 – and he had no hand in the amazing story of development of the P-51B. In the few surviving quotations he allowed, he seldom mentioned the Mustang because it outclassed the P-38 by a wide margin.

The In-Line Engine Fighter

In 1936 the Air Corps was ready to flight-test an aircraft powered by the V-1710 mated to a turbo and chose a Curtiss P-36 to be modified as the purely experimental XP-37. It flew at a respectable 340 mph but its greatest influence upon Air Corps fighter design was that it achieved a 20 percent reduction in drag over that of the P-36. The XP-37 was not produced for a variety of reasons. The streamlined nose, when compared to that of the blunt-nosed P-36, was literally the shape of the future. However, "...during 1938, about a year before delivery of the turbosupercharged XP-38, XP-39, and YP-37s, the Army became convinced, largely by the arguments of Allison, Curtiss, and Bell, that it was unwise to risk everything on the turbosupercharger, and that medium-altitude fighters should be developed." [16]

One such fighter was the P-40 and although it might have had a turbo, its V-1710 was fitted with a low-altitude rated integral supercharger and the original belly scoop was moved forward to be under the spinner. For a long while, the P-40 was the largest production program in the Air Corps.

Project C – The Twin-Engined Escort

Having the V-1710 in production allowed aircraft designers to offer a wide range of fighter prototypes which flowed to Wright Field like a flood. Following the XP-37, P-38, P-39 and P-40 came the useless XP-46 and, later, the XP-51, all powered by the V-1710. But the most anticipated prototype using the V-1710 in 1936, was a twin-engined escort and multi-mission fighter known as the Bell XFM-1 (Fighter, Multi-place) Airacuda. It was expected to satisfy three needs: the Army's, because it mounted two 37 mm cannon; escort advocates, because it was an escort; and bomber barons, because it carried bombs. Kelsey had anticipated it. It was a failure because it was slow and underpowered. Nine YFM-1s and three YFM-1As were ordered but the first of these did not fly until eight months after the XP-38 flew for the first time.

The Lockheed P-38 Lightning

Clarence L. "Kelly" Johnson and Hall Hibbard offered six design alternative layouts, all of which had two engines and one of which became the design basis for the famous and strikingly beautiful XP-38. Few people remain aware that several layouts featured pusher props or that pusher props were then very desirable designs. When the XP-38 was rolled out, Kelsey was allowed to make the first flight in January 1939. A month later, while making a one-stop refuelling, cross-country flight from the west coast to Wright Field, he was greeted by General Arnold. Arnold pressed Kelsey to take off

Left: Photographed on 16 August 1937, the XP-37 is seen here with tufts of cotton attached to study airflow in flight. Three features tested on the XP-37 led the way to the XP-38: an in-line engine, a turbo and a very streamlined nose. A 20 percent decrease in drag over that of the basic airframe of the Curtiss P-36 sparked a revolution in Air Corps fighter design.

Right: This view of the Curtiss XP-37 reveals some of the promise the experimental fighter offered to the Air Corps in 1937 because of its streamlined nose. Seen here in front of Wright Field's hangars, the XP-37's success led to the design of the great Lockheed P-38.

Below: The XP-37 photographed sporting the Wright Field emblem — an arrow with the word "Wright" on it. This aircraft was a modified Curtiss P-36 and its streamlined nose was literally the shape of the future.

as soon as possible after refueling to try to break Hughes' non-stop, cross-country flying time record by quickly reaching an East Coast airfield. He crashed near Mitchel Field on Long Island.[17] Official timers were not present but Kelsey did not break Hughes' record as he had not flown non-stop.

Despite the loss of the prototype, Arnold knew the plane was a winner and made it clear he wanted as many P-38s as possible. Kelsey's crash, P-38 complexity, and production delays slowed development. Later, in October 1939, 13 service versions were ordered. Lockheed were producing a wide variety of aircraft for which British and French purchasing commissions came to the US to buy aircraft to counter the war with Germany which many people thought was inevitable. There was brief interest from the RAF to buy Lightnings and some were exported. These were supplied without turbos, forcing the few RAF Lightning Is to be tested as low-altitude fighters. No further aircraft were purchased as the US refused to export aircraft with their precious turbos installed. None of the early models – XP-38, YP-38, P-38, XP-38A, P-38D, P-38E or the British export model 322 (Lightning I) – were suitable for combat. It was not until the P-38F was produced in 1942 that a model of the Lightning was worthy of the name "combat fighter." There was no P-38B or C.

Conclusion

After applying advanced technology to bomber development, the Air Corps waited until 1937 before demanding the same from industry for fighters. From 1931 to almost the end of the

From left to right: Major General Oscar Westover, Brigadier General George Brett, and an unidentified officer. Westover downgraded fighter development and Brett, as Chief of Materiel, initially gave the XP-46 top priority following Westover's death in 1938. The aircraft is a Northrop A-17 Nomad.

decade, officers struggled indifferently with the concept of the escort. They began with slow two-seaters having some guns aimed to the rear and ended the decade with an ungainly twin-engined, all-purpose fighter that was obsolete when war began. Intentions to rely on the V-1710 and turbo resulted in the P-38 which, after a period of development, became one of the main fighter types including the P-38, P-39, P-40, P-47, P-51,

The North American XP-51 (serial number 41-38 or 1038) powered by an Allison V-1710-39 engine.

and P-63 used by the AAF during World War Two. Bomber invincibility, though the main topic of instruction at the ACTS, was an unproven theory now hedged by attempts to conceive the definitive escort. But the glamor of the fast-climbing interceptor needed for air defense was to overshadow the ill-defined and controversial escort type of fighter. Concurrent with all attitudes was the notion that no fighter could fly as far as a B-17, and therefore the B-17 was expected to fight through enemy defenses all by itself in tight formations.

Right: These two Colonels – Cass Hough (left) and Ben Kelsey – were deeply involved in finding a solution in recovering control of a P-38 after it encountered compressibility. Although Hough's idea of using trim tabs to bring a P-38 out of an uncontrollable dive was satisfactory, an article in a 1944 magazine labelling him as the "fastest man alive" soured relations with Kelsey and others who had not discovered the trim tab method first. This photograph was taken on 9 September 1944, long after the P-38 was taken out of service as an escort in the ETO.

Below: General H.H. Arnold (right) talks to William Knudsen (wearing white hat). They are at the Lockheed factory inspecting the YP-38. Note that the canopy top section at that time opened to the side.

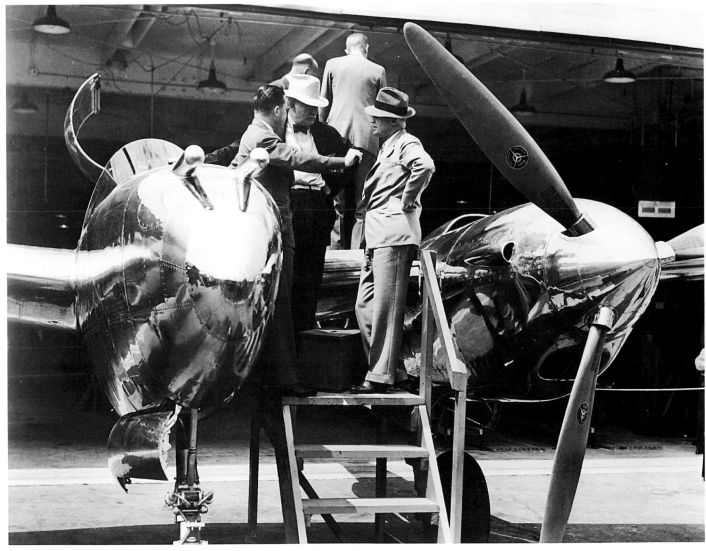

Chapter 2

"Bombardment invincibility irked me no end..."

Early Prototypes

The Great Depression in the early 1930s hampered much of American life, including fighter aircraft development. During the late 1930s, America had isolated itself from the wars being fought in distant parts of the world. However, when these countries were forced into war, they turned to America's industrial and technological might to buy their aircraft. Foreign purchasing commissions, who spent millions in the US for modern aircraft, provided a welcome investment for plant construction and expansion of aircraft production which eventually led to America's wartime output miracle. A new healthy aircraft industry with improved design staffs, was soon able to provide the Air Corps with better and more modern aircraft.

By the last months of 1937, and certainly no later than January 1938, France and Britain realized that Germany was mobilizing for war. The two countries ordered aircraft from American manufacturers in 1938. and two purchasing commissions from France and Britain, returned again in February 1939 to increase orders.

President Roosevelt also wanted to improve his air forces and on 28 September 1938 held a conference in the White House, during which he authorized the unheard of increase in production to 10,000 aircraft in a single year and wanted industry to be capable of producing 20,000. By January 1939, Congress trimmed the figure to 5,500 for Fiscal Year 1940 but this displeased Roosevelt who, on 16 May 1940, asked Congress for 50,000 aircraft. This astronomical request resounded like a thunderclap on the sensitive ears of Air Corps officers who, in the previous year, had fought for every extra airplane they could get their hands on.

To an Air Corps subsisting on near handouts, the organization of the Corps was suddenly tasked not only with finding ways to build itself up, but also had to contend with being patient while giving away a large percentage of US production to foreign buyers. This monumental change in procurement made the year 1940 the most difficult of the war for staff planning officers, some of whom did not like seeing precious American aircraft go to British or French buyers.

Roosevelt's cornucopia of opportunity inspired Arnold, who had become Chief of the Air Corps in 1938. Within months of Westover's death and Arnold's ascension, the Army Chief of Staff, General Malin Craig, was replaced by General George Marshall. Both Arnold and Marshall were far more interested in air power than were their predecessors. These great leaders were able to guide the Air Corps through the maze of fundamental changes in 1940. Arnold created interest in fighters.

"Hap" Arnold is still remembered today as a unique figure because his foresight coincided with the beginning and the peak of growth of the Air Force. He had been taught to fly by the Wright brothers and at the end of his tenure as Chief, also witnessed the development of the jet aircraft and rockets. He was so highly regarded as a General officer that Marshall later named Arnold to be one of three Deputies in the Army High Command. Arnold was a formidable personality who looked like everybody's grandfather because he had white hair and a smooth-complexioned, smiling face. His nickname "Hap" did not mean "happy" and he could not be approached casually. He wore his uniform smartly and his cap was pulled down low over his eyes, the way cadets at the Academy wore theirs. Arnold stood erect, demanded results and had a quick temper, was impatient and replaced officers summarily. He was not the grandfather type but he led the AAF into greatness.

Although the Air Corps budget was increased, most completed aircraft went overseas. On 21 October 1940, General Arnold complained to Materiel saying "…we have paid millions for accelerated delivery" yet industry was slow to supply aircraft. In December 1940, a report stated that no deliveries had been made on orders for the P-38, P-39, P-43, P-44, A-20, B-24, B-25, and B-26, and "…*the original contract provided for deliveries of 443 combat airplanes by December 1, 1940. Actual deliveries on the 5,500 program, as of November, total 316 airplanes over contract schedules.*" [1]

Irving Brinton Holley, Jr. described it best in his book entitled *Buying Aircraft: Material Procurement for the Army Air Forces* in which he lamented about "…the awful summer of 1940." The Air Corps operated not many more than a few hundred modern combat aircraft, yet it had to prepare for war. In May 1938, France had put a near stranglehold on production and ordered 1,000 P-36s and in 1939 some P-40s. A total of 291 P-36s reached France and were used against the *Luftwaffe* before France capitulated. Most of the French order, which stood at some 4,000 P-40s, was taken over by Britain. The Air Corps received only third best claim on production in its own country. The P-40 was the third-most produced fighter in America during World War Two, with Curtiss being America's most relied upon aircraft manufacturer in 1940. Foreign sales brought in a lot of money which funded significant plant construction but the Air Corps was not party to that largesse, as a large part of production still went overseas. The Air Corps was unprepared for what was about to happen: America could not defend itself or fight a war because it did not have enough equipment.

To accelerate development of new aircraft, the government approved a policy to use the money from sales to foreign customers to finance the development of better aircraft for specific use by the Air Corps. [2] Agreed in March 1940, the rule allowed companies leeway to interpret for themselves just what was a better type. NAA (North American Aviation) used this rule which led to development of the

Mustang. A foreign customer was also required to report back to the US on the combat suitability of its American-made products. French and British-flown US aircraft were used in combat during 1940 and American manufacturers received first-hand reports on how their designs had stood up to enemy aircraft. The Air Corps watched on the sidelines as other countries continued to take a large percentage of production.

From Twin to Single-Engined

Six months after the first flight of the twin-engined XP-38, the Air Corps was satisfied that it would have the world's finest twin-engined design, and it now also wanted a single-engined interceptor. On 25 July 1939, Brig. Gen. George Brett, Chief of the Materiel Division, and Maj. (later, Brig. Gen.) Franklin O. Carroll, Chief of Experimental Engineering, asked for a massive Research and Development program known as Project 71, and in sub-section 71-1 the *"single place, single engined, pursuit interceptor"* was given a requirement. Project 71-1 provided that the Air Corps would have dozens of squadrons with Curtiss P-46s. The reason for the new specification was because the Air Corps had declared that the YP-39, P-40, and YP-43 were unsatisfactory as interceptors. Three weeks prior to this, Circular Proposal CP-39-770 had been offered by Brett to Arnold "...in order that designs other than the XP-39 may be considered."

The P-39 was the first Air Corps fighter design to employ an engine in mid-fuselage. Other prototypes had engines at the rear driving pusher props. The first flight of the XP-39, also fitted with a turbo, was on 6 April 1938. When the XP-39B was built and flown in November 1938, the turbo was not fitted, confining it to low-altitude operations. The sleek-looking P-39 also suffered from unstable flying characteristics and of the thousands that were produced, most were sold to Russia. The P-39 was at first attractive to the Air Corps mainly because it carried a 37 mm cannon firing through the prop spinner. To get a better interceptor, CP-39-770 brought forth designs for the Curtiss XP-46, Republic XP-47 (not the prototype of the much different XP-47B), and the Douglas DS-312A. The XP-46 and XP-47 were to be armed with machine guns but the DS-312A uncorked a serious attempt to employ heavy armament in fighters.

XP-46

On paper the XP-46 was placed third on CP-39-770 but on 1 September 1939 – the day Hitler invaded Poland – Brett

In mid-1938, Brigadier General Barton Yount was the Assistant Chief of the Air Corps. He and General Arnold demanded and won priority from the NACA for wind tunnel testing of the XP-46.

recommended development of the P-46 and dropped the other two.[3] The XP-46 was to be the improved fighter reserved for the Air Corps and paid for by foreign sales of P-40s, none of which were fitted with a turbo. When the two XP-46s reached Wright Field they received top priority. French combat experience with the same manufacturer's P-36 resulted in their influence in some aspects of design. Procurement of two – the XP-46 and XP-46A – was approved on 17 January, 1940. However, months prior to then, Brig. Gen. B. K. Yount had told the National Advisory Committee for Aeronautics (NACA) that XP-46 wind tunnel work had a higher priority than for any other project and ordered a drag-reduction study to be made.[4]

The urgent need to get a fighter as fast as the German Bf 109 prompted both Curtiss and the NACA to design "...a pursuit airplane around an Allison V-1710 having a speed of 400 mph."[5] The Curtiss design was preferred and they built a full-scale wind tunnel model for the NACA to test in a drag reduction study, which, in the main, centered on investigation of the belly scoop – then not much more than a hindrance to high speed. At the same time, the NAA was in the process of designing their Mustang with a belly scoop. General Arnold had established a list of eight manufacturers he thought capable of experimentation in fighter design. However, NAA were not on the list as they were expected to build P-40s for Britain. Arnold required that NAA pay Curtiss for their NACA belly scoop study, which they did on May 14, 1940. Around May or June Curtiss had asked the government for reimbursement for their wind tunnel model costs. An officer replied to Curtiss on 14 May – the day Atwood of NAA paid Curtiss – stating:

"Inasmuch as the Army A.C. has had none of the expense in constructing the full scale model of the XP-46 airplane, the M.D. (Materiel Division. author) agrees with your contention as outlined in the ref. letter. Mr. Roche of the office of the M.D. Liaison Officer at Langley Fld. is being informed. (Letter 5-7-40) Request received by telephone from Mr. Roche calling from Langley Fld. In which he requested that a letter be forwarded to the Mat. Div. giving authority to the A.C. and to N.A.C.A. to conduct tests on the full scale model of our CP-39-13. The Army Development Recovery negotiations set up the policy wherein the Army A.C. was to be given 'in kind' in the total

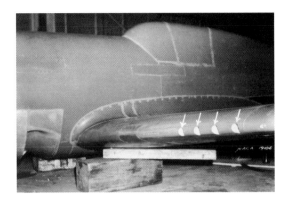

Left and right: The XP-46 wind tunnel model which underwent examinations as part of fuselage and wing gun drag investigations.

Below: Both the NACA and Curtiss conceived a fighter to fly at 400 mph. The Curtiss design was selected and a full-scale wind tunnel model was built with the designation XP-46. In a series of configurations intended to keep drag low, before intakes and scoops and armament ports were incorporated, the bullet-shaped model was extremely smooth. It was from this shape that tests and subsequent reports were made following each slight modification. The eventual XP-46 aircraft achieved a speed well short of 400 mph and was not as fast as the XP-51. For scale purposes, note the technician kneeling at the entrance to the wind tunnel.

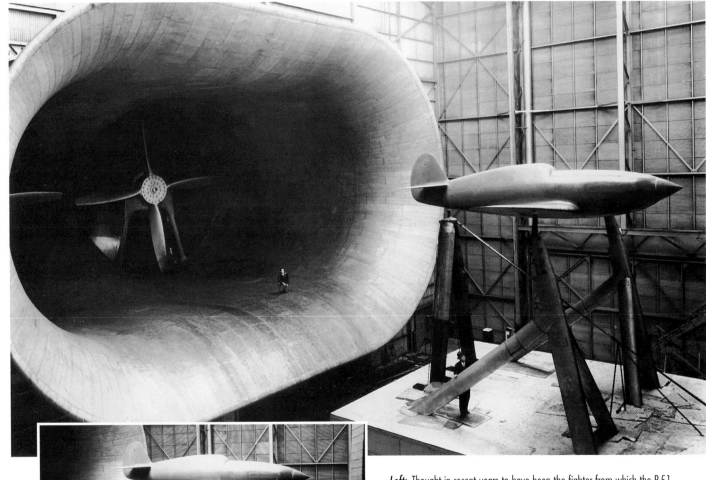

Left: Thought in recent years to have been the fighter from which the P-51 Mustang was copied, the XP-46 is seen here in its elementary form at the Langley wind tunnel awaiting modifications from the NACA in an attempt to improve its chances of winning a significant contract for Curtiss. The NACA labored for months to improve the poor aerodynamic characteristics of the small but heavy fighter and although some fundamental research was carried out on the belly scoop design, the scoop proved inadequate. Insofar as similarity is a factor in copying, the XP-46 resembled the XP-47 – not the XP-51. As can be seen in this photograph, the first drag investigation centered around lowered landing gear and flaps. Note that there are no scoops, intakes or guns on the model.

Left: The NACA tried three types of inlets above the spinner on the XP-46 wind tunnel model. All are shown here. The exhaust stacks were also given variation in testing. A flat windshield was tried but Curtiss rejected that option.

Right: This XP-46 wind tunnel model shows a variation of the scoop under the spinner designed by the NACA. "Prestone" was the name of a glycol coolant applied to any scoop offering ducting leading to a radiator used to cool glycol.

Far right: The nose scoop was enlarged and its drag characteristics investigated.

Below: Either Curtiss or the NACA, or both, attempted to employ wing leading-edge ducts and top-of-wing exhaust outlets on the XP-46 wind tunnel model.

amount which you had paid for Pursuit development with Curtiss up to and including the XP-46 contract. The question of crediting or recognizing development cost which the Curtiss Co. expended was never recognized by the AC and efforts to sell the full scale mockup to the AC were met with the statement that the AC did not feel justified in paying for it, resulting in the feeling that the mockup be considered Corporate property. N. American recognized this model the property of Curtiss-Wright and have taken steps to pay a sum of money to partially reimburse this Co. The Curtiss-Wright Co would feel at fault by making a bonafide arrangement with N. American and then allowing competitors of Curtiss and N. American to receive information at no expense to them. As an alternate, should the Government feel that this provject (sic) is of sufficient interest to warrant purchase of this model, thus saying the C-W Co and allowing them to refun (sic) monies to M. Amer. (sic), the C.W Co would be glad to negotiate with the Air Corps." [6]

Top and above: In a competition with the XP-47 and DS-312A, the XP-46 — shown here — was the third-place winner. However on the day Hitler's armies marched into Poland, the Air Corps gave the XP-46 top priority for production in 1942. Even though the XP-51 was a contemporary of the XP-46, the XP-51 was ignored because it was a British project. When America went to war, the XP-47B was chosen for production. Note a total of four scoops seen in outline. Even with the masterful assistance of the NACA, Curtiss was unable to design scoops providing adequate cooling for the XP-46. The XP-46A, which had guns and other military equipment, was slower than the XP-46.

After this the matter was probably closed for a while. Curtiss was paid and NAA were privy to the NACA data. The XP-46 was to be among the most desired new fighters until 1942. Project 71-1 mentioned a future of squadrons of P-46s. Schlaifer and Heron recorded "…the British also ordered a large number of an improved model of the P-40 known as the P-46, which existed only on paper. Later in 1940, the airplanes on order were: 500 P-40s, 1,000 P-46s, 200 P-39s, and 800 P-38s." [7] Urgency was applied to produce P-46s. The first flight occurred on 2 February 1941 with two XP-46s arriving at Wright Field in September 1941. Testing was terminated in March, 1942 because neither aircraft cooled satisfactorily. They became ground instruction tools at Chanute Field. It was in April that Col. Oliver P. Echols, Assistant Chief of Materiel Command, attempted to stop the Mustang after the RAF contracts were fulfiled.

The NA-73 (XP-51) flew for the first time on 1 May 1941 and its unexpected success later prompted men who in 1941 had thought it did not fit into USAAF plans, to come forward after the war to express bewilderment its success. Retired Brig. Gen. Benjamin Kelsey, who had been subordinate to Echols in the Materiel Command, was interviewed in 1981 and stated that, in 1940, he and Echols "maneuvered hard" to get the P-51 into production but the Air Corps could not pay for it. [8] The author who interviewed Kelsey stated – perhaps on advice from Kelsey – that NAA adapted the XP-46 into the

design of the XP-51 and the team at NAA conceived the Mustang from "basics" best known at Curtiss. Kelsey or that author discounted expertise at NAA and Kelsey also suggested that the P-51 could not go into production for the AAF because of "problems." That same author stated that the AAF ordered Mustangs on 7 July 1941 "long before" America's war began. He also stated that the AAF had no need for dive bombers. In fact Echols tried to stop the P-51 and Kelsey's only contribution to the P-51 was to say it was faster than the P-40E.

What links the two fighter prototypes is the NACA drag-reduction study. The study was conducted on a mock-up of the XP-46 in 1939 and the report was dated 11 January 1940. [9] After that, NAA shared in NACA data although most probably, only the belly scoop data mattered to NAA. Edgar Schmued, the P-51 designer, and Edward Horkey, NAA's Chief Aerodynamicist, stated they did not use the design of the

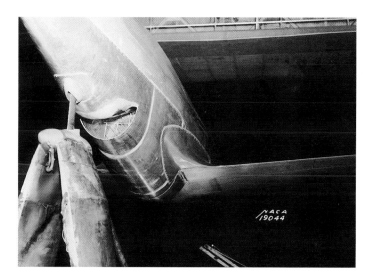

Top and above: Before November 1939, the Air Corps asked the NACA to help "provide adequate engine cooling" on the XP-46, and a full-scale wind tunnel model having no inlets or scoops was provided. From the uncluttered shape a variety of scoops and inlets were designed and tested. Besides a "Prestone" scoop under the spinner, carburetor inlets above, and wing leading-edge ducts associated with top-of-wing exhaust outlets, the mid-fuselage belly scoop was given extensive development. The NACA designed inlets known as A, B, and C. Inlet A "... was tested with two upper duct surfaces" inside the belly scoop. Inlet B was "... smaller and further forward (and) was rotated 30 degrees down about a point 20 and one-half inches back of the duct leading edge producing a large inlet scoop much like the jaws of an alligator." The last arrangement tested, Inlet C, was the original sloping inlet provided by the Curtiss Company.

XP-46 and that the belly scoop was a feature of the XP-51. NAA wanted it to have low drag, so why not look at the NACA study? Placement of a scoop on the belly containing the engine coolant radiator was being examined, tested, and produced in several countries. The British Hawker Hurricane of 1937 was one of the first aircraft to employ a belly scoop. Curtiss had tried it on the XP-40 and had discarded the idea but tried it again on the XP-46. Belly scoop drag had to be addressed. The NACA was in the business of assisting industry and had readily agreed to Yount's request because building a library of basic research was what the NACA was all about.

Blueprints now discovered, reveal that the full-scale XP-46 wind tunnel model was examined with three different belly scoops. Curtiss was unable to get it right and NACA belly scoop design did not progress sufficiently to provide proper cooling within the radiator. When the XP-46 was flight tested, its systems were not cooled properly. To prevent delays in production, Curtiss fell back on its reliable P-40D design.

The Final Report of the XP-46 said "...*in June, 1940 the Curtiss Company was permitted to delay the project one month in order that all of the Contractor's efforts might be devoted to the P-40D development which had more definite production possibilities.*" [10] The P-40D was brought to prominence mainly because it had self-sealing fuel tanks. A blow to the future of the little XP-46 had come during the Battle of Britain. Air Corps observers sent to Britain to report on advances in aviation in British and German aircraft demanded changes to Air Corps fighters. Better armament, self-sealing fuel tanks, and armor plate had to be added to all fighters.

Left and inset: The XP-40 first flew on October 14, 1938. During the initial test flights, the radiator scoop was installed at three locations; first on the belly aft of the wing, then under the cowl and finally, placed directly under the spinner as seen on the production P-40.

Air Corps Pressure Upon the NACA

Yount demanded that the NACA give high priority to the XP-46 study was not followed by a demand that it test the XP-51. The NACA had four major wartime research projects: airfoils, drag clean-up, compressibility, and handling.[11] Drag clean-up applied the expanding new science of aerodynamics to increase speed in a design by examining full-scale aircraft in the NACA's new wind tunnel. Drag clean-up was initiated in 1938 when the Navy asked for help in increasing the speed of the barrel-shaped, slow Brewster F2A Buffalo. After that, the Air Corps dominated the program. Eighteen Air Corps aircraft were sent through drag clean-up by November 1940 and seven were Curtiss products. The XP-46 had the only belly scoop of the 18 tested.[12] If the Air Corps had asked that the XP-51 be tested, the NACA would have discovered very low drag in the Mustang in 1940.

North American Aviation, Inc.

When the Air Corps sent the British Purchasing Commission (BPC) to NAA to supply Britain with more fighters, the Air Corps was not reversing its official attitude that NAA was judged to be incapable of experimentation with fighter design. The Air Corps simply expected NAA to build P-40s. That was the cookie-cutter view, that by handing plans to NAA, the firm need not conceive of new ideas. In 1939, General Arnold had created interest in fighters and made "...a list of manufacturers – recommended as qualified for construction of experimental Pursuit Aircraft."[13] Arnold left NAA off the list. The eight preferred companies were "...Curtiss, Bell, Seversky, Grumman, Vought-Sikorsky, Lockheed, Vultee, and Consolidated." Four companies were later added to the list but NAA was not one of them.

NAA was formed as a holding company in 1928 but in 1935 it became a true aircraft company. Prior to Edgar Schmued becoming associated, NAA was formed from Fokker of America and the General Aviation companies. Ray Wagner – author, historian and archivist – has described how German-born Ed Schmued credited his dentist father for a portion of his education in aviation technology when young Schmued was given any aviation technology book he asked for, because there was no money for a formal education. He apprenticed at an engine factory and spent part of World War One as a mechanic. After the war, Schmued attempted to build an airplane inside his father's house but due to the restrictions imposed by the Treaty of Versailles, it was soon confiscated. Poor economic conditions led him to leave Germany in 1925 to go to Brazil and he attempted "...to arouse interest among Brazilian capitalists for an aviation venture (which) failed miserably. He joined the service department of General Motors in Brazil"[14] and "...decided to emigrate to the US" and departed in 1930. "I

applied at Fokker Aircraft as a designer and persuaded the engineering management to start a preliminary design department." The Fokker of America company was on the East Coast, and after four weeks Schmued was appointed head of the department. Schmued said it was "...the first preliminary design department in the US." The General Aviation Corporation, created by General Motors, took over Fokker of America. Schmued was Project Engineer on the big General Aviation YO-27 of 1932 and the GA-43 airliner. The General Aviation company became the North American Aviation company which was relocated from the East Coast to California in 1935. Schmued became an American citizen in 1935.

NAA undertook some fighter design work after 1935, modifying its BC series of trainers into a single-seat fighter for Peru known as the NA-50, and another for Thailand known as the P-64 in 1940. For his part, Schmued knew he could design a better fighter than the P-40 or XP-46. Schmued headed Preliminary Design at NAA and he designed the P-51 Mustang. He was an ideas man, a man with a genius for concepts. He wanted to keep the front third of the P-51 free of protuberances and thickness. The slimming of the fuselage was a concept similar to that of refining the laminar-flow wing. One look at the P-40 and XP-46 reveals drag-producing front thirds both fuselages and fat cross-sections. The P-51 is clean.

Breaking away from large and heavy designs, Edgar Schmued led America and perhaps the world during World War Two in creating the concept of the lightweight fighter. On 26 June 1942, test pilots in NAA's Engineering Flight Test Division advised J. Leland Atwood, Vice-President of NAA, that the P-51's rate of climb was inferior to that of the Bf 109. They said "...to thoroughly compete against this airplane, the P-51 weight must be reduced 800 to 1,000 pounds even at a sacrifice of top speed." By September, the USAAF formally introduced a weight reduction program on the P-51. Schmued's XP-51F was one of the first aircraft designed from the start with a mind to making

North American Aviation Inc. offered its Model NA 35 trainer – seen here – to Japan prior to the Second World War. Left to right: Vance Breese, a for-hire test pilot; the Japanese representative; and Ed Schmued, NAA design team engineer. The prototype made its first flight on 9 December 1939.

light weight a modern goal in fighter design. The XP-51F made its first flight on 14 February 1944. (Later, when he was Vice-President at Northrop, Schmued helped conceive the N-102 Fang lightweight jet fighter concept which led to the T-38/F-5 series of jet aircraft designed by Welko Gasich.)

One of the issues debated by Atwood and Schmued was who placed the belly scoop where it was – more than a third of the distance back from the nose. Schmued stated categorically: "I evolved a design concept which involved placing the coolant radiator back of the wing." Schmued wanted it to have a belly scoop to serve an aft-mounted radiator to balance the weight of the engine up front.

"I located the radiator scoop because of reduced interference drag at this location. I alone made the decision where to place the radiator (installation)." Schmued gave credit to Dr. Beverly Shenstone of Great Britain who "...suggested dropping the lip of the radiator inlet to form a so-called 'gutter'."

When Atwood took control of NAA following James "Dutch" Kindelberger's death, he and Raymond Rice showed adverse attitudes toward others, including Schmued and Ed Horkey, aerodynamicist at the company. Horkey resigned and Schmued was ousted in 1952. Atwood led others to believe he and not Schmued designed the P-51, and both men went to their graves competing for credit decades after the war. In an age when it is not disputed that 'Kelly' Johnson designed the P-38, some dispute who really designed the P-51. Once Schmued was outside of the company, he was portrayed as the rebel and the headline-grabber. Schmued said: "Atwood didn't even know what the Meredith Effect was, until Dr. Shenstone told him." He added that "...Raymond Rice was not a member of the design team. He never made a drawing! L.L. Waite was at the time of the design of the Mustang still employed by McDonnell Aircraft."

NAA ignored Curtiss data concerning the P-40 and P-46 but may have accepted NACA drag studies. Horkey stated "...the standard procedure in those days was to have Ed Schmued and his group make an inboard profile and three-view drawing and the start of a specification." [15]

The Air Corps required NAA to purchase data from Curtiss since the organization was expected to produce fighters because Arnold had declared NAA unable to experiment in fighter design. The NACA scoop study should have been available for free, as was the NACA laminar flow wing study. On 14 May 1940 J.L. Atwood paid Curtiss $56,000.00. Ever since that transaction, some writers link the XP-46 with the XP-51 by comparing side views to give evidence of copying. Any single-engined, low-wing fighter powered by a V-1710 and having a belly scoop would look similar to the XP-46 XP-47 and XP-51. Side views of similar aircraft cannot convey scientific originality. The XP-46 was a failure and the XP-47 was never built. The XP-51 eventually proved to have the lowest drag of any

J. Leland Atwood (left), the number two man at NAA, congratulates Don Gentile, one of the highest-scoring Mustang aces while touring America on a War Bond tour.

contemporary fighter. The XP-46A flew no faster than 355 mph, while the XP-51 flew at 382 mph. Curtiss was not surprised. The wartime Chief Engineer at Curtiss went so far as to write in a company newsletter to employees to say that their efforts resulted in a justifiable claim for the success of the Mustang! [16]

XP-51

The British Purchasing Commission which had been purchasing trainers asked Curtiss to build P-40 fighters. The Air Corps expected that by giving NAA a customer, the company would produce any type of aircraft just to make money. Rather than build the P-40, Schmued designed the Mustang. On 11 April 1940 the BPC signed a Letter of Intent to purchase "...400 aircraft, type NA-50B." [17] Although the prototype Mustang was the NA-73, the original contract specified the NA-50B – this being, at the time, the in-house designator for a line of fighters. The NA-50B design went through changes and at the time of roll-out the prototype was redesignated NA-73.

The full design story of the Mustang may never be known but James "Dutch" Kindelberger, Chairman of NAA, did give Schmued credit for designing the Mustang. Schmued and a team of newly hired scientists, fresh out of the California Institute of Technology, played a greater role in drag reduction in NAA fighters than was evident in the results from other companies' design staffs. NAA had brought in scientists and changed the way aircraft were designed. After the successful P-51, NAA went on to design the best low-drag fighters. The Korean War F-86 was the first American production jet fighter to go supersonic in a dive. The F-100 was the first mass-production jet to go supersonic in level flight. (The Navy's Douglas F4D Skyray beat the F-100 by a few days but was

NAA personnel (left to right): L.L. Waite, Technical Engineering;
Raymond H. Rice, Chief Engineer; and Edgar Schmued, Design Engineer.

produced only in a small quantity.) Science – not engineering – was the key to reducing drag.

Ed Horkey – foremost among scientists in his field – was hired in 1938 and had spent time making studies in Cal Tech's Guggenheim Aeronautical Laboratory's wind tunnel alongside "Kelly" Johnson and others. Horkey, a very tall and down-to-earth, quiet, practical man had studied under Professor Theodor von Karman who impressed upon his students the teachings of Sir George Cayley, some of whose papers were published in 1809 and 1810. Cayley described natural precedents for studying ways to delay the point of pressure build-up on a body affected by flow in a fluid. Natural creatures (birds and fish) evolved by adapting to moving through a fluid (air and water).[18] Cayley's and von Karman's theories made Horkey pay as much attention to the aerodynamic efficiency of the rear of a shape as others in the past had paid only to the front. The smooth movements of fish and birds were not due entirely to their forward shapes. The thickest part of a bird or fish is near its center but the thickest part of the P-40 was at its front. The streamlined shapes of natural creatures presented a discovery to Horkey who became Chief Aerodynamicist at NAA. Horkey put Schmued's concepts to blueprint.

The point of pressure build-up on a wing or fuselage is affected by resistance of the fluid. Pressure build-up on a steeply curved, front-located upper surface of a wing causes drag when air behind the thick point becomes turbulent. Until approximately 1940, when the theory of laminar flow

was advanced, the thickest part of the wing was near the leading edge to generate lift. Drag was not studied intensely in the USA until the late 1940s. In an effort to reduce drag, the NACA produced a formal paper suggesting that the thick part be moved toward the center of a wing. Horkey said "…total airfoil drag is made up of pressure drag, as well as skin friction." If a wing's trailing edge surfaces are cusped, "…positive pressures create thrust. Negative pressures perpendicular to (a) surface, create drag." [19]

The NACA had made airfoil studies for laminar flow wings but had not built one even though its studies were available to industry. The NA-73 was designed with a standard wing, but Horkey saw the NACA study and convinced Raymond Rice, Chief Engineer, to use a laminar flow wing even though the NA-73 was already built and rolled out. The XP-51 had the world's first laminar flow wing and although it was probably not the best design, it had lower drag than all that had come before. True laminar flow is still a theoretical goal which designers attempt to reach.

Ed Schmued and Ed Horkey wanted to keep the front third of the fuselage of the Mustang free of protuberances and thickness, so the logical place for the scoop was under the belly since thickness was kept toward the center of the fuselage.

Control of Plants

When Col. Oliver Echols, Assistant Chief of Materiel, learned of NAA's decision not to produce Curtiss' design he sent an

Taken post-war, this photograph of Professor Willy Messerschmitt (left) and Edward Horkey, shows two of the men responsible for some of the greatest aircraft designs in the world. Horkey's achievements in the aerodynamics of the Mustang helped create the lowest-drag airframe of the Second World War.

The NA-73 wind tunnel model being inspected by Larry Waite who worked in Advance Design at NAA. The model displays a non-cuffed, three-bladed propeller.

angry telegram to Brett, questioning:

"... the advisability of permitting the French and British to go into these plants at this time and enter (into) contract for (a) completely new development. If this is permitted, they can take over the engineering staff of all our manufacturers which will prevent us from obtaining any development whatsoever. It is (of) doubtful advisability to permit foreign nations to undertake to design completely new airplanes which are improvements on the models which we now have, and which our manufacturers are trying to sell (to) them." [20]

Echols had a point. An embarrassment to Arnold occurred in 1938 when the crash of the Douglas DB-7 prototype injured a French buyer on board. Roosevelt had given his Secretary of the Treasury, Henry Morgenthau, the power to oversee procurement for the Air Corps. Injury to the French buyer in an accident revealed that foreigners were involved in procurement much too early in the design process. The Air Corps had allowed illegal access and tested Morgenthau's power. General Arnold was singled out as the officer causing embarrassment to the Secretary. Roosevelt threatened Arnold with exile to Guam or Alaska. NAA had welcomed the British, and why not?

From that point on, NAA's fighter production was earmarked entirely for British orders and the Air Corps would receive B-25 bombers and AT-6 trainers until the contract for Mustangs was fulfilled in late 1942. The Air Corps had embarrassed NAA when it tried to force the company to produce P-40s and it caught the AAF off guard by building the NA-73. Arnold may have kept NAA off his list but foreign sales and the rule to have a buyer finance a better fighter for the US

resulted in the P-51.

The British limited aileron travel on its Mustang I and Mustang IA, and also wanted four 20 mm cannon. NAA built the Mustang to Air Corps standards using the Handbook of Instruction for Aircraft Designers (HIAD) as used by all US manufacturers. The Mustang was a completely American project. It did not deviate from the HIAD. What angered Echols was that Materiel seemed to lose control of NAA. The rule was that the Air Corps would receive two aircraft free from all foreign orders and NAA gave it two XP-51s. The Air Corps was not interested in the Mustang but simply wanted control.

R-40C

General Arnold heartily agreed to a revolutionary new fighter design competition which ended a decade of downgrading fighters. "Request for Data 40C" or "R-40C" was an attempt to jump-start the dying art of fighter design. The high-horsepower, in-line engines put into development in the 1930s were believed to be ready for mass-production by the early 1940s. War demanded better fighters for the generation following those powered by the V-1710 and cannon armament decisions dictated having noses free of props and engines. The Douglas DS-312A had led the way in armament choices and the logical way to install cannon was to place engines in mid-fuselage or at the rear. In setting a new competition for fighters, Arnold expected that industry would receive those more powerful engines. In November 1939, Brig. Gen. Yount asked Col. M.F. Harmon, Assistant

Clarence "Dutch" Kindelberger, Chairman of NAA, and Senator Claude Pepper examine the cockpit of a production version of the Mustang.

NAA model NA-73 was designated XP-51 even though the Materiel Command had no interest in purchasing Mustangs until after April 1942. Here, the XP-51 painted with Air Corps rudder stripes and with insignia under the wing, awaits an uncertain future.

Commandant of the ACTS, about the lack of fighter theory taught there, to which Harmon replied: "*…bombardment invincibility irked me no end. Pursuit instruction reached its all-time low during the period 1934 to 1936. The actual time devoted to Pursuit instruction was far short of that shown in the approved program.*" [21]

Two years later, Arnold and Eaker authored a book in which they wrote "*…there was a time in this country, and to a lesser extent in the air forces abroad, when many held that the fighter plane had passed from the picture.*" [22] Arnold tried to make up for the error and ordered R-40C which stemmed from Confidential Technical Instruction (CTI) Number 7 of December, 1939 (a CTI was a brief, written statement distributed to alert senior officers of a major decision recently taken in Washington, DC). CTI-7 requested a "Single Engine Pursuit Competition, Advanced Design" and R-40C was formalized in February, 1940. R-40C was General Arnold's attempt to advance fighter design in one great leap. CTI-7 led to extremely radical fighter design based upon the unbuilt Douglas DS-312A design. The DS-312A was a pusher-prop featuring a nose free for the installation of multiple cannon.

It may be said fairly that R-40C hampered the war effort but helped fighter design. In gearing up to fight a war, the Air Corps might have served itself better by focusing upon improving conventional designs rather than allow armament choices to dictate design.

Interest in mounting cannon in fighters had been the basis for design of the P-38 and P-39. Lockheed's P-38 layout of a small center fuselage and two booms freed the nose for carrying the most lethal arrangement of armament in use in

1939. Few historians recall that "Kelly" Johnson and Hall Hibbard offered six design alternatives for the P-38, several of which were pusher-props. All had two engines. The P-38 was a waypoint on the road to R-40C.

The eight manufacturers thought capable of experimentation were notified. On 1 February 1940 Maj. E.M. Powers, Chief of the Engineering Section, wrote R-40C and filled half a page about the Douglas DS-312A. Maj. Gen. Arnold wrote to Robert Lovett, Assistant Secretary of War for Air, on the same day and also spent half a page on the DS-312A. Both Arnold and Powers appeared to explain the DS-312A away with a torrent of words but, in fact, were asking for an improved version! Arnold wanted to "*…determine a possible replacement for the Douglas proposal in this year's R & D program. Funds are now available for the purpose of obtaining preliminary design information of advanced designs, for experimental development in F.Y. (Fiscal Year) 1941, in order to meet quantity production requirements of F.Y. 1942.*" [23]

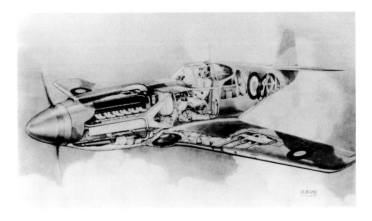

This 1940 artist's cutaway sketch of the Mustang by Al Algier shows the short upper scoop, six guns and British markings. The first Mustang Is had four wing guns and two in the cowl which fired through the propeller arc.

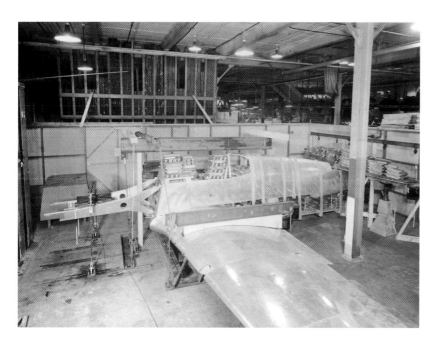

Left: Taken on 13 January 1941, this photograph shows the "low angle of attack loading on (the) fuselage" of the NA-73.

Below: This rare photograph shows the NA-73 mock-up with a rounded windshield, set-back carburettor intake, and an unusual weapons placement. Ed Schmued and Ed Horkey had a better grasp of aerodynamics than did Donovan Berlin at Curtiss and the ultimate performance of the XP-51 exceeded that of the XP-46 by a very wide margin. There is no resemblance between the two.

Above: A rare close-up of the canopy of the NA-73 mock-up. It has no metal supports, was curved and was ultimately rejected by the Air Corps. The carburettor downdraft intake was raised from the cowl's upper surface and was ducted all the way back to the windshield. Later the intake was modified and fitted flush with the cowl.

Right: The cockpit of the NA-73 mock-up was made of wood and was so lacking in detail that it almost bore similarities to a child's funfair vehicle!

Left: The prototype NA-73 in civilian registration being run-up. Note the open intake and exhaust ramps serving the belly radiator. Parked behind are three SNJ/AT-6/Harvard trainers.

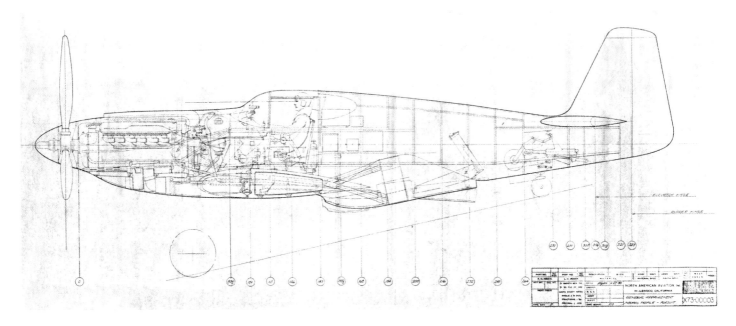

Above: This drawing produced by Al Algier of the NAA NA-73, dated 27 June 1940, may be one of the earliest drawings of the Mustang.

Above: This photograph of the NA-73 is significant for the set-back upper nose intake and what appears to be retouched insignia and a deletion of the tail wheel strut, all done to make a display print probably in order to impress an official.

Above: The NAA contract to produce Mustangs exclusively for Britain required two of them to be given free to the Air Corps. S/n 41-039 was the second of them and was later was painted in AAF markings and camouflage but it never left the U.S. and was declared "unnecessary" in 1942. However the NACA tested the Mustang I — also known as the XP-51 — long after 1942.

Powers said R-40C would probably bring "...100 different designs" ranging from conventional-type small airplanes to "...non-conventional tail first, pusher types." Furthermore, the X-1800, XIV-1430, R-2160, H-3130, and V-3420 in-line, liquid-cooled engines were expected to be available. With words put to paper in 1940, the Air Corps planned to have tail-less, pusher-prop fighters mass-produced in 1942. Although R-40C gave the single-engined interceptor its biggest boost by the Air Corps' most senior officer, the off-course effect of introducing radical, pusher-prop fighters seriously delayed attention to the P-51. R-40C failed to field a fighter. Luckily, the P-38 was being produced in 1942 and the sudden development of the P-47B promised success.

Briefly, R-40C brought forth the Bell XP-52, Vultee XP-54, Curtiss XP-55, Northrop XP-56, Bell XP-59, McDonnell XP-67, and Republic XP-69. Only one of them had a prop in the nose and none had an engine in front of the pilot. (Note that the XP-59 and XP-59A were two entirely different designs submitted by the same manufacturer. The XP-59 was a pusher prop and the XP-59A was America's first experimental jet aircraft. Similar designations were afforded for reasons of secrecy.) Although the Vultee XP-54 won the competition, none of the experimental types in R-40C was judged worthy of production because of a lack of good engines and because war had begun.

Stop-Gap Fighters

When Japan bombed Pearl Harbor in December 1941, war forced the realization that the USAAF had no world-class fighters to take into combat. The P-39 and P-40 were all that was to be available until the end of 1942, a year later. Stop-gap fighters were called for. From that urgent search came the

magnificent XP-47B. The P-47B was fast, but slow-climbing and it became possible only because the Air Corps allowed a substantial change in engine production from in-lines to radials at Pratt & Whitney. Besides the P-47B, the USAAF encouraged Curtiss to develop its stop-gap types, the XP-53/XP-60 Series and the bulky XP-62.

The R-2800 Engine

Following Hitler's drive into Poland, Mussolini had vanquished defenseless Ethiopia and Japan had staged a genocidal war in China. It was apparent that fascist regimes intended to rule the world. The Materiel Division realised that the Air Corps would soon be drawn into war without having a single-engined interceptor worth sending into combat before 1942. The in-line engine development program and R-40C were not going to produce results quickly enough. In May, 1941 Brett told his Division to study: "...*the possibility of the utility of the air cooled engine in pursuit aircraft. The directive was the result of a discussion with Mr. Lovett, apparently indicating the Allison engine was a washout and that the Air Corps should now immediately take advantage of air cooled possibilities.*" [24]

Even today, this pre-war statement is astounding. The Air Corps had relied upon the decade-old V-1710 in-line program, and had no other in-line engine of unquestioned reliability with which to power its next fighters. Assistant Secretary of War for Air, Robert Lovett, gave advice which was ignored and the "washout" V-1710 was continued.

From seemingly out of nowhere came a miracle. The firm of Pratt & Whitney (P&W) had been developing a variety of in-lines, especially the much sought-after X-1800. By the middle of 1939 it still was not ready. P&W declared itself unfamiliar with in-lines and in early 1940 asked for and received a release from further development. Around 1930, P&W had hired L.S. Hobbs, a research engineer and he and others had solved the matter of getting the air stream to cool more than one row of cylinders. As a result, P&W had built the R-2800 radial which was soon achieving the amazing output of 1,850 hp, nearly twice the horsepower of the V-1710. The R-2800 was the greatest American aircraft engine of World War Two. It saved the USAAF fighter development program from stagnation. On 1 October 1940 the Navy's Vought F4U Corsair powered by the R-2800 was the world's first radial-engined fighter to reach 400 mph in level flight. The AAF sat up and took notice.

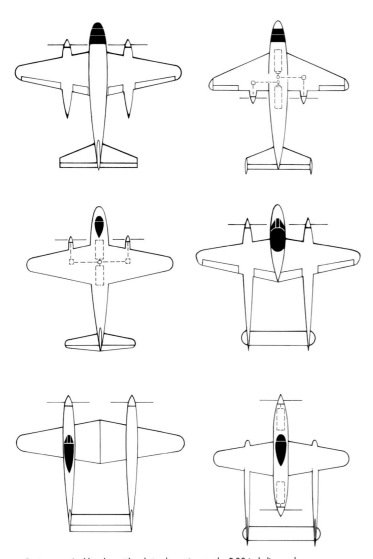

Designers at Lockheed considered six alternatives to the P-38 including pusher-prop, push-pull, mid-fuselage, and tractor-prop which was to lead to R-40C and the pusher-prop design revolution.

P-47B

The Republic Corporation – formerly Seversky – had offered the XP-47 design which was to have been powered by the V-1710 if built. However, when the P&W R-2800 became a definite possibility, Republic quickly offered its XP-44 interceptor, designed to be powered by that magnificent engine. The XP-44 looked so promising that the Air Corps ordered 80 and on 9 September 1940 the project was announced. Days later it was dropped and the somewhat similar XP-47B was put under contract on the 13th. The first XP-47B interceptor was rolled out in November 1941 and at 412 mph, was faster than the 395 mph P-38! The old radial-versus-in-line controversy was resurrected.

Intended to be the stop-gap fighter to fill a void between the P-38 and whatever in-line-powered fighter might come next, the P-47B Thunderbolt excited Air Corps officers because it had a turbo. Careful work by Alexander Kartveli and his masterful design team, produced a great fighter large enough for a turbo and eight wing-mounted .50 caliber machine guns. The immediate success of the P-47B allowed fighter development planners to draw a relaxed breath. However, despite the use of a turbo, the P-47B proved not to be the fast-climbing, single-engined interceptor on everyone's mind, and so the search continued.

Air Defense

General MacArthur's support for an intercontinental bomber in 1931 and Claire Chennault's success in 1933 in countering friendly bombers in an exercise, were benign events compared to a shooting war. It was time to think about defending America. The real reason why American air defense got a boost was because in 1938, Germany, then involved in intimidating confrontation with neighboring countries, sent its extremely long-range Focke-Wulf Fw 200 *Condor* four-engined airliner on an around-the-world demonstration tour. It flew non-stop from Germany to America. The flight certainly alarmed Arnold, who reasoned that the *Condor* could be made into a bomber, which it was. General Marshall authorized Arnold to create an air defense system. Maj. (later, Maj. Gen.) Gordon Saville devised a new form of air defense and in early 1940, Arnold invited Saville to speak at a gathering of senior officers at Mitchel Field to convince the Army to support it. A year later Saville wrote a paper entitled *Air Defense Doctrine*.

Saville pointed out to his captive and unfriendly audience that in World War One it had been normal to keep a large number of fighters aloft in a "search patrol" or on an "air alert" and those methods had increased maintenance, burned up fuel and tired pilots. Saville's most convincing contention was that aircraft have mobility and can be flown to any point to provide defense. Anti-aircraft artillery and barrage balloons were immobile and static. With availability of the P-38, air defense seemed viable to the Army and an air defense system was created. By 1943, an organization of squadrons of fighters was called a "Group," but in 1940 it was known as an "Air Defense Interceptor Group."

The search for a single-engined interceptor, which began with the XP-46 and was jumped ahead to the XP-52, then progressed through a series including pusher-prop types reaching to the XP-69 in sequence, was but one unsolved problem faced as war began. Other projects crowded in upon each other as the Air Corps struggled to identify, define, and give priority to deserving programs. With so much emphasis aimed elsewhere, the XP-51 was ignored. More importantly, escort development became mired in inconsequentiality.

Above and inset: Inspired by the Douglas DS-312A design, the Curtiss XP-55 Ascender was a radical but flight-proven answer to R-40C and the question of how to install more guns in a fighter's nose. Note the canard on the nose and the wing-outboard vertical stabilisers and rudders. The wing was swept for reasons of balance, not speed.

Left: The angle of this photo emphasises the XP-55's forward canard, swept wing, and outboard vertical stabilisers and rudders.

Below: The "business end" of the XP-55. The guns are installed in the nose and the protuberances forward of, and on the canard are pitot tubes.

Above left and above: The Northrop XP-56 flying wing fighter runs-up its engine. Powered by the R-2800 radial engine, the XP-56 was not a success due to an aft center of gravity and slow speed. The photograph above shows the aircraft's gull wing to advantage.

Left: Northrop technicians refuel the XP-56. Nose-to-nose with it, is the Vultee A-35 Vengeance dive bomber which the AAF disliked intensely.

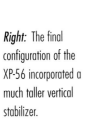

Right: The final configuration of the XP-56 incorporated a much taller vertical stabilizer.

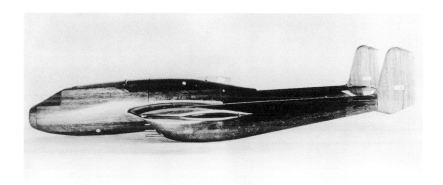

Left: R-40C inspired many pusher-prop, buried-engine and twin-boom fighter designs. Bell's XP-52 and XP-59 — neither were ever built — were the first to utilize those attributes so that heavy armament could be placed in the forward areas. In this case, the left-side grouping of six cannon is apparent. The XP-59 is not to be confused with the jet-powered Bell XP-59A Airacomet.

Left: The Republic XP-69 three-quarter scale wind tunnel model was as far as development of that airplane progressed. The AAF preferred development of that company's XP-72, a 490 mph prototype which flew but which was not produced.

Below: The Republic XP-69 in the NACA Langley wind tunnel. Note the contra-prop and the huge belly scoop.

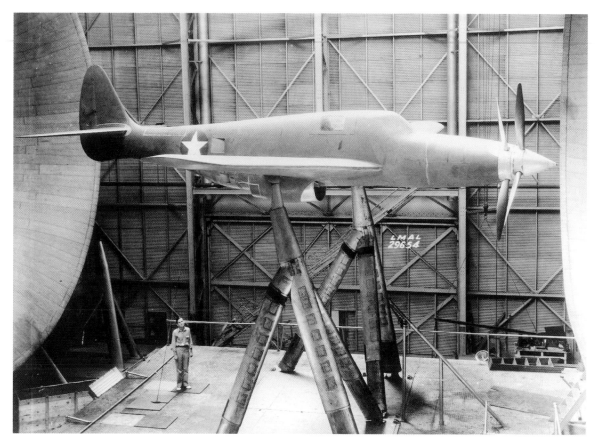

Above: Bearing similarities to the Lockheed SR-71 Blackbird, the McDonnell XP-67 Moonbat had its fuselage and nacelles blended into the wing to form a very elegant head-on view.

Left: Perhaps the most striking and most promising of all R-40C designs, the XP-67 was a triumph for the McDonnell Aircraft Corporation which, up to the construction of the XP-67, was a parts manufacturer. The XP-67 featured wing-body and wing-nacelle blending, similar to that designed on the SR-71 Blackbird.

Right: McDonnell's XP-67 in a close-up photograph shows its clean lines and aerodynamically aesthetic appearance. The aircraft was an incomparably masterful achievement for its designers and for the company's owner, whose creations are still flying today.

Above, left, and below: The McDonnell XP-67 Moonbat had a single exhaust duct on each engine; ducting all exhausts from each engine into a single rear efflux provided some jet-type thrust. Unfortunately, in September 1944, the Moonbat suffered an in-flight engine fire and made an emergency landing, but burned up once on the ground.

Below: The McDonnell XP-67 design originated with an engine mounted in mid-fuselage driving shafts through angled gearboxes to the propellers, but later was built with two engines.

Right, below left, and below right: Three views of the winner of R-40C, the Vultee XP-54 (41-1210).

Above, and left and bottom: With the Vultee emblem beneath its cockpit visible in the photographs above and at bottom, the slim, elegant XP-54 — winner of the R-40C design competition — appeared to be a very promising fighter, but it was overrated and its various "improvements" simply resulted in it becoming overweight with a subsequent drop in performance. In 1940, the Air Corps planned to install cannon in the noses of single-engined fighters and thus forced the development of pusher-prop and mid-fuselage-mounted engine types of designs. The twin-boom layout on the XP-54 afforded the placement of its pusher prop at the rear, so freeing the nose for heavy cannon.

Chapter 3

'I do not believe escort fighters can be developed..."

Defining the Escort Type

The vast Materiel Division, with its home at Wright Field in Dayton, Ohio and its Commanding General in Washington, DC, was like an octopus stretching tentacles of power to the farthest corners of the Air Corps. After Spaatz, Chief of Plans, had proclaimed escort was virtually unnecessary, Materiel was asked for its opinion in March 1940. Brig. Gen. Brett, Chief of the Materiel Division and no expert in tactics or a war of maneuver in the air, but an officer whose decisions were loftier than those of ordinary pilots, said the escort would provide *"...accompaniment for protection of bombardment aviation"* by the *"...interposition of itself between the enemy and the bombardment formation."* The escort would repel enemy fighters *"...by effective long-range fire power."* Guns were to be concentrated in *"...the rear hemisphere"* of an escort. [1]

Brigadier General Oliver Echols photographed when he was commander of the Materiel Command in 1940.

Three ideas emerged while the war raged: escorts would stay close to bombers, would fire against the enemy at long range, and guns would be concentrated toward the rear. Of the three, firing at long range meant creating automatic fire control systems, having more than one crew and not maneuvering. Spaatz repeated his previous statements: "I do not believe escort fighters can be developed to accompany medium and heavy bombers over their tactical radius of operations which will be different in overall dimensions than the bombers they accompany. If better armament can be devised for escort fighters for this purpose, the same armament should be put on the bombers." [2]

It was a common belief that only an escort carrying an incredibly large amount of fuel could fly with a bomber and it would have to carry inordinately numerous defensive weapons for a fighter aircraft; but the attempt had to be made. There was an underlying fear of facing a situation which promised high loss rates, since American officers were well aware of RAF losses over Europe in daylight. The mid-1930s belief that bombers were invincible had begun to lose credibility. Hitler's *Luftwaffe* was by then knocking down from the skies virtually any type of RAF bomber operating in broad daylight over France and Germany.

On 27 March 1940, two very important letters were written dealing with the escort issue. Brett wrote to General Arnold and Arnold wrote to the Adjutant General. Brett's set of Military Characteristics governing the escort fighter was agreed upon by Arnold. Arnold stated that the multi-place twin-engined aircraft had to have a range of 1,330 miles and a speed of *"...not less than 425 mph."* Arnold wanted the guns *"...to obtain the maximum fire power in all directions with the heaviest concentration to the rear hemisphere. A minimum of eight weapons are required, at least two of which shall be automatic cannon."* [3]

Arnold intended the characteristics to be "effective" for Fiscal Year 1941. With the range of medium bombers standing at 1,000 miles, Brett suggested a 500-mile minimum for an escort, but Arnold asked for a 2,700-mile range. Arnold knew that not just medium bombers, but also the B-17 and B-24 'heavies' would need protection. He endeavoured to get his subordinates to produce an escort that could fly to Berlin and back to Britain. The *Luftwaffe* had made RAF daylight bombing almost impossible. The AAF had two years to prepare before its bombers could make their first mission to a German city, and that was not enough time. Brett asked Spaatz about the characteristics of the escort and on 26 April 1940 Spaatz said the characteristics *"...were drawn on the assumption that medium bombardment requires accompanying protection. This assumption is open to question particularly when it is noted that weather often will prevent arrival at the objective in formation. If it is thus impracticable for bombardment airplanes to maintain their formation, obviously it is impossible for them to be convoyed by accompanying fighters. Moreover, the present probability of technical advance in providing each bombardment airplane with increased defensive armament makes it desirable that protection for bombardment airplanes be built into the airplane itself. To produce a result which requires intimate coordination between two separate units in the air is a well-known difficulty. Built-in protection avoids this major disadvantage. It is realized that increased defensive firepower built into bombardment airplanes can be accomplished only at the expense of disposable load – gasoline or bombs. In the case of light bombardment airplanes it is likely that the total useful fuel load is not sufficient to provide the desired range, a worthwhile bomb load, and necessary defensive armament. Hence this appears to be, at present, the only clear case in which accompanying fighters may be required."* [4]

In June 1940, General George Marshall, Army Chief of Staff, and the most respected man in uniform in the US, suggested to Arnold that he consider an *"...air cruiser type of aircraft - capable of performing both combat and bombardment missions - fighting in formation to diminish pursuit attack."* (5)

Marshall's words had the force of an order and they came shortly after the time the Lockheed XP-58 was chosen to become the escort that would satisfy Brett, Spaatz, Arnold, Marshall, and above all – presumably – bomber crews.

Bomber Destroyer Escort

As mentioned, Spaatz did not believe escort by small fighters was possible. He was the second-most powerful General in the AAF. No matter, because no officer would have believed in 1940 that a fighter the size of the P-51 could fly to Berlin and back. The P-51 did not have guns aimed to the rear or automatic fire control turrets and never would have. Brig. Gen. Millard Harmon had become recognized as Chennault's heir-apparent as the fighter expert. Arnold was not convinced by Spaatz' escort theories and hedged his bets. In April, Arnold asked Harmon if there should be one type of fighter to destroy bombers and another to escort friendly ones. In May Harmon responded: *"...while the mission of the escort fighter is primarily defensive, its tactics may be either offensive or defensive. When (enemy) pursuit finds it no longer profitable to attack bombers on a collision course from the rear because of defensive strength of either the bombers themselves, or of escort fighters, the development of the long-range gunfire attack from a parallel course or the bomb attack from overhead, may be expected. The escort fighter must be prepared to assault and drive off or destroy forces attempting such attacks and must, therefore, be prepared to operate offensively."* (6)

Left to right: General H.H. Arnold, General George Marshall, Admiral Ernest King, and Bell Test Pilot Bob Stanley inspect an XP-59A. In June 1940, Marshall supported development of an air cruiser, which eventually became the XP-58. Thus, before war began, the Army (and its Air Corps) committed itself to having a longer range in a multi-purpose fighter rather than supporting range extension in smaller fighters such as the P-47.

Harmon added his voice to the chorus asking for a multi-mission fighter. However, he envisioned a fighter which would destroy enemy bombers when ordered, and escort AAF bombers when called upon. He believed that the new type of aircraft – the bomber-destroyer – should also be outfitted as an escort. To require an escort to destroy bombers was not asking much more of it, he assumed. Harmon added that the escort had to have *"...100 per cent fire in any direction; two cannon capable of covering the entire upper hemisphere, (and) provision for using manual control in case of failure of remote gun fire control."*

The escort had to have a speed equal to that of a bomber, an equal radius of action, an equal rate of climb and armament *"...with emphasis on fire in the rear hemisphere. The mission of this type of aircraft will be executed in part in areas in which enemy interceptor fighter aviation will be*

operating." The aircraft would require a defense against *"...at least three hostile units"* and to have fire power *"...at least three times as great as that of the opposing aircraft types."*

This was when Chennault's expertise with the use of maneuver could have been useful. Despite Spaatz' view that the bombers could protect themselves, Arnold, Brett, and Harmon had created a need for a huge fighter that would be weighed down with inordinately large and unwieldy equipment and, therefore, would be as vulnerable as the bombers it would protect. If Marshall's ideas were agreed upon, it would carry bombs. Despite these impossible requirements, the Air Corps went ahead in 1940 with developing an escort which had no future in war. The type of escort fighter imagined was to provide a static defense, like a moat around a castle, and to wait for the enemy to come to it. Kelsey's twin-engined, overload concept once again emerged in fighter design.

On 11 January 1945, General Carl "Tooey" Spaatz (center) was given a tour of the Packard plant by George Christopher (left). Five years earlier, Spaatz created the theory of bomber escort which resulted in the overweight, twin-engined XP-58. He also supported development of four-engined escorts.

XP-58

The Lockheed Corporation's success with the big P-38 was its ticket to selection for designing, developing, and producing the bomber-destroyer escort. In Februar, 1939, Brett suggested to Arnold that CP-39-775 be let, for another twin-engined interceptor, and two X-1800 engines were purchased for the future XP-58. Lockheed built the XP-49 powered by two XIV-1430s which was a modification of the XP-58. The XP-49 flew on 11 November 1942 but it did not perform well and was canceled. By May 1940, the XP-58 had been designated. The Air Corps did not have to pay Lockheed for the XP-58 because a Foreign Release Agreement approved on 17 April 1940 was entered into between the Government and Lockheed whereby an improved version of the P-38 would be developed and delivered without cost, in return for the release of the P-38 for sale to the British. [7]

The RAF had bought a few P-38s but found them unsuitable and never used them in combat, but having bought them, they had also paid for the first XP-58. Design of the XP-58 changed immediately because weight escalated. The XIV-1430s were to replace the X-1800s with the R-2160 and H-2470 being considered. The original weight estimate of 18,500 lb grew to 33,785 lbs and two R-2800s were the next engine type suggested. Eventually the flyable XP-58 weighed 40,294 lbs. The final engine actually used on a flyable XP-58 was the Allison V-3420. First flight took place on 6 June 1944, on D-Day when Allied troops landed in Normandy! The XP-58 experiment not only was costly and late, but the P-51B had been flying in combat for seven months before its first flight, yet no one cancelled the XP-58 until October 1944.

The Lockheed XP-49 was a re-engined P-38 designed and built to satisfy those who wanted a more powerful version of that aircraft. Originally designed with the X-1800 engine, the XP-49 received two XIV-1430s but it was not successful and was canceled in favor of the same company's XP-58. Note that the rear vertical crane support is mounted ahead of the horizontal stabilizer. The reason for this test was to ascertain the strength of the landing gear.

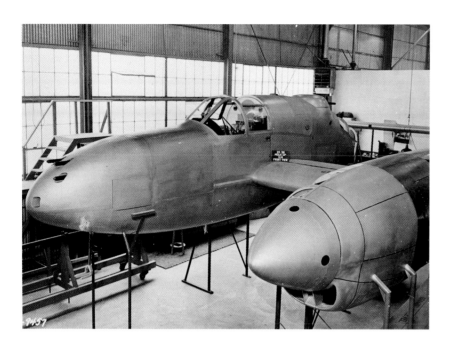

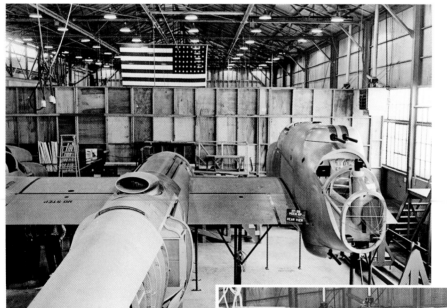

Four views of the XP-58 mock-up, bearing resemblance to the P-38. These close-up photographs indicate the great size of what was to have been the primary AAF escort fighter, but the XP-58 became too heavy and unmaneuverable. However, so long as it was given high priority, other developments were given much less attention. The rear views show the underside, rear-facing gunner's compartment and the upper, automatically controlled turret. The photograph above shows the rear gunner's station; in the back, protruding above and below the housing is the periscope for the remote-controlled turrets.

Above and below: The Lockheed XP-58 was intended to be the AAF primary escort fighter and was the result of much theory in 1940. Expressly required were firepower to the rear, automatic cannon, and a policy of close escort. Continual changes forced excessive weight onto the XP-58 and its lengthy development saw it surpassed by the P-51B, which was far more maneuverable and faster. In the in-flight shot, a test crewman peers from the rear gunner's compartment while his turret — minus its guns — is above and behind him.

Above: The Northrop P-61 night fighter was developed with a variety of weapons including a remote-controlled revolving upper turret which could be directed to the rear. A rear-facing crewman, seated behind the Plexiglas dome aft of the crew compartment, made the design compatible with the need for a bomber-destroyer. The layout of the P-61 is not very different to that of the Lockheed XP-58 bomber-destroyer. Eventually the upper turret was either fixed facing forward or removed and the rear crew seat was unused if the radar operator/gunner seated upward and behind the pilot was the only other crewman.

"Kelly" Johnson had the same problems as did other aircraft designers in finding ways to counter the newly discovered phenomenon of compressibility. As an aircraft in high-speed flight pushes into the air ahead of it, the air becomes dense and compresses. When air over the wing of a World War Two fighter entered the transonic range, the aircraft reached its Critical Mach Number (CMN). Exceeding the CMN could cause attachment of a shock wave and a steep rise in drag occurred, often followed by loss of control and/or break-up of the aircraft. Johnson's P-38 reached its CMN at .67 of the speed of sound – at approximately 450 mph. The P-38 had the lowest CMN of the three main wartime AAF fighter types, which restricted its diving characteristics. The XP-58 was similar and suffered from a low CMN.

The XP-58 was not the only type of bomber-destroyer offered. Hughes Aircraft offered the D-2 which evolved into the D-5. Both were designed to have guns facing to the rear. Ordered in October 1940, the famous Northrop P-61 has been rightfully described as America's first aircraft to be designed from the start as a night fighter. Yet one look at the huge rear-facing Plexiglas enclosure and the moveable upper turret which was remotely controlled, indicates that the P-61 was first designed as a bomber-destroyer escort.

The XP-51 had the highest CMN of AAF fighters which could be dived to extremely high speeds and it was also used as an experimental aircraft after 1945.[8] Models of NAA jet fighter designs were mounted on top of the Mustang's wing and dived to 0.8 Mach. Airflow over the top of a wing is faster than underneath and airflow over instrumented models attached to the XP-51 reached Mach 1.4.[9]

From 1940 to late 1943, American tactical theory was unchanged and an escort fighter pilot was not expected to maneuver or leave the side of bombers. Tactics were changed in late 1943 by group commanders who were dismayed by policy which prevented the destruction of the *Luftwaffe*. Until changes were made, P-47 escorts chased enemy fighters away from bombers and returned alongside quickly, but enemy fighters on the offensive held the initiative – and the advantage. While theory of tactics remained fixed, definition of what the pure escort type itself should be, was not resolved until 1944. The slim little Mustang eventually took over the job only after all other possible fighter alternatives were first given a chance.

XP-71

A last word is in order about the pure bomber-destroyer type. Once the German Focke-Wulf *Condor's* non-stop flight had alarmed the Air Corps and during development of the "escort" XP-58, the Air Corps embarked upon a project for a pure bomber-destroyer. It handed the job to Curtiss, as was customary, after "…considerable concern was entertained lest the Germans attempt to use long-distance heavy bombers of the Focke Wulf type against the United States." [10] Never completely built, the design of the XP-71 was so impressive that it staggers the imagination today. It was to be powered by two four-row, air-cooled R-4360s engines driving pusher props and have a wingspan jusr 20 ft less than a B-17! It was designed from the beginning to carry one 75 mm and two 30 mm cannon. Firing a fixed-mounted artillery piece in the sky at moving targets was considered to be normal in 1940. When asked how it was to be done, on 11 September 1941, Lt. Col. (later, Maj. Gen.) B.E. Meyers told the Army's Chief of Ordnance: "…*the airplane pilot puts the airplane approximately on target, directly astern and at the same level.*"

The pilot was to hold the XP-71 steady, the cannon crewman took range, used a

Major General Bennett E. Meyers — retired on 31 August 1945 — was Echols' spokesperson in 1942 when Echols and Meyers expressed dislike of the P-51 Mustang.

computer to calculate elevation and fuse settings, made final corrections to the flight path through the autopilot auxiliary controls, "… *and at the proper time fires the piece.*" [11]

The concept of the XP-71 as a flying artillery emplacement may appear to have been short-sighted but the threat of enemy bombers was real. Had Germany based bombers in South America, round-trip flights to the USA were possible. Other 75 mm cannon-carrying developments involved the B-25C, XA-26B and XA-38. Eventually a later model of the B-25 carried that cannon but it was used air-to-ground. At the time of interest in using a 75 mm cannon against enemy bombers, all the aforementioned types were considered as "fighters" and development was pushed with vigor.

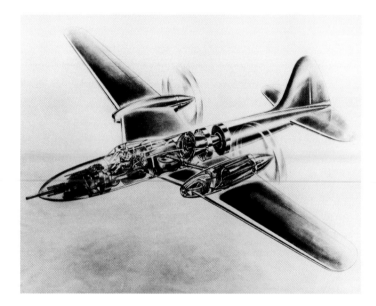

Above: Cancellation of the XP-71 did not end the plan to put a 75 mm cannon in a twin-engined "fighter" and the B-25G and H (seen here) were used in combat against ground targets in the Pacific and European Theaters of Operations.

Above: This artist's cutaway view of the unbuilt XP-71 designed by Curtiss shows the second crewman and the two 30 mm cannon above and behind the 75 mm cannon.

Right: The Curtiss XP-71 never passed the stage of having a few components manufactured, but this wind tunnel model provides a hint of what would have been its massive size, extremely powerful engines and very long wingspan. It was to have been powered by the same engine utilized in the Convair B-36 and the Navy's Goodyear F2G Super Corsair — the R-4360.

The AAF and RAF agreed that development of four-engined bombers into escorts was possible, and in 1941 the Air Corps initiated development of a B-24 into this XB-41 "escort." The XB-41 proved to be unsatisfactory and was not used in combat.

The first alarm of war affecting America's neutrality had been sounded almost simultaneously with the call to develop pusher-prop types of fighters. Trial and error in fighter development was the only pay-off for years of neglect and of higher priority given to bombers. The single-engined interceptor and bomber-destroyer were relatively easy to define and to build prototypes for, but the escort was to continue to bedevil the staffs at Wright Field.

XB-40 and XB-41

While the XP-58 was being developed, the AAF decided to pursue what seemed like the most logical course of action and convert four-engined bombers into escorts! What better escort could there be than the same type of aircraft having the same range? In 1940 the British lost so many daytime, unescorted bombers sent on deep penetrations of the European Continent to the *Luftwaffe* that it was forced into night operations and advised the AAF to do the same. The British did not plan to develop a single-engined, single-seat, long-range escort and thought it could not be done.[12] But Britain and the AAF agreed that a four-engined bomber could be modified into an escort. Even though Britain never tried it, the USAAF did. After Japan bombed Pearl Harbor and brought America into the war, the AAF began a formal program to develop four-engined escorts.

CTI-571 dated 16 April 1942 directed development and in August, Spaatz approved the project. A B-17 was converted and designated "XB-40" and in September a B-24D was ordered for conversion. The B-24, designated XB-41, was a failure when it was tested in 1943 and was dropped.[13] The USAAF proceeded urgently with the XB-40 and a few service-test versions of the YB-40 were flown in combat from Britain starting in May 1943. They were withdrawn shortly afterward.

Conclusions

Following years of opinion that bombers were self-defending, the declaration of a need for escort is dated from 27 March 1940 when the characteristics of the escort were written.

The AAF modified two types of four-engined bombers as escorts. This is the YB-40, a version of the famed B-17 Flying Fortress. In May 1943 several YB-40s were flown as "escorts" on successive combat missions, but this overweight and slow conversion was quickly removed from combat use.

Three years later, bomber crews were sent over Germany without escorts, still believing in the self-defending bomber.

Nothing attempted proved successful until the very end of 1943. Although General Arnold pressed for development of an escort in 1940, planners lost sight of the fact that a fighter pilot's air war is a war of maneuver, as it had been in the First World War. Instead of examining methods of increasing the ranges of single-seat fighters, mass-produced then or later, planners gravitated toward developing types of large, twin-engined escorts carrying very heavy armament and several crewmen, all of which required ever-greater fuel loads. From repeated failure came the fear of never having an escort. Desperation in mid-1943 over the situation led to the character-assasination and replacement of Brig. Gen. Frank O'Driscoll Hunter, Commanding General of the Eighth Fighter Command (VIII FC).

The P-35 and P-36 were obsolescent. The P-39, P-40, and P-43 were becoming obsolete. The XP-52, XP-54, XP-55, XP-56, XP-59, XP-62, XP-67, and XP-69 would not be produced. (The XP-53/XP-60 Series and XP-75 will be discussed later.) The P-38 and P-47 remained as the best fighters in 1943. They were forced to be the escorts of choice. Slowness of production at Lockheed, and demands by Army generals upon the AAF to provide P-38s in all theaters of operations particularly where Army troops were present, prevented there being enough P-38s to go around. If Germany was to be beaten first and bombers were to be operated continuously from Britain to destroy German-held targets, P-38s should have been sent there immediately in 1942 and kept there. They were not. As will be shown, the missed opportunity to operate P-38s in the European Theater of Operations (ETO) through all of 1943 led to high losses of bombers and their crews.

Chapter 4

"Getting all that is possible..."

The Packard Merlin

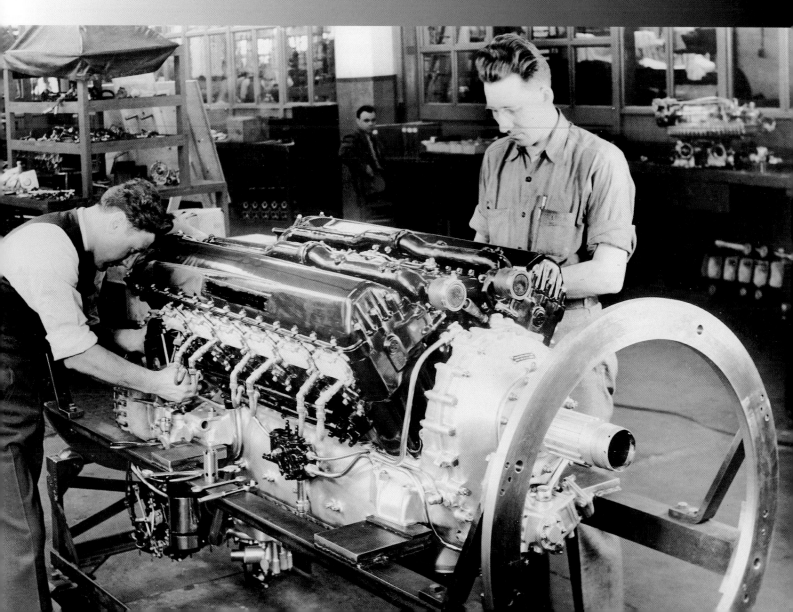

It is accepted that the ultimate escort fighter of World War Two was the P-51 Mustang, but few people know why a British engine powered the best version, or, indeed why that engine was produced in America. The story of the Packard Merlin engine is one full of surprises, even today.

Although consecutive letter designations separate the P-51A from the P-51B, there is a world of difference between the two models. The P-51A and others before it were powered by General Motors' Allison Division's V-1710 and those Mustangs achieved only a modest performance. The P-51B and models after that were driven to incomparably greater performance levels by the Packard Merlin.

In early 1940 Robert Lovett, Assistant Secretary of War for Air, believed the V-1710 to be a washout. Lack of good engines jeopardized improvement of the Air Corps' fighter program because so many developments were based on in-lines and turbos. No American in-line other than the V-1710 was to be available within a short time. However, war and broader thinking took into account previous wishes by American manufacturers to produce Merlins in the US. The lack of other American in-lines was apparent when the Air Corps asked Curtiss to follow the P-40D with an improved version of the aeroplane and the USAAF was forced to consider obtaining a license to produce the Merlin to give to Curtiss. On 17 June 1940 the Advisory Committee to the Council of National Defense helped write CTI-65 which ordered provision "...*for the production of (the) Rolls-Royce Merlin XX as a stop-gap engine in the 1,200 hp class. The Merlin XX will be a substitute for the V-1710 engine in 373 Pursuit Fighters and 885 Pursuits scheduled on the 3,000-airplane program for Fiscal Year 1941.*"[1]

The 1,258 fighters were to be the P-40F and L. Actual orders for the two totalled 2,011. In 1940, the P-40 was the only AAF fighter worth the name. Delivery of the first P-40F came in January 1942 – at about the time the XP-46 was canceled and the XP-51 was not wanted by Echols. Re-engining aircraft was a very carefully considered program because it was expensive, time consuming, and often it did not greatly improve the basic design. However, when re-engining was considered for the highly regarded XP-58 and the XP-60, there was no limit to the number of types of American engines considered. Many officers thought the P-38 should have been re-engined with the Merlin, but the AAF had no intention of doing so despite problems with the V-1710. It would have caused re-design of the engine compartments and slowed an already slow production process. The XP-49 powered by XIV-1430s was an improved P-38, but it was a failure. The designer of the P-40, Donovan Berlin, later complained that the P-40 would have benefited from the Packard two-stage Merlin. The V-1650-3 was not available until mid-1943 and by that time the P-51B was more important.

During the important conference held in Casablanca in January 1943 to discuss the planned Allied strategic bombing offensive against Germany, Lieutenant General H.H. Arnold met with Air Chief Marshal Sir Charles Portal. Arnold held a comparatively lower rank than Portal at the time.

The first contract for the Packard Motor Car Company to build Merlins specified 3,000 units for the Air Corps and 6,000 for the British. Even after Lovett declared the V-1710 a washout, the AAF had no plans for Merlins beyond the 3,000-unit program. In October 1941 the Right Honorable J.T.C. Moore-Brabazon, in charge of Britain's Ministry of Aircraft Production (MAP), received a letter from Arnold who wrote: "*I see no reason why the Packard Merlin production should change from the original plans, that is, with your getting all that is possible.*" [2]

However, it was considered that Packard would produce Merlins only for Britain once the USAAF had obtained 3,000 engines. In January 1942, Arnold told Air Chief Marshal Sir Charles Portal, the British Chief of Air Staff: "*As things stand now though, I see no reason why you can't have all the Packard Merlin contract after the 9,000 contract is finished.*" [3]

(AUTHOR'S NOTE: Arnold was effectively "moving the goalposts"; the 3,000 engines under contract were agreed before the US was drawn into war. Following Pearl Harbor, Packard Merlin production was increased.)

Packard had a fine record in serving the needs of the Air Service in World War One and the company performed just as admirably during World War Two. Jesse and Charles Vincent were brothers who made the Packard name as famous among USAAF fighter pilots as they had among car owners. Jesse was born in Arkansas and in his teens repaired tools on the family farm, including his brother's riding cultivator. He became interested in cars and studied engineering through correspondence courses, then worked for the Burroughs

Corporation in 1903 when Alvan Macauley worked there. Vincent created such a rapid and economical change to the manufacture of adding machines that he was made Superintendent at Burroughs. By 1910 his patents filled a book. He repaired company cars because he wanted to own one some day and he became entranced by cars and engines.

Macauley left Burroughs to work for Packard and persuaded Vincent to join him in 1912. Three years later, Jesse Vincent created his "Twin-Six", a 12-cylinder car engine at a time when six cylinders were normal and Cadillac's eight was thought to be the height of luxury. The smooth and quiet Twin-Six brought a fortune in sales. Packard cars were the epitome of perfection. Its 1936 cars rank among the most sought-after antique vehicles in the world.

Jesse Vincent was a cheerful-looking man of medium height who had an air of genius about him and who could not be confounded by the most complex engineering detail. He was fond of golf and Scotch and was a very-hard working, easy-going man who also skied, flew aircraft and owned a yacht. He drove Packard-powered speedboats and won the Gold Cup in 1922. He died in 1962, one month before Packard ceased to exist as a company.

Charles H. Vincent was born in Missouri in the late 1880s and lived to be 98 years old. He learned to hunt small animals with a rifle to bring meat to the table. He also worked for Burroughs and because of asthma, asked to be allowed to

Charles H Vincent photographed in his ham radio room at his home on the proving grounds of the Packard company in Michigan. Vincent, also a top marksman, was responsible for the final road-testing of every Packard car.

travel west to dry-air states to demonstrate and repair the company's products. He spent 14 months in West Texas as a cow-puncher. He worked for several car makers in Detroit and in 1911 worked for the Hudson car company where he invented the variable venturi carburetor, making it work perfectly by 1915 when he became known as the "father" of

Jesse Vincent loved speed and all things mechanical. The proud man stands before his Stinson Reliant and car on 4 August 1937. He was also a Lieutenant Colonel in the Air Service and as co-designer of the Packard Liberty aircraft engine during the First World War, he was commissioned to oversee its production, establishing the Engineering facility at McCook Field.

Alvan Macauley (right) was Packard's Chairman and his company's V-1650-3 Merlin transformed the Mustang into one of the great developments in aviation history.

the Hudson Super-Six engine. After an absence he worked for Packard and was involved with the Liberty aircraft engine.

C.H. Vincent's home was on the Packard proving grounds in Utica, Michigan where he had a complete Ham radio station. His first love was competitive shooting and he set national records, one of which was a civilian record in the Wimbledon Cup matches which stood for twenty-four years. He became Manager of the Proving Grounds in 1927 and then Superintendent. As Service Manager during Merlin production, Vincent trained the Field Service Representatives who roamed the theaters of war where Packard Merlins were in use. He retired in 1948 as Consulting Engineer.

During World War One, Packard had initiated the writing of a contract to produce America's first combat aircraft engine,

The "Round the World Flight" of 1924 used aircraft powered by Packard Liberty engines. A Packard car is parked at far left.

the Liberty. Foreign delegations came to America in May 1917 to see what they could use in their aircraft. Jesse Vincent of Packard told the Chairman of the company, Alvan Macauley, that having different American companies produce a variety of aircraft engines wasted a good opportunity to make a standard one. America's companies were subsequently organized to produce the Liberty. To ensure standardization, the Air Service commissioned Jesse Vincent as a Lieutenant Colonel. He then created the Engineering Section at McCook Field in Dayton, Ohio and later commanded that Section.[4] McCook Field and its Sections were the beginning of Wright-Patterson Air Force Base and the Materiel Command.

After World War One, Packard produced the LePere biplane for the Air Service, won the Collier Trophy in 1929 for its diesel aircraft engine, and produced some of the finest marine engines in the world through World War Two. No company had a better history of production for the military services and its automobiles were also among the most luxurious in the world. Packard of all America's car makers, performed best in the field of aviation.

When World War Two began, Britain needed many more Merlins than its factories could produce. Britain tried to support French production of the Merlin at the French Fordair company, a subsidiary of the American Ford Motor company, but France was overrun in May 1940. When the American government gave approval of awarding licensed production of the Merlin, the Rolls-Royce of America Corporation had its representatives meet with Brett and Admiral John Towers. One of the representatives met with General Arnold and William Knudsen, Chairman of the General Motors (GM) corporation and Roosevelt's right-hand man, who also headed the Office of Production Management (OPM). Production in America was assured when Knudsen agreed to it.

Henry Ford, Chairman of his company, was approached to build Merlins but Ford was an isolationist and believed that the British would be conquered by Germany and when asked, he refused to build the engine.[5] Knudsen talked with Col. Vincent in June 1940 and Packard agreed to build them. Packard formed its Aircraft Engine Division with Jesse Vincent as Vice President of Engineering; his brother, Charles was named Assistant Service Manager.

After the war, Jesse Vincent wrote a report of Packard's Merlin production. He recalled when Packard was sobered by the enormity and complexity of the engineering problems to be faced in producing the engine: "...we started with the understanding that we were to build the same engine for both governments and ended up with the decision to build engines for the British which were installationally interchangeable with British-built units." [6]

Merlins in Spitfires and Mustangs were not identical. The greatest challenge facing Packard was adapting its assembly-line methods to producing Merlins which Rolls-Royce had produced using time-honored hand-method production techniques. Moreover, differences in the drawings, in basic engineering and in manufacture between the two countries lengthened Packard's task in tooling up for production.

In August 1940, a team from Rolls-Royce arrived in Detroit and told Vincent that Packard "...*should tool up for this improved two-piece*"cylinder block which was not then in production in Britain! After discovering two types of Merlin were to be produced side-by-side and that Packard was to produce a block Rolls-Royce had yet to produce, Vincent and his partners realized the magnitude of the situation Packard had accepted. There was more to come.

In November, Packard made basic drawings but not production drawings for the Merlin XX which became the Merlin 28 in Britain. In the US, the Merlin XX became the V-1650-1 which had a single-stage, engine-driven integral supercharger. In general, the Merlin 28 and V-1650-1 were similar. Packard had to "...*reverse all projected views and include much production information not found on the British drawings*" which "...*did not correspond with the current production parts being used by*" Rolls-Royce. Sample castings sent from Britain "...*were considerably heavier than called for in the drawings.*" Subassemblies, machined tolerances, types of machined finishes, and dimensions of tubing were not included on drawings. Oral instruction and craft expertise were among the shop practices at Rolls-Royce. Bolt tightness at Rolls-Royce was assured by experience and practice. Packard devised a match between printed requirements and tool torque indications.

The most exasperating task in producing engines for the British involved screw thread engineering. "*We found it absolutely impossible to obtain complete engineering information covering these (screw) threads, and it was necessary for us to use our own judgement to a certain extent in arriving at standards.*" Packard measured "...*the actual threaded parts of a British-built engine*" and was comfortable using standardized American screws and bolts in AAF Merlins though the contract specified using British Association (BA), British Standard Fine (BSF), British Standard Whitworth (BSW), and British Standard Pipe (BS), and right and left-handed screws on Merlins destined for the RAF. Thread pitches and threads-to-the-inch on bolts

Using a convoy of Packard saloons (*top*), on 7 May 1941, a group of OPM (Office of Production Management), British Purchasing Commission officials, and US Officers and Ordnance officials visited Packard's Detroit plant (*middle*) to inspect the company's first Rolls-Royce Merlin aircraft engine (*above*).

and screws varied by as much as four values. Changing over to manufacturing dozens of types of screws and bolts by the tens of thousands not found anywhere in America is a story in itself. Packard-built British Merlins presented difficulties to Packard. Such was the stuff of licensed production!

Packard established "...*satisfactory shop practices to eliminate much of the British hand fitting (which) was a task of such magnitude as to constitute one of the very important problems that had to be handled*." Rolls-Royce put a symbol on a drawing indicating a change, without noting where the change was made on the piece drawn. The individual on the shop floor made the change from past experience. Packard made detailed instructions on drawings which eliminated guesswork by American workers.

In the beginning there had been fewer exchanges of information but Vincent recalled "...*starting approximately April 8, 1942, however, the interchange of information was established on a sort of recipirocal basis.*"

The first V-1650-1 was delivered within a year of the contract date. Used on the P-40F, it had an altitude rating of 18,000 ft and a horsepower of 1,150 which later grew to 1,600 hp. The better engine did not improve the top speed of

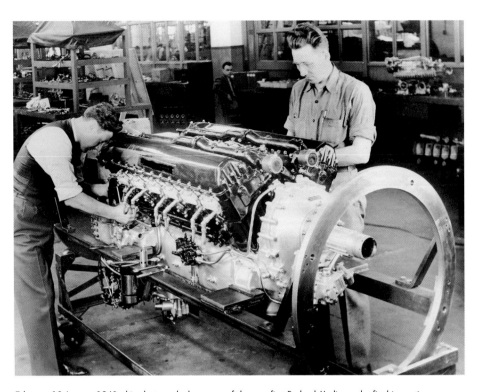

Taken on 13 January 1941, this photograph shows one of the very first Packard Merlins under final inspection.

the P-40F over the P-40E Warhawk and rated at 366 mph the P-40F was 2 mph slower than the P-40E! Weight between the three models was nearly the same at about 6,400 lbs. The Warhawk had too much drag.[7]

The development which changed the air war was the Rolls-Royce Merlin 60. The two-stage, two-speed supercharger in the Merlin 60 which - as the V-1650-3 - drove the P-51B to fame, was a new development made simultaneously in two countries. According to Jesse Vincent: "...in the early part of 1941, Packard and Rolls-Royce started individually to design a two-stage supercharger to achieve the desired altitudes." Packard then "...conceived the idea" of its planetary drive which "...when used with a pre-determined aneroid altitude setting made supercharger impeller changes automatic." On 9 October 1941 Packard proposed to the AAF to develop it, was given a contract, then built and tested the unit. It was installed on a test engine in May, 1942. Packard developed its own two-stage supercharger drive used in the V-1650-3 because the Rolls-Royce engine was in need of "...*extensive consideration of lubrication for front and rear bearings due to the extremely high heat factors imposed by this type of construction. The main supercharger distributing tube was promptly re-*

Packard was one of America's finest automobile manufacturers, but following the outbreak of war, car production ended on 9 February 1942.

designed to ensure adequate lubrication." Vincent stated in his report: "Supercharger planetary pinion bearing wear was found to be excessive in service, causing excessive replacement and some engine failure."

After the war, British experts credited Packard with improvements to the "...carburetor, silver-lead indium bearings, planetary supercharger drive mechanism, and modifications to the coolant pump and camshaft drive." [8]

The two-stage supercharged Rolls-Royce Merlin 60 and Packard V-1650-3 were phenomenally advanced, in-line, liquid-cooled engines. The AAF had started out wanting only 3,000 single-stage engines in the 1, 200 hp class, but no one in the AAF anticipated that Packard would make available a more-powerful two-stage Merlin. Its emergence changed the course of the air war for two English-speaking countries. After Rolls-Royce developed the Merlin 60, General Arnold quickly decided not to give all Packard production to Britain. General Arnold's early and overly generous attitude was revealed in the second contract of 31 June 1942 which called for 14,000

Aircraft assembly at Packard; the photograph was taken on 5 August 1942.

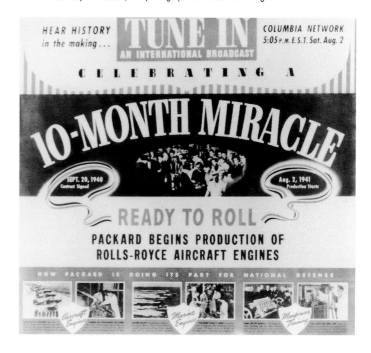

A line-up of Merlins awaiting shipment. These were not V-1650-3s because the date of the photograph was 3 November 1942.

Merlin 28s and only 34 V-1650-1s. But when Rolls-Royce developed the two-stage Merlin 60 which powered the British Spitfire IX and Packard and NAA installed the V-1650-3 in the P-51B, Arnold gave Packard a new contract which

revealed a USAAF need for the two-stage Merlin. On 24 June 1943, Packard's third contract called for 13,325 V-1650-3s. Thousands of British-type Merlins continued to be produced at Packard but by that date, the amazing story of the P-51B Mustang began to unfold before the disbelieving eyes of officers at Wright Field.

The horsepower of the V-1650-3 engine began where the V-1650-1 left off, having the earlier engine's final horsepower of 1,600 at the start which was raised to 1,720 in the V-1650-7 for the P-51D. The V-1650-3 had an operational ceiling of almost 40,000 ft and its full-throttle height was well over 20,000 ft. The first V-1650-3 was shipped to NAA on 17 April 1943 but during that summer, delays affected production which, in turn, slowed production of the P-51B.

Rolls-Royce *designed* the Merlin, not Packard, and aside from Packard's improved supercharger there was Rolls-Royce's intercooler. Rolls-Royce historian, David Birch, stated the intercooler increased "…the pressure ratio and also the charge density" and "…reduced the temperature of the charge on leaving the supercharger. The Allison had no such device." The intercooler had its own liquid-filled jacket and radiator and when the fuel-air mixture left the first stage of compression it entered the intercooler and its temperature

Before the fuselage of the P-51B was deepened to accommodate piping and to achieve smooth aerodynamics, the fuselage of the XP-51B had a pinched-in waist ahead of the belly scoop.

was dropped and the mix entered the second stage. Packard faithfully produced intercoolers for its V-1650-3s.

In mid-1942, British authorities discovered low drag in the airframes of the Mustangs it was operating in combat. The British government wanted to determine if a Rolls-Royce Merlin 65 could be fitted to the engine compartment without major structural changes in order to develop a medium-altitude fighter to complement the high-altitude Spitfire IX. The simplicity and ease of re-engining the Mustang became one of the greatest aviation achievements of the entire war. Birch states the length of the two-stage Merlin was "...just a few inches" longer than a one-stage! It fit almost without modification to the Mustang except to the engine mount! [9] The best in-line engine of the war would drive the previously-maligned Mustang I to become the best fighter of the war.

Major General Charles Branshaw commanded the Materiel Centre at Wright-Patterson Field by 1943.

The Allison used a downdraft carburetor and the Merlin, an updraft. The Merlin's greater horsepower required a larger engine-coolant radiator. Larger-diameter coolant-carrying pipes necessitated a deepening of the fuselage beneath the pilot's seat. The differences between the Allison-Mustang and Merlin-Mustang were far greater than cosmetic.

Replacing the Allison V-1710 with a Merlin 28 would not have provided a broad jump in performance and Rolls-Royce proceeded directly to re-engine a Mustang with the Merlin 60 Series. Allison had considerable difficulty in developing a two-stage supercharged version of the V-1710. It did not appear until 1945 and the length of the two-stage Allison would have been too long for the engine compartment of the Mustang. The NAA P-82/F-82 Twin Mustang was powered by 1,860 hp two-stage Merlins. In 1947, the F-82E version had less powerful two-stage Allisons.

By 1944 Packard produced the V-1650-3 almost exclusively for AAF Mustangs. The total of all Merlin contracts was 75,986 but Packard produced just over 50,000 by war's end. In August 1944, at the height of the air war, Packard exceeded schedules by 25 percent and was congratulated by the AAF. Seven models were in production in that month. British plants produced approximately 150,000 Merlins.

During 1943, Packard's production was slowed, seriously affecting P-51B production. In March, the Air Service Command gave a higher preference rating to spare parts for the one-stage Merlin than for the engines themselves. That forced removal of 100 two-stage engines from production to make room for spare parts production. Col. John Sessums, Jr., told Echols there would

be a delay in two-stage production and that spare parts "...would cost us 1,200 complete engines." [10] Spare parts for the V-1650-1 in the obsolescent P-40F and L delayed the far more superior P-51B. At about the time the V-1650-3 was to be mass-produced, 2,000 Packard workers staged a walk-out on 26 and 27 May 1943 and the entire workforce struck from 3-8 June. Echols told Arnold that 600,000 man-hours were lost, as well as 240 one-stage and 150 two-stage engines in June and July. [11]

When the AAF finally recognized the superiority of the P-51B, it ordered Packard to increase production beyond its capability. However, when the AAF realized Packard was producing to its limit, it began an unsuccessful search for other manufacturers to produce Merlins. Maj. Gen. Charles Branshaw, Commanding the Materiel Center at Wright Field, told Echols, whose office was in Washington, "...*three thousand additional single-stage engines have been added to (the) Packard schedule for production to start in March, 1944. This eight-hundred a month single-stage production will decrease two-stage production by (the) same amount and will delay two-stage expansion.*" Engines produced for Britain and a new schedule put into effect by the Joint Aircraft Committee (JAC) on 10 June 1943 "...*added additional Packard engine requirements to a program already in arrearage. Production planning by Packard (was) an impossibility. Failure of (the) engine sub-committee to provide for (the) diversion of Packard capacity from (the) British beyond six hundred two-stage engines per month indicates lack of coordination between committees.*" [12]

A low preference rating had been given to both the Merlin and the Mustang with top priority going to the P-38, P-47, V-1710 and R-2800. Because of this, machine tools were not afforded equitably and in a timely manner. The Technical Executive in the AAF told Echols that hope lay "...*in raising (the) preference rating of P-51B airplanes to at least group two. Suggest further the possibility of placing 1,000 P-51B airplanes on a special project in preference group one in order to further insure (sic) tool deliveries to Packard.*" [13]

Casting difficulties arose in making parts for superchargers on the V-1650-1 and -3. Aluminum castings required a special Materiel Specification and Packard made its own, after believing "...*our forgings showed appreciable weight saving over the same parts made by others, and with grain flow carefully controlled to make the most use of available material.*" Packard told the JAC that difficulties "...*are due to*

Left: 19 October 1943: a female inspector at Packard examines the jewel-like precision applied to the manufacture of the twin turbines for the compressor mounted on a common shaft for the Merlin's two-stage supercharger.

Below: By 19 October 1943, the Packard aircraft engine assembly plant was in full production of Merlins.

Right: The plaque above the Packard Merlin needs no explanation. Thousands of Merlins were produced for British aircraft at the Detroit car maker's plant.

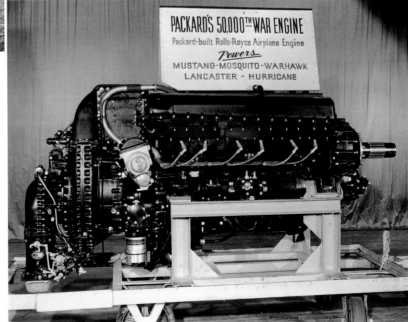

In September 1943 at Willow Run Airport, the workers of the Packard company presented P-51B "Sky-Clipper" (s/n 43-12484), the Mustang they paid for from their own pockets, to the AAF. The aircraft was marked with its serial number, inscription, and an engraved metal dedication plaque bolted to the armor plate. It went on to serve in Europe with the 354th Fighter Group where it was flown by Lieutenant Bruno Peters from Michigan. The Crew Chief was Laurence A. Wood, Assistant Crew Chief was S/Sgt. Joel O. Scruggs, Armorer was Sgt. W. Clifford, and Assistant Armorer was E.C. Cagley. In the photograph (*below*) Captain Brill, the pilot sent to receive the Mustang, shakes hands with a Packard official.

the complexity of the V-1650-3 castings and somewhat to the nature of the alloy being used." By August, 1943 Packard was finding difficulty in getting additional subcontractors "...*for anti-friction bearings, sleeve bearings, castings, forgings, carburetors, and magnetos.*" Until Packard's preference rating was raised, it was afforded second-best treatment.

By now, the P-51B was almost recognized as potentially one of the best fighters in the world. It was being tested but had not entered combat and was not considered as an escort type. Yet plans to produce 500 more P-51Bs required Packard to produce 700 more Merlins per month and that was impossible. Lt. Gen. Barney Giles, Chief of the Air Staff, was told by Echols that Merlins for 500 more Mustangs, added to production for the British, called for "...*a production rate of 3,500 Merlin engines per month from United States production. The all-out capacity of Packard is 2,700 a month.*"[14] Britain reduced its needs for two-stage Merlins and by late August 700 Packard Merlins per month were allocated only for P-51Bs.

Machine tools still were needed in August for V-1650-3 production and W.M. Packer of Packard told Col. (later, Maj.

Gen.) Benjamin Chidlaw that the low urgency rating and spare parts production would cost the "...*equivalent of 1,050 engines a month.*" There was a $44 million dollar backlog of work and spare parts production was greater than "...*38 percent of engine money value.*" [15] By late August Chidlaw said the P-51B was placed in "*Group II of (the) Aircraft Preference List*" and Packard began to receive machine tools. The P-47 was dropped to Group III.

Vincent took pride in world speed records established during the war by aircraft powered with Packard Merlins. On 12-13 May 1944 Col. Clair A. Peterson flew a P-51D from Los Angeles to New York City in six hours, 31 minutes and beat Howard Hughes' record of seven hours, 28 minutes set in 1937. Two Mosquitos set a trans-Atlantic record flying from Labrador to the British Isles in six hours, 46 minutes. They were powered by Packard-built British Merlins.

The intolerable engine situation which was apparent in 1940 improved by 1943 with the R-2800 and the Merlin. The story of the Packard Merlin precedes that of the North American P-51 simply because change was made to engine production prior to when change came to the Mustang itself.

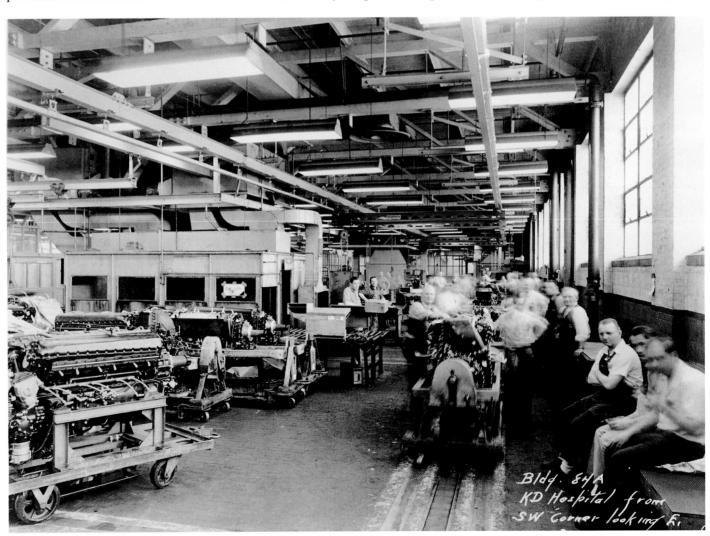

25 May 1945: the war in Europe was over but fighting continued in the Pacific and at Packard on that day, the Merlin production line was still running.

Chapter 5

"Unsatisfactory for combat"

Echols' Resistance to the Mustang

In 1940 Oliver Echols was angered by NAA's agreement to design a fighter rather than build P-40s. One of the facts of life is that military organizations control sections of industry and many manufacturers owe their existence to military contracts. The Materiel Command in 1940 had lost control of NAA and Echols neither forgot nor forgave that. When the Mustang became the subject of a possible buy for the Air Corps in 1942, Echols tried to stop NAA's production of fighters for the US. It may be recalled that the Ryan company built Charles Lindbergh's famous aircraft, but in the year prior to Lindbergh's famous flight, T. Claude Ryan flew his monoplane M-1 in a sporting race against Air Corps De Havilland biplanes and beat them. Ryan – a Reserve Lieutenant – was told by a General that he would regret having upstaged the best fighters the Air Corps had. Despite the superiority of the M-1 and Lindbergh's aircraft, the Ryan company was refused contracts for many years.[1] In 1942 Echols followed a precedent because he wanted to "punish" NAA.

Oliver Echols was described in 'Who's Who' as a trouble-shooter.[2] He graduated from the Virginia Military Institute in 1913, joined the Army, was trained in Field Artillery, and became an Aerial Observer who saw combat in World War One. From 1926 he began a series of assignments as a student. He later became Chief of Technical and Engineering Facilities and spent nineteen years in and around Dayton, Ohio and Washington, DC. He was a pilot who relished control of other men. In September 1944 the merger of Materiel with the Air Service Command formed the Air Technical Service Command (ATSC), headed by Echols' old nemesis, William Knudsen, who had been commissioned straight out of civilian life as a Lieutenant General. Echols' higher military aspirations were ended and he found he was in control of only a portion of the newly-created ATSC. Echols' final job in uniform was as an official in General Dwight Eisenhower's Military Government in Germany after the war. As a civilian, he became Chairman of the Northrop Corporation in the early 1950s and, strangely, hired Ed Schmued who became Vice President there. While at Northrop, Schmued created the concept of the lightweight jet, the N-102 Fang, which was not built but led to the T-38/F-5. Echols and Schmued were replaced by a new leadership at Northrop in 1957.

Major General Oliver Echols attempted personally to stop production of the P-51 following the end of initial supply to the RAF.

Five months after the NA-73 made its first flight in October 1940, the Air Corps sent Capt. Morris J. Lee out to California to fly it. On March 22 1941 Lee's report was used by Materiel to indicate its disinterest in a fighter having modest armament and low-altitude capability. The Air Corps wanted the P-40F. Lee's entire report, brief and to the point of being a snub, stated:

"1. In case of turnover, exit difficult.
2. With left 10 mph crosswind take-off not satisfactory.
3. Controllability too stiff and very little movement to get action.
4. Windshield gives distorted vision due to curved glass.
5. Unsatisfactory for combat.
6. No rear vision." [3]

A British Project in America

The Air Corps had given the V-1650-1 to Curtiss for installation in the P-40F. Rolls-Royce and Packard had begun to develop the two-stage Merlin 60/V-1650-3 for production and the Materiel Division was aware of the exact physical dimensions and weight of the proposed engine a year and a half before Packard sent the first one to NAA. While at Curtiss, Donovan Berlin wanted the V-1650-3 for his P-40. In January, 1942 Echols wrote Arnold that *"...the P-40 series cannot feasibly accommodate the present Rolls-Royce Merlin 61 or the proposed stepped-up Allison engines without major modification to the aircraft design."* [4] Echols' letter came just before the month in which he tried to stop the Mustang. The AAF would have put the V-1650-3 in a P-40 if it had fit. Through the long summer of 1942, British favor for the Mustang together with the availability of the Merlin created a superb match in timing. It was a coincidence that the Mustang and the V-1650-3 appeared simultaneously.

In 1940, the NA-73 was a British project and the XP-46 was all-American. According to Project Pilot, Capt. (later, Lt. Gen.) Ralph Swofford: "I had Pursuit and we had one project, the XP-46."

Swofford was interested in the NA-73 and he "...met a number of times with Ed Schmued and other NAA personnel to keep in touch with progress and problems. I do not know who made the initial decision that the AAF 'had no requirement' for the P-51; I just know that those were the words we received." When asked if procurement of the P-51 was considered, he replied: "…we made our recommendations, often in a loud voice, but they were not always approved. With specific regard to the XP-51, since this was a British project, our role was limited and understandably so." [5]

Shortly after Capt. Lee's report downgrading the P-51, the Air Corps was renamed the Army Air Forces. The Air Corps did not want the P-51. The initial British order for 400 Mustang Is had been signed in early 1940. The BPC ordered another 220. In 1941, to handle foreign orders, an office at Wright Field known as Defense Aid was created in response to President Roosevelt's view that "…the defense of the United Kingdom is vital to the defense of the United States." The office was opened in May 1941 and was superseded by the Office of Lend-Lease in Washington, DC in October of that year. Defense Aid "procured, stored, issued, and transported supplies and equipment for beneficiary foreign governments." [6] When the BPC asked for a further 150 Mustangs, Defense Aid Contract DA-AC-140 was signed on 30 June 1941. These were to be Mustang IAs with four 20 mm cannon. On 9 September 1941, General Arnold wrote to General Marshall recommending to Roosevelt that "…*the Anti-Axis Pool shall receive all aircraft produced under Defense Aid.*"

Eventually, 57 Mustang IAs from DA-AC-140 found their way into the USAAF. As of 1 June 1942 "…*two hundred fifty-seven P-51s were scheduled for delivery to Great Britain.*" On 15 June the Directorate of Crew Training – AFACT – reported: "*On the basis of April 30th, RM-80D estimates that this will permit delivery to the AAF of 57 P-51s*" for the Directorate of Ground Support – AFGRS. Writers have asserted that the Defense Aid contract for 150 Mustangs is proof that the USAAF had ordered 57 P-51s before war began and that the USAAF had always wanted the Mustang. That is not true. Shortly after the Japanese attack on Pearl Harbor, the

US took possession of a few dozen aircraft sold to foreign buyers in the interest of national defense but later let most of them go to buyers. In mid-1942 – after General Arnold kept the Mustang production line going for the USAAF – 57 Mustang IAs were retained in order to familiarize USAAF personnel with an aircraft which was to be produced for the USAAF starting in very late 1942. Writers use contract DA-AC-140 as proof that Mustangs had been under a USAAF contract all along. From DA-AC-140, 92 Mustang IAs went to the RAF, 57 were kept and one was unaccounted for in records. The Mustang IA was designated P-51 in the USAAF.

In 1941, the USAAF did not want the Mustang but the government's Release for Foreign Sale rule required that the AAF receive two Mustang Is for free from NAA which were designated XP-51. The USAAF had so little interest in one of the two that it handed serial number 41-038 to the NACA in December, 1941; 41-039 sat at Wright Field awaiting testing of the XP-46.

XP-60

Glenn Curtiss and his company had impressed the Army and Navy with his fine aircraft early in the 20th century and Curtiss himself is as revered in the US as are the Wright brothers. By 1940, the Curtiss company was almost automatically handed new contracts, while other companies pleaded for business. In the same month – October 1940 – in which the NA-73 made its first flight, Curtiss received orders for two prototypes for what was to be a stop-gap fighter design designated XP-53. General Arnold had realized that the fighter situation was not going to improve because production would not make fighters available until 1942. Arnold needed a stop-gap fighter that would fill a void until more P-38s arrived.

The Curtiss P-36 and P-40 were already production items and the XP-37, XP-42, XP-46, XP-55 – and now the XP-53 – were experiments Curtiss was allowed to try. NAA had been forced to pay Curtiss for NACA belly scoop technology, but Curtiss did not have to pay the NACA for laminar-flow wing design technology used on the XP-53. The Air Corps decided the XP-53 should be re-engined even before it was completed. The unfinished XP-53 was to have been powered by the XIV-1430 but the AAF gave Curtiss the Packard V-1650-1 and redesignated the airplane as the XP-60. The XP-60 made its first flight on 18 September 1941. The USAAF handed unlimited opportunity to Curtiss to jump itself into the modern age with fighter design, but Curtiss did not and the P-40 was its last "good" fighter. Shortly after the war, a failed Curtiss jet fighter was the very last design and the company went out of business.

Some indication of how highly the AAF thought of Curtiss is shown by a contract that was signed on October 31, 1941 for 1,950 P-60As, a full year before the XP-60A flew for

As a captain, Colonel Ralph Swofford was Project Pilot on the XP-46.

Above: This Curtiss XP-60 (Model 90) was derived from the XP-53 (Model 88) which was not built and was to have been an improved version of the failed XP-46. Curtiss' designer, Donovan Berlin, was given use of the two most recent features – the laminar flow wing and the Packard V-1650-1 engine – with which to come up with a winner, but he failed.

Below: The Curtiss XP-60 with Packard V-1650-1 Merlin engine.

the first time! In the entire history of the Army and Navy to that point in time, no other aircraft design had been promoted in advance with such confidence and no other aircraft was promised such vast military funds in advance. The fervor engendered by the contract drew officers into believing the XP-60 would be the new wonder weapon. The XP-60 was the USAAF's way of helping Curtiss over the problems with the XP-46. Probably on orders from Materiel, Capt. Lee had extinguished interest in the Mustang in order to enable Materiel to provide funding for the Curtiss P-60As.

The first Republic XP-47B was rolled out two months after the flight of the XP-60. It was an immediate success. In January 1942, the AAF realized the potential of the XP-47B, canceled the contract for P-60As and told Curtiss to produce P-47Gs. Despite having the greatest aircraft production capacity in the US, Curtiss could build no more than about 500 P-47s. The reverse of what had been expected of NAA – to produce another manufacturer's designs – fell upon Curtiss.

High-ranking AAF officers lobbied forcefully for re-introduction of the cancelled P-60A. The XP-60 series was spun off into an endless list of prototypes, no two of which looked alike. Some of the XP-60 series were adapted for consideration by the Navy as the XF14C-1 and XF15C-1. Five possibilities of powerplants were assigned by the AAF to the XP-60 series: V-1710, V-1650-1, XIV-1430, XIV-2220, and R-2800. The XP-60A first flew in November 1942; the XP-60C in January 1943; the XP-60E in May 1943, and the YP-60E in July 1944. Cancellation of the XP-60 in 1942 did not mean the AAF was without compassion for Curtiss. The Curtiss XP-62 was contracted for, in Arnold's office. It also failed.

War Begins

Within days of Japan bombing Pearl Harbor, General Arnold understood that he had to have more aircraft and not necessarily the best ones. He could not afford to wait for the XP-54, winner of the R-40C competition, or for P-60As. The P-47B was given high priority. Arnold issued a directive stating: "…*we will err on the side of having more of the older models on order than*

Left: Yet another in the XP-60 stop-gap fighter series. This is the XP-60 (Model 95B) which was not significantly different to the XP-60C.

Below: This rare photograph of the XP-60A shows the installation of experimental "Bucholtz" landing gear. The aircraft's resemblance to the P-40 is apparent. The landing gear may have been nothing more than a contraption suited to moving around aircraft that were awaiting "real" landing gear.

Below: The Curtiss XP-60A shown on 14 October 1942. Curtiss designers changed from use of a belly scoop on the XP-46 to a return to the chin-mounted scoop seen on an earlier Curtiss fighter, the obsolescent P-40. Merely on the strength of the reputation of Curtiss, the AAF ordered 1,950 P-60As before this first one flew. Conversely, because Arnold had little regard for NAA's ability to experiment with fighter design, when the Mustang was re-engined with the Merlin, no Merlin-Mustangs were ordered. The P-60A was eventually canceled and Curtiss was ordered to produce P-47Gs.

Brigadier General Patrick W. Timberlake is seen here receiving a decoration whilst serving in North Africa. By 1944 he had advanced his responsibilities following his tour in Materiel.

appears to be necessary to cover the gap between termination of present orders and the production of new models." [7]

When the AAF gave the V-1650-1 to Curtiss for the P-40F and XP-60, the XP-51 – powered by the V-1710 – was excess. The AAF had no plans to order Mustangs for itself once production for the RAF ceased towards the end of 1942. In February 1942, James Kindelberger, president of NAA, wrote to Arnold saying of the 770 British Mustangs ordered: *"...approximately 220 have been delivered and the production rate is now 78 per month. It is our duty to point out that the time has come, if not actually past, when continuity of production of this model can be maintained. If additional airplanes are ordered at once, the new features can be engineered and incorporated and comparatively little loss of production will result. If such an order is not forthcoming, arrangements will be made to dismantle and store the tools and the plant will be re-arranged to produce only B-25 airplanes."* [8]

Sometime near the end of 1941, NAA had allowed pilots from the nearby 79th Pursuit Squadron of the 20th Pursuit Group to fly Mustang Is. Maj. Thayer S. Olds, CO of the squadron, reported on 2 January 1942 to the Commanding General of the IV Interceptor Command saying he and his pilots had nothing but praise for the Mustang. Two pilots of

the 79th PS – Louis S. Wait and R.C. Chilton – later became test pilots at NAA. Lt. Homer Sanders liked it so much he later criticized the USAAF over the Mustang. The Army wanted ground support aircraft and after receiving Kindelberger's letter, Arnold decided to keep the NAA line producing some versions of the Mustang for the AAF.

The Mustang Should Not Be Continued

General Arnold may not have been aware immediately of all the actions of his Chief of Materiel, Echols, or perhaps Arnold had delegated supreme authority. Despite Arnold's December 1941 directive to err on the side of producing older models, Echols retained an attitude of opposition toward the British for the largesse of Lend-Lease, and to NAA for confounding the plan to produce P-40s for the BPC. Oliver Echols was not only proud of running the huge and powerful Materiel Division, but he was also willing to contest the opinions of everyone around him.

On 3 March 1942, Lt. Col. P.W. Timberlake, Echols' Assistant for Procurement Services, told his Chief in the Production Engineering Section that a cable from London said all Mustang Is were temporarily grounded because a control column clevis had failed. [9] On 4 March a representative of NAA wrote to Echols to propose *"...a Ground Attack version of the P-51"* to the AAF. NAA was producing four P-51s and four B-25s per day at the time of the letter. NAA expected to complete production for the RAF in *"July 1942"* and if the AAF did not want the P-51, *"...certain stages of production will be discontinued within sixty days."* NAA believed the AAF did not want the P-51 because *"...it will interfere with B-25 production."* [10] The letter did not reach the Materiel Division in time to prevent Timberlake from trying to stop Mustang production altogether.

In late February or early March 1942 the Air War Plans Division (AWPD) required NAA to produce Mustangs as dive bombers. The head of the AWPD was Col. (later, Maj. Gen.) H.A. Craig. Lt. Col. Timberlake, sent a memo dated 5 March 1942 to Craig intending to stop the Mustang once British contracts were fulfilled. Timberlake wrote:

"1. As a result of investigation of the proposal to a board of officers in your office last week with the view of utilizing the P-51 as a dive bomber, the following is submitted. 2. It is the opinion of the Materiel Division that the production of the P-51 airplane at Inglewood should not be continued for the following reasons: a. No engines are immediately available due to the planned increase of production of Bell P-39s to 600 per month. b. A potential loss of two B-25s per day would result if the P-51 line is continued at Inglewood. c. A development project is

required to convert the P-51 airplane to a dive bomber, requiring special study of the dive brake design, bomb racks, and cannon installation. 3. The Materiel Division is making a study with the view of setting up the P-51 production line in Kansas City when engines and GFE are available.[11]

Timberlake did not explain why Mustang production would have affected B-25 production or why P-40s built at NAA would not. When NAA had been handed the job of building P-40s for the BPC, it was never thought it would affect B-25 production.

Lt. Col. Ford Fair, recorder for the President of a Board of Officers, sent a memo to Timberlake on 9 March, stating: *"...the following additional information relative to the P-51 adoption as a dive bomber is requested to amplify statements in your memorandum March 5, same subject."* Where Timberlake said no engines were available, Fair asked: *"...would engines be available by August, September or later and approximately what month?"* Where Timberlake said two B-25s per day would be lost, Fair asked: *"...would the potential loss of two B-25s per day appear in 1942 or 1943 and approximately what month?"* Where Timberlake wanted a development project, Fair asked: *"...is a development project mandatory on the adoption or could manufacturer's guarantees of performance be accepted?"*[12]

On 22 March Timberlake changed his views and pronounced 500 Mustangs could be produced as A-36 dive bombers after the British contract ended late in the year. Timberlake had run up a trial balloon and had given Echols time to firm up his own case for terminating the Mustang. Timberlake warned Craig that *"...from past experience it has been found that manufacturers will guaranty (sic) indiscriminately when they are attempting to make a sale."*[13]

He had a point. Aircraft companies often overstated a design's capabilities in order to secure a production contract. The XP-46 and P-39 were touted as 400 mph fighters and the Douglas drawings for the DS-312A stated it would fly at 503 mph if built. No mass-produced, piston-engined fighter ever exceeded 500 mph (views that the one-off, XP-47J reached 504 mph are open to question.)

Echols Tried To Stop The Mustang

CTI-538 ordered procurement of 500 Mustangs to be manufactured as dive bombers. On 7 April 1942, Col. T.J. Hanley, Assistant to the Chief of the Air Staff, sent a memo to his Chief, Harmon, advising:

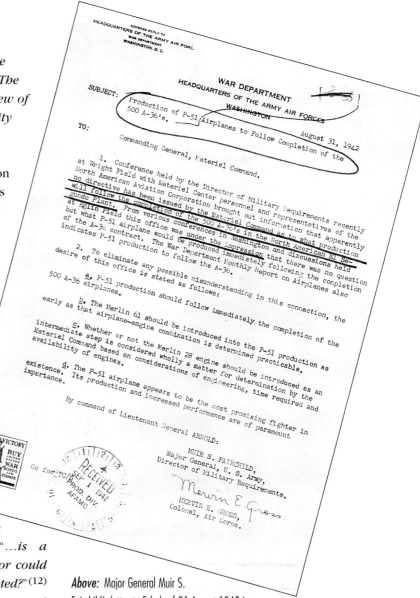

Above: Major General Muir S. Fairchild's letter to Echols of 31 August 1942 in which he stated P-51 production should follow immediately after the completion of the initial order for 500 A-36s.

"a. The maximum number of dive bomber types procurable in 1942 on present contracts was 842.

b. The only possible source of additional interim planes in 1942 was a ground attack dive bomber modification of the NA P-51." Hanley recommended that Echols *"...be directed to initiate a conversion project for the P-51 to a dive bomber type with a view toward augmenting dive bomber production during 1942."*[14]

Harmon approved it. On 16 April Hanley's directive was sent to Echols and on 19 April Maj. Gen. Muir Fairchild, Director of Military Requirements, sent a formal Requirement to Echols to procure 500 A-36s saying: *"...it is desired that the P-51 airplane be converted to an interim dive bomber, without waiting for completion of the dive bomber conversion project."* Fairchild hoped to have some Mustangs produced as fighters: *"...those produced without dive brakes can be used as fighters, fighter bombers, observation airplanes or in operational training units.*" [15] Fairchild had shown brief interest in the Brewster XA-32 dive bomber but on 14 April Fairchild reversed himself and got in line to have A-36s instead. Echols told Fairchild: "...*the procurement of (the XA-32) type is to be made in lieu of other types, such as the A-24, A-25, A-31 or the dive bomber version of the P-51.*" [16]

In the chain of command, Echols took direction from Fairchild. Shortly after, Echols received orders from two superiors to have NAA build A-36s. Echols relented and the A-36 was put under contract. Maj. B.E. Meyers, ever loyal to Echols, who after the war paid dearly for indiscretions, told the Technical Executive that a directive from Fairchild was not "...*iron-clad in any way*" and Materiel's plans would be final. [17] What that meant was Echols would follow to the letter the order for 500 A-36s and ignore the opportunity to produce some Mustangs as fighters.

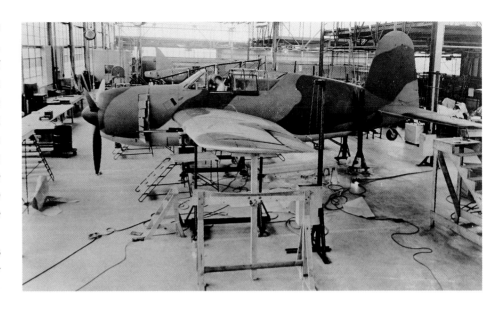

Above: The mock-up of the Brewster XA-32. The date on this photograph — 9 May 1942 — indicates that Echols tried to stop the Mustang before its replacement, the XA-32, was flying. Noteworthy are the vertical stabilizer, the placement of the horizontal stabilizer, the absence of exhaust stacks, British-style camouflage, and fixed tailwheel. The three-bladed prop was replaced by a four-bladed version. The AAF was transitioning from dive bombers to attack fighters, and from Observation types to Tactical Reconnaissance aircraft. The XA-32 represented both transitions. On 30 April 1943 the specification for a dive bomber was changed to that of a ground support type, and AAF dive bombers were a thing of the past, except in the tactical deployment of P-47s and others.

Below: The Brewster XA-32 made its first flight in 1943 and in this photograph the resemblance to Brewster's Buffalo is apparent. Note the four-bladed prop and the Brewster-style retractable main landing gear. Multiple exhaust stacks and high, horizontal stabilizer placement are noteworthy, as is the AAF paint scheme. Heavy armament distinguished the XA-32 from the XP-51.

A-36 and other Dive Bombers

The Air Corps had operated dive bombers but wanted better ones. The Navy operated the best dive bombers and the Air Corps was able to share in production. In October 1940 Meyers told the Adjutant General that the Air Corps wanted *"...160 Navy dive bombers of the SBD-2, NA-44, 2-PA, and NA-50 type."* [18] Two were NAA designs. Douglas SBDs were purchased and redesignated A-24s. In January 1942 when America went to war, President Roosevelt told Morgenthau, his Secretary of War, that he wanted 11,000 *"...light, dive, torpedo, and scout bombers."* [19] One month later, Meyers involved the USAAF in a reciprocal agreement with the Navy for *"...3,000 Curtiss A-25 type aircraft at the same time (the Navy) contracts for 3,523 SB2Cs."* Meyers said the AAF wanted an aircraft *"...that more nearly fits the needs for a ground support weapon"* indicating that he and others were less interested in the dive bombing technique of putting bombs on targets using single engined aircraft. [20]

With the outbreak of war, the Army and its AAF sought its own designs and did not want to rely upon the Navy. One

NAA test pilot Bob Chilton demonstrates the dive brakes on the A-36 for the photographer. Note the "alligator-jaws"-type of belly scoop. The upper half of the dive brake appears from this side view as a white line under the cockpit.

officer, Col. Kenneth B. Wolfe, Chief of Production Engineering, liked the high speed of the NA-73 and said it should replace the slow Vultee A-35 dive bomber. In response, NAA created the A-36 (model NA-97). The high speed of the Mustang drew Wolfe's everlasting support.

The USAAF wanted dive bombers that were fast enough not to have to be escorted by fighters. A-24s, which entered combat in February 1942 and A-25s, were too slow. A total of 863 A-24s and 900 A-25s were taken out of combat zones and used as trainers or target tugs. The same fate awaited 583 A-35s used by the AAF. The withdrawal of what were supposed to be front-line attack aircraft left a void which had to be filled.

The AAF separated itself from procuring Navy aircraft and ordered prototypes of two dive bomber designs meeting USAAF specifications. The Brewster XA-32 was powered by the R-2800 and was flown in 1943. Two Vultee XA-41s ordered in the winter of 1942 were powered by the huge R-4360 and first flight came in February 1944. On 30 April 1943 the dive bomber and fighter programs were combined as fighter-bomber missions. Neither the XA-32 nor the XA-41 were put into production.

After the issue of whether or not to procure Mustangs was resolved, a contract for 500 A-36s was signed. On 1 February 1943 Col. Ralph Stearley, Director of Air Support,

asked the IV Support Command to conduct a flight comparison examination between an A-24 and an A-36. The March 1943 report stated that the A-36 was 200 mph faster than an A-24.[21] The Army gave great support to procuring the A-36, a fast air support type of fighter, and paved the way for future Mustangs. Two combat groups of A-36s operated in the Mediterranean Theater of Operations (MTO) in 1943 and 1944.

P-51A

The A-36 might have become the main ground support aircraft of choice in the AAF but NAA made steady improvements to the basic design and before the end of 1942, offered the P-51A (NA-99) fighter version of the Mustang armed with machine guns. In August 1942, Kindelberger offered to change "... *the 500 A-36 airplanes to the P-51 type.*"[22] On 9 August, Arnold decided that the first 500 Mustangs would be A-36s and P-51As would follow. The USAAF was less interested in the P-51A as a low altitude fighter than the Army. A contract for 1,200 Mustangs had been signed on June 25 and it absorbed the 500 A-36s but the contract did not specify what model would fulfil the remaining 700 specified. The P-51A was now in great demand because the Army wanted thousands of some type of ground support fighter. Two thousand dive bombers that were failures had to be replaced because the USAAF had depended upon the A-24, A-25, and A-35. Army pressure to have a fast ground support type placed pressure upon mass-production of the P-51A.

Friction

The Materiel Command grew inordinately large and powerful as the war spread into a global conflict. Holding firmly to its prerogatives, Materiel fostered thorough testing of the XP-46 and let the XP-51 gather dust until approximately April 1942. It was Materiel's responsibility to supply new aircraft to the large Air Forces Proving Ground Command (AFPGC) at Eglin Field in Florida. Once engineering tests were completed at Wright Field, Eglin Field was supposed to receive fighters to test them for combat suitability. Echols refused to delegate authority to Eglin. Until late 1942 or early 1943, the P-51 was not given a second opinion outside of Wright Field which had expressed its displeasure in Capt. Lee's

The report prepared by 4th Interceptor Command on the test performance of the Mustang in trials conducted with the P-40 and P-66. It is noteworthy that USAAF pilots were flying the P-51 in late 1941.

COPY OF A COPY

CONFIDENTIAL

OFFICE OF THE COMMANDING GENERAL
4th Interceptor Command
Riverside, California

EL

SUBJECT: Performance Report on North American Mustang Fighter

January 8, 1942

"A"

TO: The Chief of the Air Corps, Munitions Building
Washington, D.C.

1. Attached hereto is a confidential report on performance of the North American Mustang Fighter as compared with Army Air Force P-38-D, P-40 and P-66 Pursuit Airplanes.

2. While not complete, it is believed that this comparative report should be of extreme interest to your headquarters in view of the fact that the figures shown are actual performance in the air under identical conditions.

3. While it is appreciated that the procurement plans for aircraft for the United States Army Air Force can not be predicted upon reports of this nature, the undersigned considers that comparative data of this type should be given serious consideration in taking over Lend-Lease Equipment scheduled for other Nations.

/s/ Wm. Ord. Ryan

WM. ORD. RYAN,
Brigadier General, U.S.A.
Command.

WOR:jh

1 Incl:
Performance report Mustang Fighter

20,000 Feet				
Mustang				
P-40	2300			
P-66	2300			
Mustang	2500	21.5		
P-40	2300	23.5		
P-66	---	25	205	
Mustang	2500	24	196	
P-40	2600		195	
P-66	2600	30	222	
	2500	25.3	210	
		29.8	238	
		32.5	215	
			220	

Note: In these tests the airplanes were flown wing to wing; actual airspeeds were the same. The large variations shown in the column for indicated air speeds do not apply to this test.

The Mustang Fighter climbed from Long Beach Airport to 25,000 feet in a few seconds less than thirteen minutes.

The Mustang Fighter indicated an airspeed of 288 MPH at 39.5 manifold pressure at 3,000 RPM at 20,000 feet altitude.

The landing characteristics of the Mustang are excellent.

In combat between the original P-40 type airplane and the Mustang Fighter, apparently the P-40 can turn very slightly inside the Mustang, but with its superior performance the Mustang can engage and break combat at will.

In accelerating from wing to wing position with a P-40 flying at top speed the rate of separation of the Mustang from the P-40, has to be seen to be believed.

- 2 -

CONFIDENTIAL

A P-51A photographed on the ramp at the Eglin Field Proving Ground Command, Florida, on 21 May 1943. Note the rear door open on the belly scoop. When Eglin Field received its very first P-51As in early 1943, this particular Mustang was one of those tested. Its ease of handling, long range and high speed prompted Eglin's test pilots to praise the aircraft, something that Wright Field's test pilots would not do. Because of friction between Wright Field and Eglin Field's Proving Ground Command, Wright Field provided the only reports about the Mustang until early 1943. The first written report issued from Eglin about the aircraft provided the first American praise written or spoken about the P-51A.

March 1941 report. One year after that, Echols tried to stop the Mustang after RAF production ended.

In April 1942, Brig. Gen. Fairchild told Brig. Gen. Grandison Gardner, Commanding General of the AFPGC to "*...test the armament installations on all production aircraft.*" Eglin would get the "*...first or second article (aircraft) produced, as soon as engineering tests are completed at Wright Field.*" [23] Materiel did not send P-51s to Eglin through most of 1942. Even though British Mustangs had been in production in the US since 1940, no Eglin test pilot got his hands on one. No AAF pilot outside of Wright Field knew if the P-51 was good or bad and Capt. Lee expressed that the XP-51 was unacceptable.

Eight months after Fairchild's directive, Gardner again asked for "*...nine older-type fighter airplanes, such as the P-39D,*" saying Fairchild's procedure "*...has never been implemented*" and "*...airplanes have not been received until production was well under way or very nearly completed.*" [24]

The situation grew so bad that sometime after March 1943 Col. (later, Brig. Gen.) Morris Nelson, Chief of the Air Defense Branch of the Requirements Division, pointed out that "as an example of the delay in the completion of reports (from Eglin Field, a report on the P-38F had been requested) the final report is dated March 6, 1943. The P-38H is already beginning to supersede the P-38G." [25] The P-38F had already been sent to a combat theater in mid-1942 but not until nine

Above: Col. Morris Nelson, seen here as a Brigadier General, pinpointed the result of the Materiel Command denying Eglin Field's Proving Ground Command the aircraft it needed to test and about which it needed to write reports. Nelson also objected to the use of fighters as bomb-carriers, and supported use of the P-51B as an air superiority fighter.

months later was Eglin's report available. The same thing happened to the P-47B.

Few remember that the P-47B was developed as an interceptor and it had short range. There is some certainty that Echols did not give Eglin time to test P-47Bs prior to combat introduction in March, 1943. Eglin was unable to prepare a timely report about actual combat radius of the P-47B and a major crisis arose when P-47s were unable to escort bombers to distant targets in mid-1943.

The friction Echols generated by building walls of non-communication between Fairchild above him and Gardner below him, was to foster widespread disinterest in the Mustang as a fighter. It attained the early, lasting, and unfavorable reputation of a ground support tactical type. Echols remained close-mouthed about the XP-51, A-36, P-51, P-51A, and P-51B and refused to allow subordinates to praise them. Those loyal to Echols found ways to criticize the Mustang. Instead, Echols was buoyant about the P-38, P-47, and XP-60 and took extreme personal interest in the General Motors/Fisher XP-75 which will be examined later.

When first produced for the USAAF as a dive bomber, the Mustang received notice as a low-altitude, tactical weapon. Through all of 1942 and most of 1943 it was never considered as an escort for bombers. Only after the British regarded it as a fighter aircraft did the AAF begin to take notice.

Above: As a Brigadier General, Major General Grandison Gardner commanded the Proving Ground Command at Eglin Field.

Chapter 6

"We are completely sold on the Mustang"

The British Requirement

As the first-user of the Mustang, the Royal Air Force appreciated the capabilities of the aircraft sooner than the USAAF. The first production British Mustang I was ready at NAA in April 1941 and in October the first machine arrived in Britain. In January 1942 an RAF squadron began receiving Mustangs and in May combat operations began. During the disastrous Dieppe raid on 19 August, an American flying with No. 414 Squadron, Hollis Hills, was the first Mustang pilot credited with an aerial victory. By January 1943 nearly 700 Mustangs were operated by Great Britain.

RAF Fighter Command had won a victory known around the world as the Battle of Britain during the summer of 1940 and although the Hawker Hurricane was available in greater numbers during the battle, it was the Spitfire which emerged as the British fighter to be reckoned with. In early 1941, Germany introduced its superb Focke-Wulf Fw 190 A which was superior to the Spitfire V. In late 1941 a Spitfire V airframe was mated to a Rolls-Royce Merlin 61 and by mid-1942, the elegant, fast-climbing Spitfire IX retook the advantage.

A Rolls-Royce test pilot, Ronald Harker, was invited by the RAF to fly a Mustang I in April 1942 and after a brief flight at Duxford one month prior to the introduction of the Spitfire IX, Harker declared that the Mustang could perform much better if it was re-engined with the same Merlin 61. By April 30, 1942 Harker had discovered a previously unknown fact and said if the Mustang had "*...a powerful and good engine like the Merlin 61, its performance should be outstanding, as it is 35 mph faster than a Spitfire V at roughly the same power.*" [1]

Even though the Mustang weighed more than the Spitfire, it used less power to fly faster. No one knew why, but the airframe had very low drag. It was not until 1951, long

A Mustang of the RAF peels off from the rest of its formation during a training flight. These high-speed aircraft, built in the USA, were used in low-level attacks on enemy territory. The photograph has been censored to exclude squadron codes, but the aircraft are possibly from No. 2 Squadron. Note yellow wing bands used for identification purposes, to avoid confusion with the Bf 109.

after the war ended, that Richard Whitcomb of the NACA discovered his area rule principle which states that an inward-curving portion of a fuselage above the wing joint will prevent the air streaming around the fuselage from colliding with air passing over the wing, causing turbulence and drag. The Mustang's fuselage had flat sides while those of the P-38, P-47 and Spitfire were fashionably rotund. The Mustang also had the highest Critical Mach Number of any piston-engined aircraft of the war and the lowest drag.

Harker's discovery was dismissed in the US because in April, Echols had attempted to stop Mustang production once RAF contracts were completed. Harker persuaded Rolls-Royce's Director and General Works Manager, Ernest Hives, to re-engine a Mustang I with a Merlin 60. In May 1942 Hives met the Air Ministry for the first time to discuss the re-engining idea but Merlin 60s were being reserved for Spitfires so the Merlin XX was considered. [2] A Mustang I was sent to Rolls-Royce's modification center at Hucknall at the very end of May.

Hives convened another conference with the Air Ministry for June 1942 Because the issue of re-engining brought forth increased communications between NAA and Rolls-Royce, one of the men required to be present was Maj. Thomas Hitchcock, Jr., America's Assistant Military Attaché at the London Embassy. Hitchcock came from that strata Americans once referred to as "high society" and was from a family which mixed socially with the Roosevelts. He was born in 1900 and by 1917 wanted to be a fighter pilot in the Great

This Mustang I, "Scrappy", was flown by Flight Officer Merlin R. (Bob) Kerher and is seen here at Gatwick on 28 June 1943.

War. His father received help from former President Theodore Roosevelt and Tommy was able to join the famed *Lafayette Escadrille*, a unit of American combat pilots in French service. During one air battle Tommy was shot down, captured, later escaped, and returned as a hero.[5] Between the wars he was the world's finest polo player. He played in all but one international competition between 1921 and 1939 and each time his team won. He became equally determined to be a fighter pilot in the Second World War and arrived in Britain in April 1942, just in time to observe the mating of the Merlin to a Mustang. Hitchcock first flew a Merlin-Mustang on 6 November 1942. Later in the war he was assigned to a staff position in the Ninth Air Force. He learned how to fly the Mustang and felt compelled to learn more about its stability problems, when it was fitted with a new fuselage fuel tank giving the aircraft a rear center of gravity. On 12 April 1944, during a test flight he was unable to pull out of a dive and died in the crash.

Tommy had calm eyes, a direct look, a frank appearance, and an unassuming and relaxed manner. He was muscular and

Thomas Hitchcock, Jr., the world's greatest pre-war polo player, was from a family on speaking terms with President Roosevelt. Hitchcock was unafraid of Echols and was prepared to confront him with Wright Field's disinterest in the Mustang.

mixed well with all types of people. He exuded determination and self-respect. Tommy was the right man in the right place to promote the Merlin-Mustang to disbelievers in America.

Witold Challier, Rolls-Royce's Performance Engineer at Hucknall and a Polish exile, began furnishing statistics and graphs starting on 8 June 1942 which demonstrated that for both the Spitfire V and Mustang I to fly at 350 mph it took 260 more horsepower for the Spitfire to achieve the same speed. Challier said a Mustang fitted with a Merlin 61 would have a "*...speed close to 440 mph at 27,800 feet and (would have) a plus-20 mph advantage over the Spitfire IX.*" [3] The Mustang was predicted to be one of the fastest, highest-flying fighters in the world, if re-engined with a two-stage Merlin. By the middle of June, Challier's facts astounded one Rolls-Royce engineer who said the Mustang "*...has a very low drag for which, so far, there is no very definite explanation.*" [4]

Later in 1942 the Mustang I was the first single-engined aircraft to penetrate German airspace from Britain, giving notice of its very long range. Maj. Hitchcock passed on to his superiors in the US all the data on Mustang operations and conferences and the penetration of German airspace should have been noted by officers at Materiel.

Word of Challier's predictions reached General Arnold who cabled Ambassador John Winant in London to say he was "*...having an immediate investigation made as to the possibility of converting Merlin 28 production to Merlin 61s, with a view of installation in Mustangs if it works out.*" CTI-710 ordered a "*...prototype P-51 equipped with (a) Merlin 61.*" [6] Tommy Hitchcock would have been informed of Arnold's cable.

Britain's officials overcame their need to keep all Merlin 60s for Spitfire IXs because Hives and others viewed "*...with alarm the fighter position for next year.*" [7] They expected that Germany would develop a fighter better than the Spitfire IX. To be prepared for that event, Rolls-Royce developed its Griffon engine, which was mated with an improved Spitfire

Left: Earnest W. Hives (second left), Rolls-Royce's General Works Manager seen whilst visiting the Packard plant on 19 October 1943. Hives, more than any other individual in 1942, was fully in support of mating a Merlin to the Mustang and was convinced that the re-engined fighter would be the best in the world. He wanted a medium-altitude fighter to complement the Spitfire IX high-altitude interceptor. It was Hives' support of re-engining which changed the course of history for the American Eighth Air Force in 1944.

Above: Distinctly identifiable as the XP-51B, this aircraft was modified to carry four 20 mm cannon, but the installation was not carried into production. Note the NAA logo on the vertical stabilizer. This is the second NA-91, later designated XP-78, redesignated XP-51B and changed to NA-101. The wheel well doors are missing and the aircraft has a pinched-in waist. Its serial number was 41-37421. Production P-51Bs had four machine guns, wheel well door and a fuller belly because the pipes to carry coolant to the radiator had to be larger since the Merlin had greater cooling demands than the Allison.

that British excitement would be carried back to Wright Field. The AAF doubted British claims for the Merlin-Mustang and asked Dr. Edward Warner to travel to Britain in August to examine the conversion and assess Challier's figures. Challier put out some new estimates in which he stated the Mustang with a Merlin 61 would have a service ceiling of 40,100 ft and full-throttle height would be 25,000 ft! These predictions astounded believers on one side of the Atlantic and were viewed with skepticism on the other side.

On 23 June 1942 the AAF had initiated a contract for 1,200 Mustangs but it was not signed until 23 August and did not mention a Merlin-Mustang! The 500 A-36s were absorbed in the contract, but Echols did not specify what was to follow them. It was at this juncture that two USAAF camps formed – one favoring the Mustang and one criticizing it. Few officers prior to 23 June would have gambled their careers to support the P-51 and many after that date continued to disparage the British project. General Arnold had initiated formal re-engining of the Mustang in the US but the job was overseen without enthusiasm or alacrity on the part of some key officers. Nevertheless, NAA, awaiting a real Merlin 61, proceeded with re-engining immediately using a mock-up. Brig. Gen. Fairchild pointedly remarked to Echols that "...*no directive has been issued by the Materiel Command as to what production will follow the A-36.*" Fairchild wanted P-51s produced as part of the contract for 1,200 Mustangs and said "...*the Merlin should be introduced.*" [10]

airframe. The redesigned Spitfire XIV appeared in late 1943. Officials were aware in 1942 that there could be a gap between the Mks IX and XIV and interest in the Merlin-Mustang became acute. Because both the Spitfire IX and XIV were high-altitude fighters, re-engining of the Mustang was to be revised to use the Merlin 65, a medium-altitude engine.

At the very end of June, 1942 Hives was "...*depressed about the fighter position, both in this country and the USA*" but he added that "...*we are sold completely on the Mustang. The Merlin 61 goes into it with no alteration to the engine cowling or to the radiator cowling.*" Hives was so hopeful that the Merlin-Mustang would prove to be a good fighter for the RAF that he wanted 250 Mustang airframes shipped from America for mating with Merlins.[8] Sir Wilfried Freeman offered to get 500.[9] Merlin-Mustangs were being test-flown at Hucknall in June.

Starting in July, Hives and other British officials invited Brig. Gen. Frank O'D. Hunter to participate in discussions so

Seven months after Pearl Harbor, a mock assault was staged upon Wright Field and the AAF high command witnessed the exercise. From left to right: General George Marshal, Lieutenant General Frank Andrews, Lieutenant General H.H. Arnold, and Major General Oliver Echols.

Dr. Edward P. Warner of the NACA was perhaps America's most knowledgeable aeronautical scientist in 1942. He was asked to travel to Britain to verify the claims of Witold Challier about the Merlin-Mustang's projected performance.

Brigadier General Franklin O. Carroll (left), as Chief of Experimental Engineering, was enthusiastic about re-engining the Mustang with a Merlin. The identity of the officer to the right is not known.

To break the log-jam of doubt – perhaps on Arnold's orders – Warner, traveled to Britain to verify Challier's claims. Echols was also in Britain in late August. It is worth repeating that the AAF had ordered 1,950 P-60As before the XP-60A had its first flight. Now, predictions of vastly superior performance in the Merlin-Mustang were greeted without mention in the latest contract. Both the Mustang and the Merlin remained in AAF minds as British projects. As if – to the British – American skepticism was not painful enough, the AAF was sending an official to inspect British predictions, indicating that the AAF did not rely upon NAA's scientists as Rolls-Royce had, with Challier. No Merlin-Mustangs would be ordered until Echols was swayed. This was indicative of an anti-British attitude among a few officers at Wright Field and in Washington, DC.

Edward Warner, then the Vice Chairman of the Civil Aeronautics Board, was America's most respected aviation authority.[11] He was a well-tailored man who had graduated with honors from Harvard in 1916, received an MA from the Massachusetts Institute of Technology in 1919, and in 1926 was Professor of Aeronautics at MIT. He joined the NACA, designed the wind tunnel at Langley Field, was the NACA's first Chief Physicist, and was head of Aerodynamics and Flight Research. Dr. Warner verified Challier's graphs, delighting the small cadre in America supporting the Mustang.

Despite Echols' disinterest, Brig. Gen. Franklin O. Carroll, Chief of Experimental Engineering, was not intimidated and on 14 August he told the Technical Executive: "*...we are proceeding full blast with the installation of the Merlin 61 (V-1650-3) engine in two P-51 airplanes. North American has estimated that the first airplane will be ready for flight by October 1, 1942, contingent upon receipt of the engine by September 1.*"[12]

British and American officials inspect the cockpit of an early-model Mustang at NAA. Note that the wing fillet is missing.

Rolls-Royce modified several Mustang Is with two-stage Merlins but included the creation of a deep chin air scoop which ruined directional stability. Mustang X (AM 121) is seen here in mid-1942 at a gathering of high-ranking officials inspecting new equipment. Rolls-Royce's independent decision to re-engine the Mustang with the Merlin was followed by General Arnold's order to re-engine the Mustang in the US. Britain's Merlin Mustang flew first.

In May and June 1942, Rolls-Royce received and re-engined several Mustangs with Merlin 65s and four months later, rolled out the first of them for ground running. The British prototypes were designated Mark X. First flight came in October 1942, one month before NAA's XP-51B flew. Rolls-Royce, not as much concerned with aerodynamics as would be an airframe manufacturer, built a deep chin scoop under the spinner of the re-engined Mustang X, degrading directional stability and requiring fin fillets. NAA re-engined the Mustang and carefully redesigned the airframe, retaining the familiar Mustang profile. NAA's Bob Chilton made the first flight on 30 November 1942. The re-engined Mustang briefly was designated XP-78 but the AAF soon reverted to XP-51B, the original designation.

One of Rolls-Royce's conversions – a Mustang X, serial number AM 121 – was handed to the USAAF's Eighth Fighter Command at RAF Bovingdon on 26 June 1943. USAAF markings and call letters VQ-R were applied.

The Meredith Effect

Those interested in the P-51 continued to debate what it was that gave the Mustang its superior aerodynamic efficiency and uncommonly long range. Six decades after the birth of the P-51, many point to what is believed to have been a mysteriously positive and powerful thrust from the belly scoop. No one has considered the area rule theory.

In 1935, F.W. Meredith of the British Royal Aircraft Establishment issued his report based on research which studied what was called the "air-pump" effect whereby air flowing through a radiator need not cause excess drag if the air exiting the radiator compensates for momentum loss. J. Leland Atwood, who was Chief Engineer of NAA at that time, said he used the report. The first belly scoop on the first Mustang had an "alligator jaws"-type variable-position inlet ramp and a variable exit ramp. The inlet orifice's upper surface was the belly of the fuselage. Atwood believed there would be an advantage in the "air pump"-effect of hot, expanded, higher-volume air leaving the radiator exhaust acting like thrust from a jet engine. Automatic control of the exit ramp was expected to close down the exhaust area at high speed and increase thrust. Atwood said the force of exhaust air "...*increases in proportion to the square of the speed.*"

This NAA company photograph shows cockpit detail on an early Mustang. Note the British-style canopy enclosure.

Test pilot Bob Chilton of NAA climbs into a P-51B-10.

Ed Schmued (left), and Bob Davis, Chief of Wind Tunnel Tests, inspect a model of the P-51B.

Above 200 mph, Atwood said, "*the faster you fly, the more help you are getting.*" [13] Others say positive thrust was achieved only at speeds near 400 mph. Mustang escort missions in 1944 were not performed at 400 mph. Only in violent combat did fighter pilots get near that speed. One author equates thrust achieved at 400 mph to the Mustang having the equivalent of an extra 200 hp. Something other than radiator thrust gave the Mustang its efficiency at speeds used in bomber escort.

Atwood stated that no wind tunnel was available at the time to test up to 400 mph but "models" were used later. Atwood "*...offered sketches and other descriptions of a design with the main radiator placed in the rear fuselage.*" Edgar Schmued claimed that he, not Atwood, placed the radiator there. Atwood claimed that the Meredith effect "*...produced significant thrust by restoring momentum to the air passing through the aircraft's radiator cooling system.*" [14] Another source said NAA "*reports very small drag but no positive thrust.*" [15] The foremost scientist at NAA – Ed Horkey – stated matter-of-factly in the late 1990s that "*...the mathematical work of a British Professor (Meredith) was never used by us at any time.*" [16] Atwood stated that a mere 3 percent loss of propeller thrust or a cost of 40 hp was caused by "his" placement of the scoop. [17] Exhaust stack ejector thrust has been added to sources of advantages in the P-51B.

The new belly scoop which appeared on the P-51B, was a great achievement. Although Dr. Beverly Shenstone suggested separating the scoop intake from the lower fuselage skin, it was Irving Ashkenas at NAA who designed the now-familiar belly scoop on the XP-51B. [18] At first, the scoop caused problems. During flight tests in 1943, Horkey said a duct rumble "*...occurred from the boundary layer air alternately going in and out of the duct.*" Test pilots were less qualified than Horkey to judge the cause of the rumble and when a new full-scale wind tunnel at Ames was available which could test a real aircraft to high speeds, Horkey volunteered to ride in a real

Irving Ashkenas designed the belly scoop for the P-51B which was copied all over the world. Appearing in February 1943, the scoop eliminated boundary layer air from causing turbulence in the orifice.

XP-51 s/n 41-039 with Wright Field's blue arrowhead insignia painted on the fuselage.

P-51B and sat in the aircraft for several runs when airflow reached 500 mph![19] The rumble was eliminated when Ashkenas's new scoop was slanted or scarfed.

No one seems to have considered Whitcomb's Area Rule effect upon low drag and high CMN of the Mustang.

"Not Invented Here"

Two camps, one praising and the other criticizing, had formed. The coming superiority of the new Mustang caught critics back-pedaling to find reason for their original lack of interest. Some committed those tissue-paper reasons to print, saying the Mustang was too heavy to be an interceptor. Rather than take the Merlin-Mustang to their heart and praise American genius, officers loyal to Echols faulted the P-51 for not having gone through Wright Field's channels of engineering scrutiny which all other AAF production aircraft had weathered. It was still a "British" project, "*Not Invented Here.*"

Control of Plants II

Until creation of the Air Technical Service Command led by Knudsen, Materiel was the proverbial 800 lb gorilla that sat anywhere it wanted. Today, no head of a USAF organization wields as much power as there once was in Echols' hands. Under Echols, Materiel set aircraft competitions, chose winners, wrote contracts, decided which companies

produced, demanded compliance from industry, and tested the prototypes. Officers in other departments or divisions which worked with Materiel depended upon Echols' approval for career advancement. No one challenged Echols except Major Hitchcock. Echols actually deferred to Hitchcock.[20]

It would have been natural for Materiel to create friends in industry and to want to control plants to the extent that a smooth-running procurement process proceeded without problems. However, Echols was of the old school of

An unidentified RAF pilot wearing the shoulder patch of the American-manned Eagle Squadron, inspects a Mustang cockpit at NAA, during a visit to the US.

engineering and did not appreciate new scientists such as Dr. Warner, Ed Horkey of NAA or Witold Challier of Rolls-Royce. It must be remembered that America was dragged into World War Two and had cherished its neutrality. Government departments such as the Materiel Command dealing with armaments production were still in their pre-war mind-set in 1942. The Navy and Army labored under an ill-defined system of procurement priorities, and those branches of the military came into conflict with each other over which need was more important. A government-imposed system of priorities emerged out of necessity in late 1942.

One of the systems in need of change was the awesome power of the Materiel Command. Coincidental with government's changes to Materiel was a rising chorus of people opposing Echols' wait-and-see attitude affecting the contract for 1,200 Mustangs and the Merlin-Mustang. Arnold, Fairchild, Kindelberger, Atwood, Schmued, Warner, Hives, Hitchcock, and others disagreed with slow acceptance of the Merlin-Mustang. When the government made its sweeping changes, Echols' power was diminished. He relented and shortly afterward agreed to produce the P-51B.

In late 1942, the government challenged the military's competency to control procurement processes because the wartime system of priorities had not been worked out satisfactorily among the uniformed services by themselves. In November the government removed some of the military's control over industry and put all production and procurement processes under civilian administrators. Roosevelt's changes caused a serious rift to Arnold's Materiel Command which he did not appreciate. Inter-service wrangling over priorities resulted in the creation of civilian overseers.

As 1942 began, so the US began its first year of a second world war. Prior to 1940, American fighter development had been slow but no one seemed alarmed. War suddenly created sharp disagreements over the quality of USAAF fighters. Senator Harry Truman, who would be President from 1944 to 1952, had chaired a committee investigating the defense industry and its first report was published in January 1942. Every aspect of preparedness and fighting ability from barracks construction to raw materials

was examined. The part of the report dealing with fighter aircraft quality was particularly critical of USAAF handling of the aviation industry. Arnold had not farmed out work and allowed the "giants" to make aircraft. The report listed 50 small aircraft manufacturers which were denied contracts. Arnold had listed eight he considered worthy of experimentation with fighters. Truman uncovered unsavory treatment. Direct refusal to offer a contract to one company which could have made one type of product cheaper than a larger company, resulted only because an officer in Materiel did not like the personality of the small company's man. The more accommodating company charged a higher price for the same item.

The media asked openly whether the USAAF had the types of fighters equal to that of America's enemies. Certain very prominent individuals such as Charles Lindbergh praised

A Packard Merlin is lowered into a P-51 engine compartment under camouflage netting at NAA.

Right: This NAA company photograph publicised the fact that Mustangs were to be employed by the USAAF. Note the large serial numbers painted on the aft fuselages.

Below: Barrage balloons float above Mines Field, home of NAA's aircraft production plants. Mines Field later became Los Angeles International Airport. The serial number on the nearest P-51B is 43-12351.

aircraft of other countries. In the worst case of negligence, a sense of racial superiority on the part of some USAAF officers delayed their believing reports stating the Japanese Zero was a superior fighter. American pilots went to war in 1942 not knowing the facts about the Zero which Chennault had forwarded from China in 1940. A war of words accompanied flawed fighter development.

British Projects

Materiel had done everything it could after the "awful summer" of 1940 to end open-armed assistance to Lend-Lease. By 1942 Materiel refused to be concerned with any project destined for Britain which had been tainted by input from British engineers. Aircraft already being produced under contract no longer caused opposition, while mating the Merlin to the Mustang may have been seen as one more example of giving-in to British genius. Materiel's hostile attitude was so unnecessary that after the Truman Committee Report was published, an anonymous USAAF officer endorsed it and wrote a report of his own which was circulated in secret because it was also critical of AAF fighters. The name of that officer is unavailable.[21]

Meyers was told to refute both reports. In August 1942 – the same month when the contract for 1,200 Mustangs was signed – Meyers, trying to justify USAAF procurement choices, exposed the inexpert processes by which an aircraft was procured, stating: "...*the decision as to whether or not the first production model of a new airplane is acceptable for military use is not made upon the recommendation of any one man. There are a number of tests which earlier models of an airplane are put through. The first production model is subjected to thorough flight testing by contractors (sic) skilled test personnel, first to determine how near the airplane meets its contractual guarantees from a purely flight performance standpoint, and the results of these tests are checked by skilled Air Force (sic) test pilots. The next phase of testing is accomplished at the Air Corps (sic) Proving Grounds at Valparaiso, Florida. The Air Corps Proving Grounds is under the Directorate of Military Requirements, and his office has the last say as to whether this particular model is sufficiently qualified to be continued in quantity production.*" [22]

Echols' Materiel Command had frustrated the AFPGC commanded by Gardner, and Requirements, commanded by Fairchild. Meyers and Echols worked hand-in-hand on issuing statements. Meyers said the Truman Committee may have

The Materiel Command disliked the Vultee A-35 Vengeance and most were sold abroad. Here, icicles hang from the wing trailing edge of one of the few used in the USAAF – s/n 41-31377, marked "WW" denoting "War Weary." To discredit the P-51 without saying so, a General officer alluded to an aircraft foisted upon the USAAF without so-called proper development. The officer spoke of the A-35, but he meant the P-51.

referred to "...*the Vultee Dive Bomber.*" Yet the reader may substitute dislike of the P-51 in reading Meyers' rebuttal which described dislike of the A-35. He stated the A-35 (or was it the P-51?) "...*was contracted for and engineered by the British, and with which the Air Forces had no connection until after it was well in production. This airplane was procured on a direct British contract prior to Lend-Lease, and the Army Air Forces were not consulted in the formulation of the initial specification, in experimental flight test, or in acceptance of the production model. This whole project was handled exclusively by the British. When re-allocation of aircraft was effected, the Air Forces found itself with a very poor airplane on its hands. Extraordinary means have been taken to modify this airplane into a usable military weapon with the least possible delay. The first production model of the revised airplane, which may not be entirely satisfactory, will be delivered to the Air Forces shortly. If the revised airplane does meet an essential military need in a satisfactory manner, it will be continued in production, otherwise, it will be dropped and a more effective weapon will be procured in its stead.*" [23]

Meyers let the cat out of the bag by saying "...the revised airplane – will be delivered – shortly." The A-35 was out of production. The Merlin-Mustang was then to be delivered shortly. As regards construction of the Mustang, NAA adhered to the Handbook of Instructions for Aircraft Designers (HIAD) and had built a far superior fighter. After Meyers got that load off Materiel's bureaucratic chest, the AAF went ahead fervently with getting the P-51B into production. The AAF began a formal

Mustang IA (AM106/G) was modified with a special "low attack" wing to carry a variety of weapons including a pair of British 40 mm Vickers "S" guns in underwing gondolas. The Air Corps (which became the Army Air Forces on 20 June 1941) was very interested in having fighters carry cannon up to 37 mm caliber and tested such weapons on the XFM-1, XP-38, and P-39, with only limited success. The next generation of US fighters generally reverted to machine gun armament.

engineering and flight evaluation of the Mustang for the first time, using a P-51A in tests at Eglin Field. The only honest criticisms of it were about the reduced aileron travel preferred by the RAF, and guns jamming. NAA had installed machine guns in the Mustang at an angle canted off the vertical and because firing stoppages resulted, Eglin Field's staff had to make changes to the Mustang's armament installation. However, Eglin's test pilots also discovered extremely long range in the Mustang and wrote a report about it!

By August, 1942 there was no interest in using the Mustang as an escort and its production had only then recently survived cessation. The AAF was still frantically searching for a single-engined interceptor. In the month following the signing of the Mustang contract, Echols

permitted a company which had never designed a fighter, to submit a design for an interceptor. General Motors' Fisher Division XP-75 will be discussed later. GM was not on Arnold's list of fighter aircraft manufacturers. Based on the history of the XP-75, what other conclusion can there be, but that Echols harbored resentment for NAA and continued to bow to preferred larger companies?

Meanwhile, the Army needed thousands of ground support fighters and the P-51A was supposedly the answer. The Office of Ground Support would claim need for every Allison-engined A-36 and P-51A, and when contracts were revised to begin production of the P-51B, the Army wanted it also. The Merlin-Mustang – a high-flyer having extremely long range – was about to become a tactical, ground support fighter.

Chapter 7

"We have nothing but the P-51..."

Without Fighter Protection

While power struggles were fought in Washington between civilian and military spheres of authority, the war continued. The issue of whether or not there was a need for fighter escort for bombers was less important than getting bombers into action. What was to become the mightiest air armada in history – the US Army Eighth Air Force – was formed on paper in America in January 1942 and grew to include over 3,500 aircraft by April 1943. The 97th Bombardment Group's B-17Es were the first of the heavy bombers to arrive in Britain on 1 July, 1942, but by mid-month, the Eighth had no more than 200 aircraft of all types in Britain, including B-24s, A-20s, C-47s, Spitfire Vs and P-38Fs. By October, more B-17 groups had arrived, including the 91st, 92nd, 301st, 303rd, 305th, and 306th. The 44th and 93rd constituted the B-24 groups. During October 1942, most bomber and fighter groups were transferred to the Twelfth AF for the invasion of North Africa, planned for 8 November.

For the short time the Eighth AF was of small size in mid-1942, it was opposed by an enemy operating some of the finest fighter aircraft of the war.

The first Eighth AF combat mission was flown on Independence Day, 4 July 1942 by the 15th Bomb Squadron (Light) using 12 borrowed and unescorted RAF Bostons sent to Holland. Two were shot down. B-17s of the 97th BG were the first of the 'heavies' sent into combat on 17 August to Rouen/Sotteville in France, escorted by RAF Spitfire IXs. There

Brand-new Fw 190 A-1s lined up at Le Bourget, having just been delivered to II./JG 26. The civilian personnel are from Focke-Wulf at Bremen sent to supervise the hand-over to the unit.

were no losses and one enemy aircraft was claimed shot down. The 97th flew more combat missions, and on 5 September, the 301st BG flew its first mission and the 92nd BG commenced operations on 6 September. The first B-24 mission was flown by the 93rd BG on 9 October.

The *Luftwaffe* was a potent force by the time the Eighth AF began combat operations. Germany controlled all of western Europe, was at war in North Africa, and had invaded Russia the previous summer. Most of Germany's numerous day fighter units were based in other theaters of war, but defense of the Channel Front remained necessary. *Jagdgeschwader* 2 and 26 were the first units to receive the new Fw 190 A, both converting from the Messerschmitt Bf 109 in 1941. The *Luftwaffe's* Bf 109s and Fw 190s opposed many missions flown by Eighth AF bombers and their RAF escorts.

By late 1942, the Bf 109 F was a formidable adversary in air fighting, but when Germany introduced the Fw 190A, it tipped the balance of air superiority in favor of the *Luftwaffe* because it was superior to the Spitfire V. Britain countered the latter when it introduced its Spitfire Mark IX in July 1942, first flown by No 64 Squadron. But the Fw 190 A remained a deadly adversary for B-17 and B-24 crews.

America's bomb groups based in Britain were escorted by RAF Spitfire IXs generally, because the four USAAF fighter groups in the Eighth AF – two Spitfire V and two P-38F – were new and inexperienced and they were undergoing training and indoctrination for most of the short time before they too were transferred to the Twelfth AF in October.

Based at Moorseele, Belgium, 6./JG 26 was the first operational Bf 109 *Staffel* to convert from the "E" and the "F"

Two mighty weapons of the Eighth Air Force! While a B-17E of the 97th Bomb Group roars over them, ground crews wave from their trusty bicycles which saved the AAF hundreds of man-hours of time on English airfields.

to the Fw 190 A in July 1941. The surprisingly excellent capabilities of the Fw 190 caused great alarm in the RAF. Restricting information here, to only Fw 190 actions because of its initial supremacy, it must be pointed out that it was German practice to split a *Jagdgeschwader* and base its *Gruppen* at various locations. The first two units to convert operated from bases all along the Channel coast to oppose the Eighth Air Force and RAF Fighter Command's escorts. By June 1941 there were approximately 144 Fw 190s defending the Channel and the figure rose substantially in 1942. Fw 190 units were based at Moorseele, Brest, Audembert, St. Omer-Clairmarais, Maldeghem, Ligescourt, Abbeville-Drucat, Le Touquet-Etaples, and St. Pol-Brias. The Eighth AF and the RAF faced a formidable foe every time the two forces went aloft.

On 6 September 1942, a pilot from II./JG 26 shot down a B-17 of the 97th BG and another *Luftwaffe* fighter pilot downed a B-17 from the 92nd BG. Losses of B-17s remained low, however. It took a lot of courage and skill for a German fighter pilot to attack one of a group of Fortresses bristling with 12 flexibly-mounted machine guns. Many gunners shooting at single Fw 190s or Bf 109s assumed kills when seeing smoke emit from German engines as *Luftwaffe* pilots

added power. Exaggerated victories claimed by gunners on B-17s and B-24s later proved to be highly inaccurate. Nevertheless, the air war had begun for the Eighth AF with an intensity which was not to let up until VE Day in May 1945. On 9 October, one B-24 and three B-17s were shot down, making it the worst day of the early period. Gunners claimed 56 kills that day but post-war records showed that only one German fighter was shot down.

In November when the Twelfth Air Force took command of most units, the reduced-size Eighth Air Force turned its attention toward strategic targets, like the U-boat pens, and also away from more tactical targets.

The most desired AAF fighter was the P-38F, and although two P-38 groups joined the Eighth Air Force in Britain in mid-1942, they were ineffective until after transfer to the Twelfth Air Force and combat in North Africa during November. The P-38s of the 1st FG arrived in June and were gone by November. P-38s of the 14th FG arrived in August and were also transferred in November. The P-38s of the 1st FG flew missions on 29 August and later flew sweeps. Not until 26 September was the P-38 intended for use as a bomber escort. P-38s took off but were recalled and an escort mission was

General Spaatz, shown here as a four-star General, touring the Packard plant on 11 January 1945 accompanied by Packard officials James H. Marks and Colonel Jesse Vincent (right). Spaatz was a Major General in 1942 and at that time declared that the Eighth Air Force did not require escort fighters.

not flown until 2 October. P-38 production contnued to be slow. Pilots had tasted combat in the Alaskan theater in August 1942 and in the South West Pacific Area in December 1942. The P-47 was not effectively introduced by the Eighth Air Force until October 1943.

Excitement felt by senior officers over completion of the first B-17 mission on 17 August without loss of aircraft or life, provided impetus to the idea that bombers did not require escort. One week after the 97th BG's very first mission to Rouen, Maj. Gen. Carl Spaatz wrote to Gen. Arnold about the mission: *"In the initial conception of Operation Roundup* (the planned spring invasion of France in 1943) *and in the absence of definite proof, it was felt that the establishment of air supremacy over Germany depended upon operating the mass of airplanes in daylight and that daylight operations could not extend much beyond the tactical radius of operation of fighters. It was under this assumption that we felt the movement of ground forces on to the continent of Europe under an umbrella of air supremacy provided by fighters, was essential to advance the blows of our air forces toward Germany. The operations of the past week, limited as they have been, have convinced me of the following: a). That daylight bombing with extreme accuracy can be carried out at high altitude by our B-17 airplanes. b). That such operations can be extended, as soon as the necessary size force has been built up, into the heart of Germany without fighter protection over the whole range of operations. c). That with the below listed forces, in addition to such as the RAF may have, complete aerial supremacy can be obtained over Germany within a year, with the resultant insurance of her rapid defeat."* [1]

Spaatz listed the numbers of bombers and fighters he needed. Because German fighter forces were predominantly based in North Africa and Russia, he was left with the impression that: *"The resultant distribution of (German) fighters on this front in a thin line with no depth opened the way to destruction of the German air resources, particularly aircraft factories, while the German air forces were elsewhere. We have no intention at this time of extending our bombing operations beyond the radius of fighter support until our forces are more highly seasoned and of sufficient numbers to overcome mass fighter resistance, but as soon as sufficient numbers have been built up, our daylight raids will be extended into the heart of Germany."*

Spaatz had declared escort unnecessary after a single heavy bomber mission. He said aerial supremacy was expected in a year. The "thin line" Spaatz spoke of, soon became a wall of resistance. Arnold replied in August and sounded as though he thought Spaatz was hasty in denying need for escorts, saying: *"My only doubt at the present time is in connection with the P-38s. I hope it stands up as well in combat as the B-17. It it doesn't, then I can see nothing in the way of a real honest-to-God fighter until we get the P-47 over to you sometime in November or December. Beyond that, as you know, we have nothing but the P-51 which will come out in about a year from now, so it looks like for the time being, either the P-38 or nothing."* [2]

Chapter 8

"The best low-altitude American fighter yet developed..."

Ground Support and Reconnaissance

The Army needed fighters to support troop actions with strafing and bombing missions. In addition, battlefield intelligence was obtained by aerial reconnaissance. The old World War One method of having a second crewman hand-hold a camera in an open rear cockpit of a reconnaissance aircraft over enemy territory was being replaced by fast, single-seat fighter aircraft carrying automatic cameras and fixed machine guns. The fastest aircraft which was to become available at the end of 1942 and the beginning of 1943 and which was suitable for this purpose, was the P-51A.

In July 1942, Brig. Gen. Muir Fairchild, head of the Air Force Materiel Planning Council, instructed a group of senior officers – including Echols – on a committee to ascertain limits of production of all fighter types. Those aircraft such as the P-38 and P-47 were not to be limited while the P-39, P-40, and P-51 -the less favored as a fighter – might have their production restricted. Fairchild asked for a recommendation as to which type of fighter offered "...*the possibility of applying the type to Ground-Air Support operations*." The P-51A was chosen for the USAAF mission of Observation, which was part of the Army's mission of Ground Support.

In October, 1942 – around the time the A-36 (NA-97) was entering production – Col. D.M. Schlatter, the Director of Ground Support, put at the top of his Routing and Record Sheet (R & R) as his subject, the issue of '*Fighter Aircraft for Observation*.' An R & R began as a single sheet of paper with the subject typed at the very top, and the officer initiating the report then typed his reasons below the subject on the first page to show why he had a valid idea. Schlatter then routed his R & R through the offices of heads of directorates who added their comments and additional pages. At the end of the line the R & R was to be returned to Schlatter who made his appeal to his superior in order to get better fighters to train pilots for ground support. The R & R became a file of papers. Schlatter started his R & R by complaining to the Director of Training (but he also had to elicit opinions from Requirements and Air Defense), saying: "*There is a complete absence of fighter aircraft availability for training of Observation units in this country... about 40 fighters of P-43, P-39, and P-40 types are in Observation units. Additional are required*." [1]

When the Army changed its requirements from fast fighter types to slow observation and tactical reconnaissance missions and forced production and introduction of the P-51A, the P-51B was also pressed into ground-support use with Brigadier General D.M. Schlatter, seen here, commanding the Directorate of Ground Support. He made it clear to the AAF that it had to obey the Army's needs. The result was that every P-51B produced between June 1943 and June 1944 was allocated either to Ground Support or Tactical Reconnaissance.

Air Defense responded first, saying that P-39s and P-63s would be added to Air Support later in the year. One month later the R & R was returned to Schlatter's desk.

Schlatter was not satisfied with the lack of enthusiasm: "*This brings out vividly the fault in the present system of airplane allocations. Observation, utilizing converted combat types as an economy measure to promote maximum production, exists on such allocations as may be made after other programs are taken care of. This is not the fault of the Director of Air Defense, who is charged with the responsibility for the fighter program and naturally cannot himself declare fighter aircraft available. It is recommended that – fighter aircraft of the P-51 and P-39 types – be allocated. If the above cannot be done, that the Army Ground Forces be notified that the Army Air Forces are unable to meet their responsibility with respect to Observation Aviation*."

By asking for P-51s as trainers, Schlatter joined those who failed to see great promise in the Merlin-Mustang. In fact Brig. Gen. Gordon Saville could and did declare fighter aircraft available. Saville allocated personally fighter aircraft to all Theaters of Operations and had the authority to send them wherever he chose. During 1940, Saville created an acceptable Air Defense system and Arnold rewarded him shortly afterward by handing him the job of Director of Air Defense. The Air Defense Directorate was active in providing fighters

Brigadier General Gordon Saville, in command of the Air Defence Directorate, had complete authority over allocation of fighters, and had great influence upon their development. He disliked the Mustang and attempted to shift it to the French and to non-fighter uses.

Right: A Mustang IA, or P-51 (s/n 41-37353), fitted with four wing-mounted 20 mm cannon undergoing a flight test by the AAF.

Left: Ship 41-37321 was fitted with four 20 mm cannon by NAA and was a Mustang IA and a P-51. Mustang IAs did not have guns in the cowl.

Below: A Mustang IA in RAF camouflage and markings has its cannon test-fired at NAA. Note the almost invisible smoke puffs just ahead of each cannon.

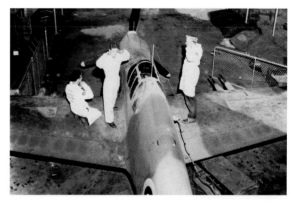

in war theaters and for bases within the US. Under Saville, the office of Air Defense supervised the allocation of fighters all over the world wherever the Army wanted them. He also sent fighters to dead-end places where less-important types were put out of the way, such as the Training Command. The system of air defense required artillery, barrage balloons, and aircraft spotters manning radios, but the heart of air defense anywhere in the world was the fast-climbing interceptor. In 1942, that interceptor was recognized as the P-38.

Saville advised in the development of new fighters. Echols, a man known for not asking advice from fellow officers, sought Saville's advice because of the great authority of the Air Defense Directorate. No AAF fighter was designed, built, tested, or produced under Echols without also receiving Saville's blessing. Under Saville, the office dispersed Mustangs unreasonably because the P-38 had to be afforded a chance to prove itself. However, Saville continued to dislike the P-51.

In November 1942, US and Allied forces had wrested control of North Africa, west of Tunisia, from the Vichy French and when the French opted to fight on the side of the US, the USAAF began giving the French American equipment. In February 1943, Saville supplied Curtiss P-40s to a French

fighter group, stating: "*Present production schedules indicate that no Packard-powered P-40s will be produced after April, 1943. Future provisions could be made to supply fifteen P-51s per month for French Forces in North Africa beginning with June production.*" [2] P-51Bs were produced that month and Saville was prepared to also supply them to the Free French Forces. The British praised the Mustang and were so vigorous in refitting them with the Merlin that their enthusiasm gave impetus to the American effort which had not existed previously. When the AAF took 57 Mustang IAs and called them P-51s, the installation of four 20 mm cannon required evaluation by the Eglin test pilots. This also included flight testing and the subsequent written reports were the first detailed evaluations made of the Mustang, which were on order for the US military. The Air Corps and AAF had made quick, poorly documented flights in the NA-73, XP-51 and A-36 but Eglin's test pilots presented a lengthy, detailed report that was filled with graphs, charts, and specific performance figures. In December 1942, after flying the P-51, Eglin Field's test pilots issued a report which contained the first official praise for the Mustang from an American source and from a source outside of Wright Field. The report stated: "*...the*

Lieutenant Colonel Ken Chilstrom, Wright Field test pilot (left), and Bob Chilton, NAA test pilot, standing against the XP-51F.

subject aircraft is the best low-altitude American fighter yet developed, and should be used as the criterion for comparison of subsequent types." Eglin's test pilots recommended that the P-51 *"…be equipped with an engine which will permit satisfactory tactical combat maneuvering between twenty-five-thousand and thirty-thousand feet"* and that the armament be changed to *"…four .50 caliber machine guns."* The P-51 should be *"…equipped with more effective aileron control."* [3]

The plans made in 1940 to have fighters carry large cannon ended with them being installed on the P-38. Schlatter saw the report but he was disinterested in high-altitude capability as his responsibility was to provide low-flying aircraft. Before the ink was barely dry on Eglin's signatures, he stated: *"…for air operations (the) maximum performance is required for lower altitudes. 25,000 - 30,000 feet operation is not necessary."* [4] Saville agreed to fulfil Schlatter's request for P-51s. and told Requirements that *"…present plans call for cessation of flow of P-40 aircraft and commencing flow of P-51 by 1 May."* [5] Saville planned to allocate Mustangs to Ground Support starting in May 1943 when the P-51B was due to be produced. Without needing to consult anyone, Saville was prepared to determine that the future of the Merlin-Mustang was to be as a ground support aircraft.

After plans were made in 1943 to invade North West Europe in 1944, the Ninth Air Force – a tactical air force – was transferred to Britain in October 1943. Saville and

Schlatter had by then set in motion the eventual assignment of the first several hundred P-51Bs to the Ninth Air Force.

In the P-51A, Eglin's test pilots had discovered superior handling, speed, and range characteristics for what they believed would be a very good fighter. The Mustang was regarded in Britain as the fighter of the future, but in the USAAF the P-38 and P-47 had been assigned to this role.

Long-Range

In December 1942, an officer in Saville's Directorate, Col. Morris Nelson, echoed Saville's plan for P-51s, and Nelson agreed with Schlatter's need for Mustangs as trainers as well as ground support types. Nelson recorded: *"…the required number of aircraft could not be made available to observation from P-51 production until October 1943 since this type is needed for pilot training and the attrition to P-40 groups now in theaters."* [6]

After P-51A (NA-99) flight tests had been carried out at Eglin in April 1943 a written report was not issued until June, after P-51B production had begun. Two months prior to then, Echols created a major change by requiring written reports on the testing of aircraft. In March, a British representative had gone to Wright Field to ask for written reports on US aircraft and there were none! Testing of aircraft up to that time resulted in the test pilot issuing brief, verbal judgements to his superior. Echols instituted what is, today, the centralization and formalization of recorded test results.

A Block System was introduced in March and a written report from Eglin was for the P-51A-1-NA where the numbers and letters indicated engineering changes within the model and at which plant the aircraft had been produced. This time the report touched upon a performance item not mentioned previously by any test pilot at Wright Field; Eglin stated that the P-51A-1-NA had *"…the longest combat range of any current American fighter (and) neared the limit of range in which a fighter pilot can undertake operational missions without excessive pilot fatigue followed by long rest periods."* [7] Strangely, this statement had no

This P-38, coded KI●B, of the 55th Fighter Squadron, 20th Fighter Group is having its guns bore-sighted at Wittering in England, five miles from the unit's main base at King's Cliffe, during November or December 1943.

effect upon those officers determining specifications for the escort fighter.

In 1944, Mustang fighter pilots frequently flew seven-hour missions. The Directorates of Ground Support, Training, and Observation all wanted Allison-powered Mustangs. New requests appeared for well over 1,000 P-51As.

P-51B

"Dutch" Kindelberger had written to the Materiel Center at Wright Field in August 1942 to "...*discuss plans for the P-51A development program*" and suggested "...*that a supplementary production line be started*" to shift to the 61 (Packard V-1650-3) "...*as soon as possible.*" Kindelberger agreed with the idea to "...*ship airplanes less engines to England*" if only to make sure his Mustangs would be produced.[8] None were shipped. The mating of the Merlin 61/V-1650-3 to the Mustang pointed toward success and because nothing specific in print said NAA would produce Merlin-Mustangs, someone had to convince Echols to go ahead with production.

One month later, in September 1942, J. Leland Atwood wrote to Brig. Gen. K.B. Wolfe suggesting the "...*production of 400 P-51B airplanes as a Special Project.*" To do it, NAA needed a high preference rating.[9] Wolfe suggested to Echols that the AAF have a "proposed contract" for the 400, assisted by Echols' putting the Mustang in Preference Group I. Wolfe promised Echols that his Production Division would "...*assign material control expediters solely to this project. It is our belief that this project is of the highest importance.*"[10]

The same month, Fairchild's Air Force Materiel Planning Council announced that limits in fighter production would be

A British Mustang IA being tested for the AAF and which, when taken over by the AAF, was designated P-51.

placed on the P-39 and P-40, but all-out production of the P-51B was not yet possible. Wolfe's September actions remain prescient and visionary even today. While some officers disparaged the "British Project," Wolfe moved ahead. He wanted to reduce P-51A production and get Materiel to move on to the Merlin-Mustang. Wolfe has never been given the credit he deserves for single-handed promotion of the P-51B. Echols did not sign Wolfe's Special Project contract until 24 November and when he did, as of the contract date of 23 December 1942, the P-51B was to be a production item. Ten were expected to be produced in March 1943, 100 in April, 156 in May, and more in every month after that.[11]

With authority in December, Wolfe told the Chief of Fighter Branch that all Mustang contracts were being changed. He was bound somewhat to please Echols and the Army by acknowledging new requests for P-51As; besides listing intended production of 400 P-51Bs at Inglewood and 1,000 P-51Cs at Dallas, 1,200 P-51As were to be produced at Inglewood and another 550 P-51As would be produced at that

This was the second P-51A-1-NA (s/n 43-6004) produced and NAA permitted the application of a name and cartoon to the aircraft while still at the factory.

BRIG. GEN. KENNETH B. WOLFE

Kenneth Bonner Wolfe is remembered most for masterminding the B-29 project to completion. It was America's most expensive, most complex program, costing more than the atomic bomb. Born in 1896 in Denver, he later graduated from the University of California in 1918, joined the Army and was trained as a pilot. His first command was as Officer in Charge of Flying Training at Souther Field until January 1920. He became Chief Engineering Officer at a principal depot and was a student at the Engineering School from 1931 to 1935. After study at the ACTS he was the Representative at the Douglas Aircraft Corporation until March 1939. Wolfe rose rapidly in rank, from Lieutenant Colonel in March 1941 to Brigadier General one year later. General Arnold had wanted a bomber like the Boeing B-29 Superfortress ever since he had dreamt about the possibilities of strategic air warfare. When Wolfe pushed the B-29 toward success, Arnold rewarded him with the rank of Major General and the job of Organizer and Commanding General of the B-29-equipped 58th Bombardment Wing before the unit went overseas and Organizer and Commanding General of the B-29-equipped XX Bomber Command in India and western China.

plant on an Acceleration Program. Wolfe placated those in favor of the P-51A by advocating the production of 1,700 aircraft, but he strongly suggested that "...*steps be taken as soon as practicable*" to have Merlins in "...*all P-51 airplanes after the first 300 P-51As.*" [12] His cooler head prevailed and Materiel at long last acted in favor of Merlin-Mustang production. Wolfe's December message contained the first indication that an NAA B-24 bomber plant in Dallas, Texas would begin production of

Mustangs. Thanks to Wolfe, P-51A production was halted at 310 airplanes. However, Directorates in need of Mustangs lobbied for P-51Bs.

Tactical Reconnaissance

By late 1942, the US had been in a world war for a full year and lessons had been learned. At just the right moment, an officer with the finest military mind – Brig. Gen. Laurence Kuter – was taken into Arnold's and Marshall's confidence.

Air Vice Marshal Sir Arthur Coningham, commanding the North West African Tactical Air Force (NATAF), wrote a report of tactical air forces under his command. The report satisfied British General, Bernard Montgomery, who placed the report in US hands. Entitled '*The Fighting Aspect of Tactical Reconnaissance by Single Engine Aircraft,*' the report landed on Schlatter's desk in December, 1942. Coningham's report was seen by Lt. Gen. Dwight Eisenhower, commanding all Allied forces in North Africa and in February 1943 Coningham was granted an appointment with Eisenhower to outline his views. Tactical reconnaissance – known as Tac-R – became a new offensive mission in the US Army. Eisenhower supported independence of air units from the Army. He created separate air, ground, and naval units under his command, freeing air units from Army Corps-level controls.

Kuter, the most brilliant theoretician in the AAF, headed the Mediterranean's Allied Air Support Command in January 1943. A tall, thin, very handsome man, he was well aware of Coningham's and

This P-51B was painted overall black as requested by the AAF for a "night fighter finish" even though the Mustang never qualified as a night fighter. The serial number was 43-7177.

This P-51A of the Cold Weather Test Detachment at Ladd Field, Alaska was modified with skis because the USAAF demanded that its aircraft be capable of operating from desert to arctic weather conditions.

Wright Field's Hangar Number 3 serves as a backdrop for a B-26 Marauder and a Mustang IA sporting a bulge in the aft left-side canopy where a camera was housed. The British demanded that the bulge be removed and the camera moved farther inside and that the aft canopy Plexiglas being returned to its original design. Following the outbreak of war in 1941, 57 Mustang IAs were kept from the British contract of 150 aircraft and the AAF designated them P-51s. By then the canopy bulge was gone. Note the "alligator-jaws"-type of belly scoop, the 20 mm cannon, and the words "Wright Field" stencilled ahead of the windscreen.

Thought to be one of the most modern observation types when it was rolled out in 1940, the Curtiss O-52 Owl had retractable landing gear but not much else to recommend it for combat use. It was not sent to the front and was used as a tug and trainer.

In 1937 the Air Corps obtained the first NAA O-47s, considered to be the world's finest observation aircraft. Obviously defenceless, the O-47 was not used operationally. In 1943 observation was changed to reconnaissance and fighter-type aircraft such as the P-51B were demanded for Tac-R. Note the crewman hand-holding a camera in the slipstream. The pregnant belly of the O-47 was covered with glass to provide a downward view.

Eisenhower's ideas and decisions. The issues of freedom of maneuver by USAAF fighters and of a less-dependent USAAF were tied to revisions made in 1943. Kuter changed the mission of Observation which had remained relatively static since World War One; it was renamed Tactical Reconnaissance. As late as 1940, the Air Corps was procuring slow, indefensible NAA O-47s and Curtiss O-52s for this role. Policy required having a second crewman stand up in a rear, open cockpit to hand-hold a camera to obtain reconnaissance photographs. In 1943 Kuter wrote: "… *observation aviation is faulty. Even when a high degree of air superiority is enjoyed, there must be…*" fighters to protect "grasshopper" types such as the O-47. Because an army's corps front in a battle became very wide, he opined, "…*there have been as many as three fighter groups in the corps front but fighter control has been practically non-existent.*" Kuter wanted to end use of fighters to escort slow observation types and asked for "…*very fast two-seaters (Mosquito type or better) or fast, able, single-place fighters (P-51 type or better). The basic element of any air command in the battle area must be the fighter elements.*" [13]

Fast Tac-R fighters were to carry cameras and guns and the Mustang was first on the list of possible candidates. Army generals required reconnaissance aircraft missions so greatly that in June 1943 General Arnold raised the priority for reconnaissance temporarily above that of fighters, but below bombers until the Army was satisfied with what was being done later in the war. [14]

Brigadier General Laurence Kuter was perhaps the greatest theoretician in the wartime AAF. He revolutionised reconnaissance and tactical air power and was adamant about using P-51Bs for escort instead of simply for tactical use.

General Marshall recognized Kuter as one of the Army's finest officers. Kuter wrote the basis for Field Manual FM-100-20, which was published in July 1943 over the signature of General Marshall. The Manual stated: "…*the gaining of air superiority is the first requirement for the success of any major land operation… Air Forces must be employed primarily against the enemy's air force until air superiority is obtained… The inherent flexibility of air power is its greatest asset… Land power and air power are co-equal and independent forces; neither is an auxiliary of the other.*" [15]

FM-100-20 changed the basic nature of the USAAF's air war doctrine in the ETO starting in December 1943. Fighters – not bombers – would gain air superiority.

Photo Reconnaissance

The F-5 was the USAAF's best photo reconnaissance (PR) type and was a PR version of the P-38F. In February 1943, the AAF began a search for a different PR aircraft because the need for more P-38s increased dramatically. Maj. Gen. George Stratemeyer, Arnold's Chief of Air Staff, asked Air Vice Marshal F. MacNeece-Foster for twin-engined de Havilland Mosquitos, saying "…*we desire to equip our PR units with them. No doubt that the purposes of our combined Air Forces would be best served if the Army Air Forces curtailed their conversion of P-38s and relied in part on your Mosquito.*" [16]

Stratemeyer was under pressure from Spaatz, Commanding General of the Allied

Above: F-6C 'Mickey' of the 107th Tactical Reconnaissance Squadron photographed at Earl's Colne, England.

Below: Two F-6s of the 109th TRS at Middle Wallop, exhibit varying ways of applying the squadron fuselage code letters "VX." The usual style was to apply the letters to the left of the star-and-bar and the aircraft letter (here "W" and "S") aft of the insignia. On the starboard side of the Mustangs, the squadron letters would be separated by the star-and-bar and the second letter ("X") would adjoin the "W" or "S", but this was not uniformly true. The serial numbers of the Mustangs seen in this picture were 43-12396 (left) and 43-12301 (right). Note camera ports to rear of the belly scoop exhausts. The Spitfire is a clipped-wing Mk V.

Above: Major Frank B. Robison of the 109th TRS wears full flight gear while posing in front of his F-6B.

Above: This pristine P-51A of the 109th TRS with its red surround to the star-and-bar insignia, appears not yet to have been used operationally.

Below: Stan Marsh flew 'Blues in the Night' in the 107th TRS. He was shot down over enemy territory in this aircraft but made it to neutral Switzerland.

Above: This F-6C of the 107th TRS, 67th RG, Ninth AF, s/n 42-103622 was flown by Lieutenant O'Keefe. 'Shoo Shoo Baby! Mk. 2' shows very little wear except to the paint on the gear doors. Tactical reconnaissance squadrons began receiving Mustangs — according to some sources — in 1942, but Merlin-powered Mustangs obviously were not supplied until 1944.

Left: This F-6 of the 15th TRS had part of its wing shot off when John Florence, Assistant Group Operations Officer, flew it. The aircraft is seen here with its cowl removed for maintenance, during the winter of 1944-1945. The 15th TRS was part of the 67th TRG, but during 1944 it was assigned to the 10th PRG. Both groups were in the Ninth Air Force.

Left: The 107th TRS, 67th TRG of the Ninth AF operated a number of P-51Cs. Technically this airplane was an F-6C-NT built at the Dallas plant. Note the camera port at the rear of the belly scoop. The serial number was 42-103375.

Above: A P-51A flown by Bob Koche of the 107th TRS parked on Marston matting somewhere in Europe.

Right: 1st Lt Elmer E. Thorp of the 109th TRS was the pilot of this bare-metal P-51C, but it had been Harry Dewall's "old ship." The 'P 32' on the vertical stabilizer denoted a manufacturer's part number.

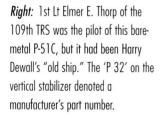

Below: P-51B "Atlanta Belle, Ethelyn" of the 109th TRS, 67th TRG, Ninth AF coded VX-Y with a Malcolm hood and AEAF stripes.

Above: Captain George James of the 109th TRS was at Middle Wallop in early 1944 when this photograph was taken. Painted below the exhaust on his aircraft, "Faith, Hope and Jollie," are photographic mission symbols. Note the "Kilroy was Here" symbols which may have meant missions flown with negative results.

Left: A 109th TRS P-51B flown by Lieutenant John W. Howard. Howard is seen here talking to one of his crew members, possibly Cpl. Schultz, at an unknown location.

Right: Lieutenant Ronald Erickson (far left) and Major Hal C. Conne, (far right), CO of the 109th TRS, photographed having a cigarette and handshake with their ground crew having just flown the 109th's 1,000th mission on 14 August 1944. Note camera symbols and "Kilroy was Here" symbols.

Above: The men and Mustangs of the 109th TRS awake to find themselves forced to a standstill because of deep snow at Gosselies, Belgium, late 1944. Not far away the Battle of the Bulge was raging.

Below: This assortment of Mustangs of the 109th TRS was photographed at Gosselies, Belgium in the fall of 1944. Due to the proximity of the front, the aircraft are guarded by armed troops. The Mustangs in the background are coded "AX" but the P-51B in the foreground has no markings. Commanded by Colonel Joe Thompson, the unit established a fine record in combat.

An F-5 of the 7th PG based at Mount Farm shows the bare-metal finish and distinctive stripes and colors of the unit. The AAF had no purpose-built photo-recon aircraft but the multi-purpose P-38/F-5 served admirably.

Air Force in Africa starting in December 1942 because Spaatz himself received urgent requests for PR from Army generals. Spaatz wanted Mosquitos and for Stratemeyer to get them, he offered to trade Mustangs.

Back in July 1942, the British Ministry of Aircraft Production had hoped to get 500 Mustang airframes from the US and the Ministry used Stratemeyer's wish for Mosquitos as bait to raise to 1,000 the number of Mustang airframes desired. Stratemeyer told MacNeece-Foster "...*the allocation of Mosquitos would be considered as a partial 'quid pro quo' within the intent of...*" a decision pending in the American-based Joint Aircraft Committee (JAC) case involving the "...*allocation of P-51 assemblies to...*" Britain. The JAC did not allow shipment of Mustang airframes.

Only a handful of Mosquitos were operated by the AAF. In late 1943 some very long-range, photo-reconnaissance Spitfire PR XIs were operated by the AAF in Britain. Spaatz suggested that Arnold ask the British for Mosquitos without engines. Spaatz was willing to give 48 Packard Merlins to Britain in exchange for engineless Mosquitos and rob Mustangs of Merlins for them.[17]

Dispersal of Mustangs

Development of the A-36 and P-51A gave the Army its ground-support type but emergence of the P-51B drove a wedge between those wanting it as a tactical weapon and others who realized its potential as a fighter. On 17 April 1943 Col. Morris R. Nelson, Chief, Air Defense Branch, Requirements Division, said the P-51B "...*will be the best fighter airplane in the world.*" Two thousand more Mustangs were contracted on 28 April. In May 1943, the first production-model P-51B was flight-tested with the report saying it achieved 441 mph at 29,800 ft and was climbed to 42,000 ft. Its rate of climb was 3,600 fpm through 5,000 ft and at 35,000 ft was still impressive at 1,200 fpm. By May, 300 P-51Bs had been allocated to Tac-R and Ground Support.

By July, Saville's allocations and dispersals reached a peak. Col. R.H. Kelly told an Assistant Chief of Air Staff that a total of 945 Mustangs were proposed for Tac-R deliveries starting that month and to last until July 1944. Kelly complained that Mustang allocation was "...*less than the number previously allocated to air support activities during 1943.*" [18]

The 945 Mustangs for Tac-R and at least that number allocated to Ground Support represented every P-51B to be produced in all of 1943 and half of those to be built in 1944. Ground Support and Tac-R had control, on paper, of every P-51B to be manufactured. However, Saville's dispersals were recorded on paper, and paper could be rewritten.

Above: Major General George Stratemeyer, Arnold's Chief of Staff until mid 1943.

Below: Colonel Elliott Roosevelt commanded the 3rd Allied Photographic Wing in the Mediterranean, the 7th PG and the 325th Reconnaissance Wing, both in Britain, and the 8th Provisional Reconnaissance Wing after D-Day. Elliott Roosevelt's personal Mosquito — marked "ER," s/n DK 315 — is seen here at the home airfield of the 31st Fighter Group in North Africa. The Mosquito was wanted for the AAF particularly by General Spaatz, and Elliott, later a Brigadier General, commanded a group in the ETO which operated the type. President Roosevelt's four sons served in uniform.

Right: Pilots of the 7th PG gathered around an F-5 demonstrate the considerable size of the Lightning.

Left: When Colonel Homer Sanders took command of the 7th PG, he felt there were limitations in the speed and altitude performance of the F-5 and wanted Spitfire XIs. So the story goes, he asked General Eaker for Spitfires, and Eaker told Sanders to compare the F-5 and a Mk. XI. In a simulated dogfight, Sanders' F-5 had a turbo explode. Using that incident as convincing evidence, Eaker went to Churchill and obtained Spitfires for the 7th PG. The date of the photograph was 8 October 1943.

Above: Colonel James G. Hall (right), was the first commander of the 7th PG. Here, he congratulates Captain George Lawson after the first mission on 8 June 1943. They are standing on the wing of an F-5.

Left: A 7th PG F-4 Photo-Lightning flown by Marshall Wayne, a 1936 Olympic diving champion. Wayne is shaking hands while his aircraft undergoes maintenance. From left to right: Lt. Harlan Fricke, Capt. J. Max Campbell, Capt. George Nesselrode, and Maj. Wayne.

Left: Two Spitfire PR XIs of the 7th Photograph Group based at Mount Farm RAF Station, England in 1944. The unit obtained the British aircraft in late 1943 to supplement reconnaissance missions conducted by Lockheed F-5s. John Blyth flew PA944, which is seen here with Invasion stripes.

Right: The 7th PG used P-51D "Outhouse Mouse" as an escort for its F-5s once Germany's fast, jet-powered Me 262s were targeted against Allied reconnaissance aircraft.

Above: One of the great reconnaissance pilots, Robert Dixon (right) returns from a mission – probably in a Spitfire XI – to be greeted by Kermit Bliss of the 7th PG. Bob Dixon went on to become a four-star General and Commanding General of the Tactical Air Command from October 1973 to April 1978.

Right: 1st Lieutenant Hoyt Warren (centre) and P-51 "Chubby Angel" together with ground crew seen at a forward base in France, August 1944. The aircraft was normally flown by Lieutenant Walton, 109th TRS, 67th TRG.

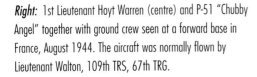

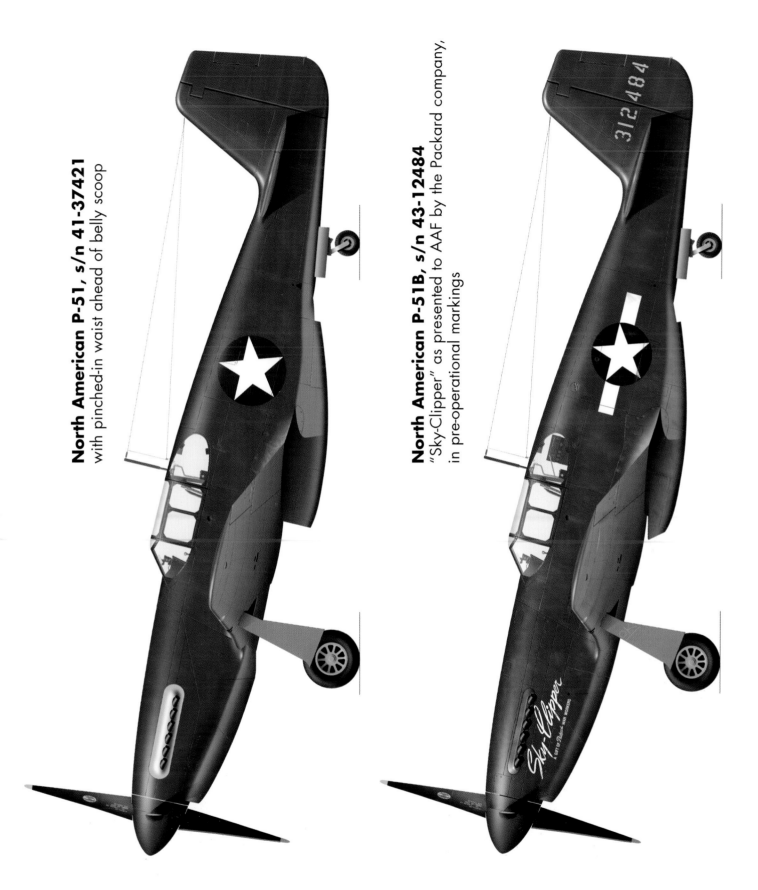

North American P-51, s/n 41-37421
with pinched-in waist ahead of belly scoop

North American P-51B, s/n 43-12484
"Sky-Clipper" as presented to AAF by the Packard company, in pre-operational markings

North American XP-51, s/n 41-039
Wright Field, Ohio

North American XP-51B (second NA-91, designated XP-78), s/n 41-37421

North American P-51A-1-NA, s/n 43-6004
"Slick Chick"

North American Mustang IA, s/n 41-37320
Wright Field, Ohio

Right: The sleek lines of the NA-73X (NX19998) with a suitably dramatic cloud backdrop to delight the company public relations personnel! The prototype was specially painted with pre-war Air Corps rudder stripes for a series of photos between the first flight on 26 October and a crash on 20 November 1940 in which it was damaged. The rudder stripes were officially discontinued in August 1940.

Below: A P-51A (left) and a P-51B parked under an almost cloudless sky at an unidentified location.

Below: Although all Mustangs were designated "P-51" generically, there was actually only one model of the Mustang designated P-51, and here its 20 mm cannon make identification immediate.

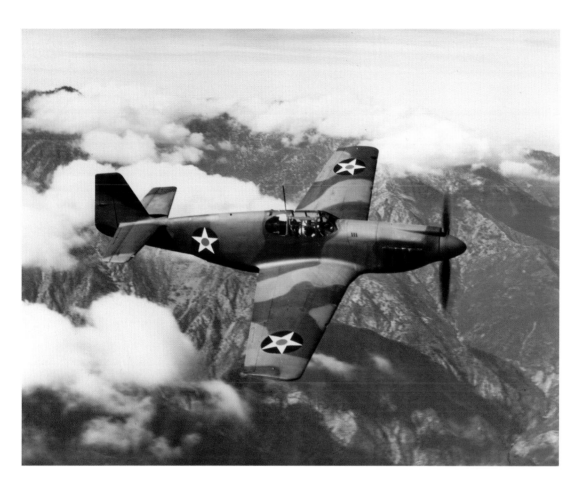

Left: The national insignia as seen on this British-camouflaged Mustang was changed shortly war was declared in America. It was thought that a red circle resembled the insignia used on Japanese aircraft, and in 1942 it was amended to just a white star on a blue circle.

Below: Visible third from left in this line-up of Mustang IIIs is an aircraft with the British serial FZ 132. The machines seen here were painted in an assortment of camouflage colours and all were given AAF insignia.

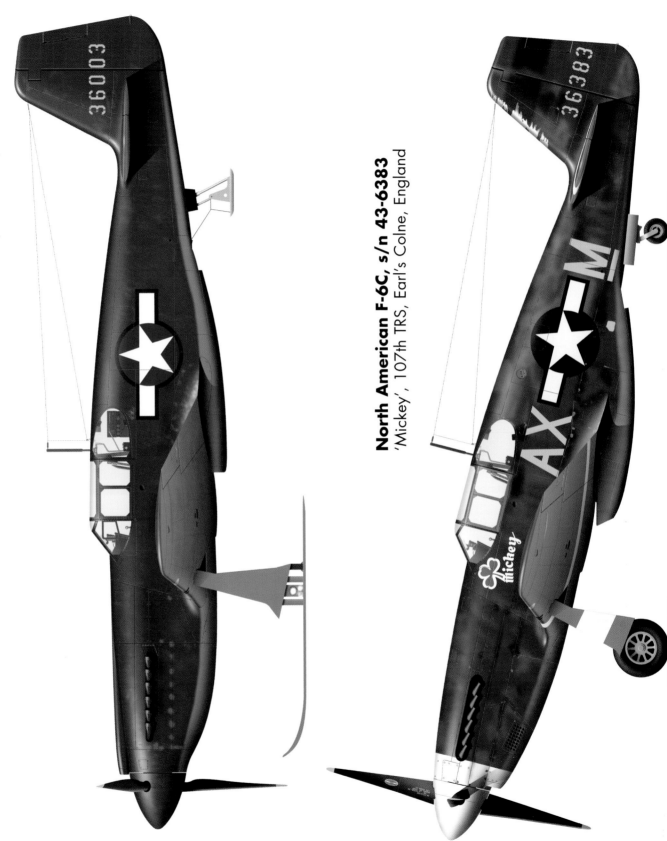

North American P-51A, s/n 43-6003
Cold Weather Test Detachment, Ladd Field, Alaska

North American F-6C, s/n 43-6383
'Mickey', 107th TRS, Earl's Colne, England

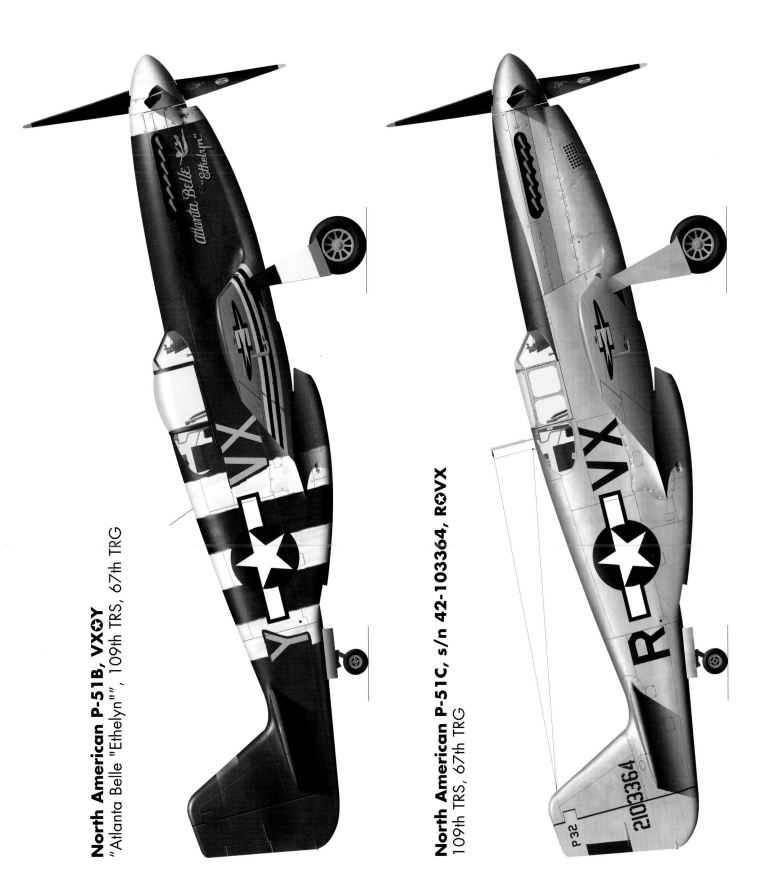

North American P-51B, VX⊙Y
"Atlanta Belle "Ethelyn"", 109th TRS, 67th TRG

North American P-51C, s/n 42-103364, R⊙VX
109th TRS, 67th TRG

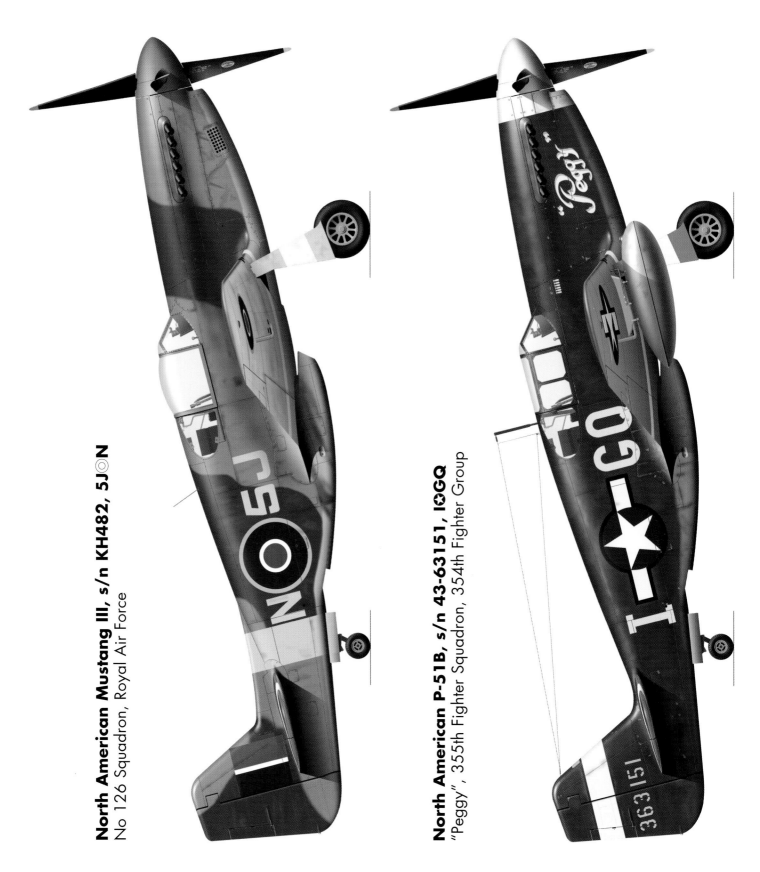

North American Mustang III, s/n KH482, 5J◉N
No 126 Squadron, Royal Air Force

North American P-51B, s/n 43-63151, I◉GQ
"Peggy", 355th Fighter Squadron, 354th Fighter Group

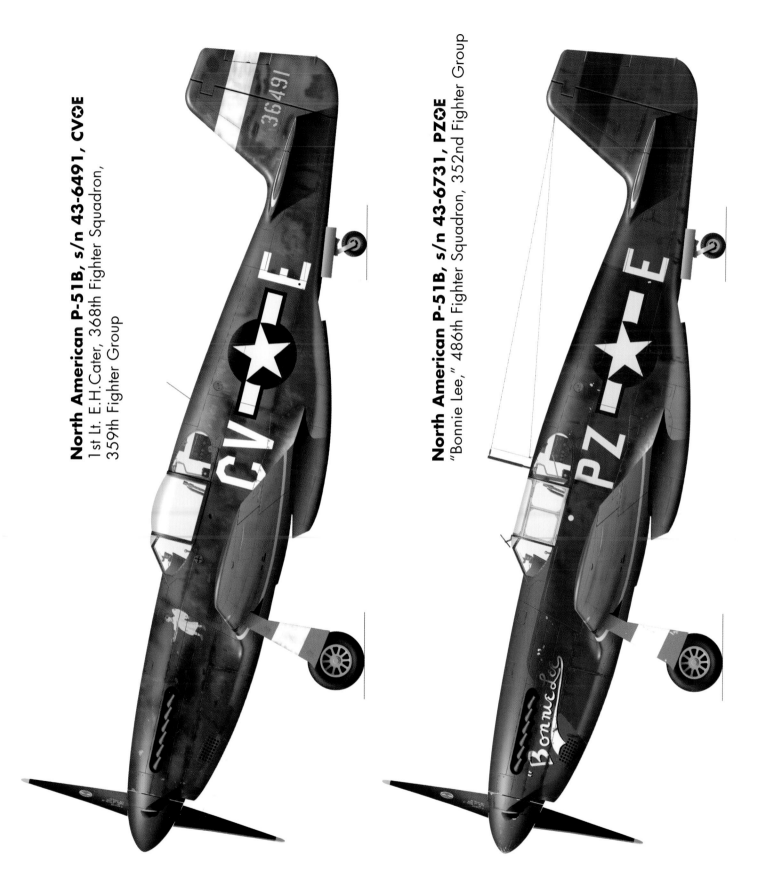

North American P-51B, s/n 43-6491, CV◉E
1st Lt. E.H.Cater, 368th Fighter Squadron,
359th Fighter Group

North American P-51B, s/n 43-6731, PZ◉E
"Bonnie Lee," 486th Fighter Squadron, 352nd Fighter Group

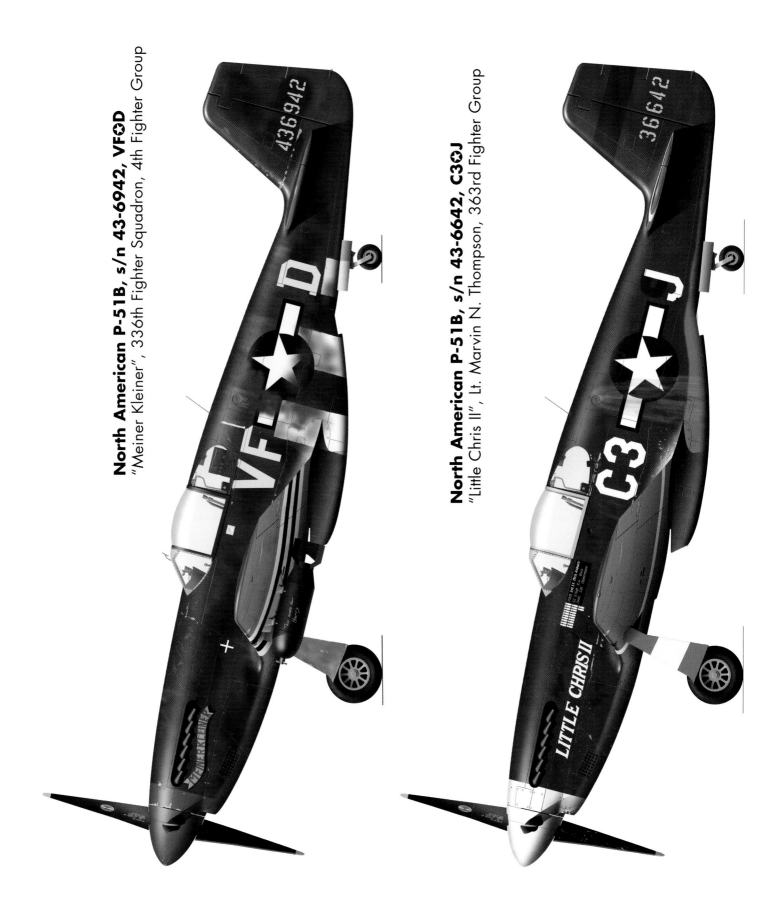

North American P-51B, s/n 43-6942, VF✪D
"Meiner Kleiner", 336th Fighter Squadron, 4th Fighter Group

North American P-51B, s/n 43-6642, C3✪J
"Little Chris II", Lt. Marvin N. Thompson, 363rd Fighter Group

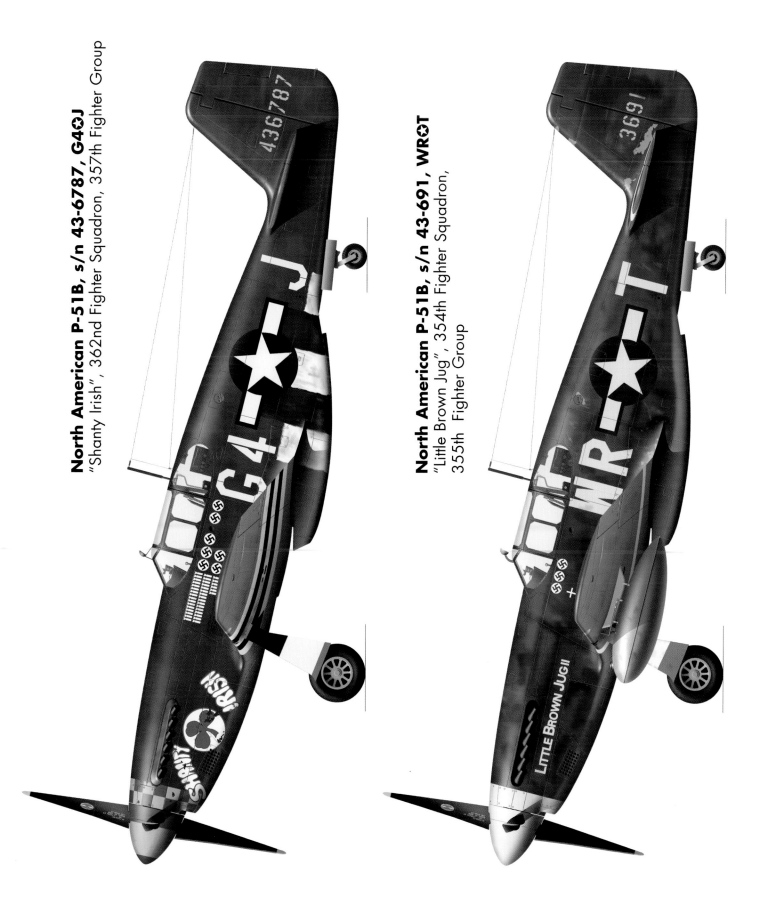

North American P-51B, s/n 43-6787, G4⊗J
"Shanty Irish", 362nd Fighter Squadron, 357th Fighter Group

North American P-51B, s/n 43-691, WR⊗T
"Little Brown Jug", 354th Fighter Squadron, 355th Fighter Group

Above: Mustang I, AG 633, of No 2 Squadron, RAF, in flight somewhere over Britain.

Right: A Mustang I, coded XV⊚U, of No 2 Squadron, RAF, shows off its impressively clean lines during an engine run-up. Note that the camera port behind the cockpit is faired with the fuselage.

Right: Capt. Duane Beeson, a 17.33 victory ace of the 4th FG gives the "thumbs up" from the cockpit of his P-51B-5 "Bee" (coded QP✪B, s/n 43-6819) at Debden on 5 April 1944.

Above and right: Captain Don S. Gentile of the 4th FG manages a smile for the official cameraman next to his aircraft in early 1944. Born on 12 June 1920, the son of Italian immigrants to the USA, Gentile was awarded many decorations for his outstanding wartime service during which he was accredited with 19.83 confirmed victories.

North American P-51B, s/n 43-6369, GQ✪Z
354th Fighter Group

North American P-51B, s/n 43-6878, C5✪J
"Pregnant Polecat", Capt. Glendon V. Davis,
364th Fighter Squadron, 357th Fighter Group

North American P-51B, s/n 43-6976, FT⦿D
"Rosey T", Haydon Holton, 354th Fighter Group

North American P-51B, s/n 43-12425, VQ⦿C
Seconded to Eighth Air Force Air Technical Section,
Bovingdon, Hertfordshire

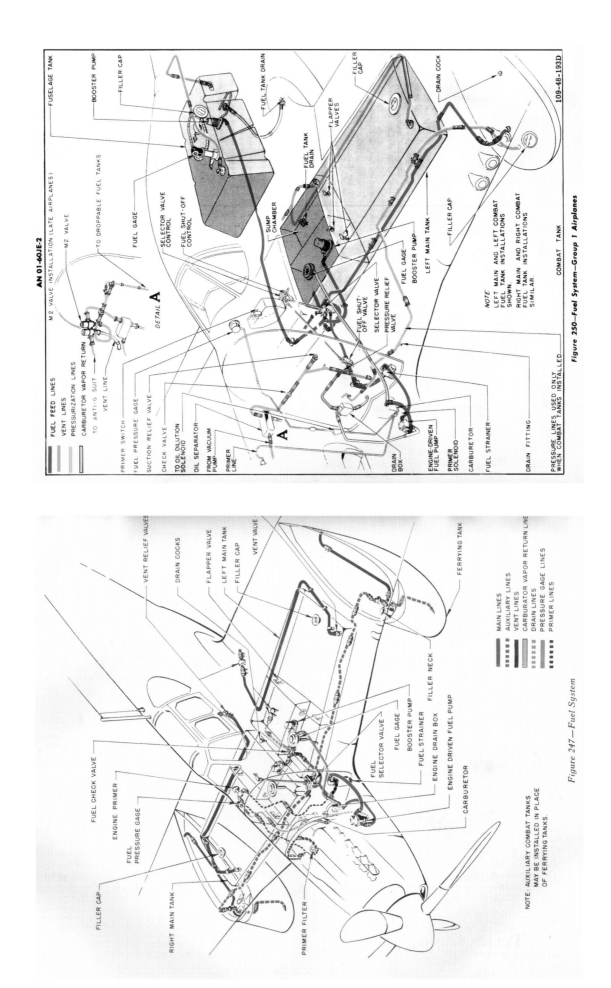

AN 01-60JE-2

M2 VALVE INSTALLATION (LATE AIRPLANES)

FUSELAGE TANK

BOOSTER PUMP

FILLER CAP

FILLER CAP

FUEL TANK DRAIN

FLAPPER VALVES

DRAIN COCK

FUEL TANK DRAIN

M2 VALVE

TO DROPPABLE FUEL TANKS

FUEL GAGE

SELECTOR VALVE CONTROL

FUEL SHUT-OFF CONTROL

SUMP CHAMBER

LEFT MAIN TANK

FILLER CAP

FUEL GAGE

BOOSTER PUMP

FUEL FEED LINES

VENT LINES

PRESSURIZATION LINES

CARBURETOR VAPOR RETURN

TO ANTI-G SUIT

VENT LINE

DETAIL A

PRIMER SWITCH

FUEL PRESSURE GAGE

SUCTION RELIEF VALVE

CHECK VALVE

TO OIL DILUTION SOLENOID

OIL SEPARATOR

FROM VACUUM PUMP

PRIMER LINE

A

DRAIN BOX

ENGINE-DRIVEN FUEL PUMP

PRIMER SOLENOID

CARBURETOR

FUEL STRAINER

DRAIN FITTING

FUEL SHUT-OFF VALVE

SELECTOR VALVE

PRESSURE RELIEF VALVE

NOTE:
LEFT MAIN AND LEFT COMBAT FUEL TANK INSTALLATIONS SHOWN.
RIGHT MAIN AND RIGHT COMBAT FUEL TANK INSTALLATIONS SIMILAR

COMBAT TANK

PRESSURE LINES USED ONLY WHEN COMBAT TANKS INSTALLED

Figure 250—Fuel System—Group 1 Airplanes

109-48-193D

VENT RELIEF VALVES

DRAIN COCKS

FLAPPER VALVE

LEFT MAIN TANK

FILLER CAP

VENT VALVE

FERRYING TANK

FILLER CAP

ENGINE PRIMER

FUEL PRESSURE GAGE

RIGHT MAIN TANK

FUEL CHECK VALVE

PRIMER FILTER

CARBURETOR

ENGINE DRIVEN FUEL PUMP

ENGINE DRAIN BOX

FILLER NECK

FUEL STRAINER

BOOSTER PUMP

FUEL GAGE

FUEL SELECTOR VALVE

MAIN LINES

AUXILIARY LINES

VENT LINES

CARBURETOR VAPOR RETURN LINE

DRAIN LINES

PRESSURE GAGE LINES

PRIMER LINES

NOTE: AUXILIARY COMBAT TANKS MAY BE INSTALLED IN PLACE OF FERRYING TANKS.

Figure 247—Fuel System

Two diagrams taken from an original handbook showing the long-range fuel tank arrangement for (left) the P-51B and (right) the P-51D.

Chapter 9

"Why build last year's airplane today?"

Weight and Stability

In November 1942 Oliver Echols offered, in writing, to resign. Until the ATSC was formed in 1944, not having advanced in command or rank, he labored under a variety of pressures and personal resentments. Emphasis upon civilian control of procurement in late 1942 was accompanied by pressure to put the P-51B under contract. The year 1943 was to begin with almost every officer still convinced that the four-engined bomber was self-defending. Threat of aerial bombardment of America and a need for better interceptors made the search for the best interceptor a continuing affair. The XP-51 was judged to have a poor climb rate preventing it from being such a type. It was in that same November that the General Motors/Fisher XP-75 interceptor was put under contract, while it was also believed that a new multi-mission fighter was needed. The P-38 was the only choice as both interceptor and multi-mission fighter in production as the year 1943 began.

Chesley Gordon Peterson, DFC, DSO, RAFVR, seen here as Acting Squadron Leader of No 71 Eagle Squadron. Peterson completed a large number of sorties over enemy-occupied territory and at all times displayed high qualities of leadership and courage. During operations over Dieppe, he destroyed a Ju 88, bringing his victories to six. He was later selected to choose the fighter best suited for the AAF to be produced in 1943. He chose the Mustang but was told it would not be continued as a fighter.

Echols' bias toward the British seldom found its way into print, but in April 1941 it did. General Arnold was planning a trip to Britain, which was at war but the US was not. Echols gave Brig. Gen. George Kenney a memo. Britain had suggested that America produce the Hawker Typhoon. Echols told Kenney: "*I think that, of course, anything that comes out of England at this particular time is a description of the Typhoon. As you know they are endeavoring to bring heavy pressure to bear upon us to manufacture the Typhoon, and (Baker's) requirement is, as you know, a description of that airplane, except that the Typhoon does not go to 38,000 feet. As you know General Arnold is leaving tomorrow for a month in England, and he will return all envisioned with English requirements as has everyone else who has returned from England, and I would not be a bit surprised if, while over there, they will sell him on the ideas in regard to pursuit armament, and, consequently, I think we should be prepared to make such variations in our airplanes as he demands upon his return.*" [1]

The US never did manufacture Typhoons and the AAF had set 38,000 ft as the requirement for its interceptors. Echols told Kenney that the .50 caliber machine gun was "*...actually equal to the present 20 mm guns.*"

Shortly before that, Echols had sent Capt. Lee to California to downgrade the Mustang. In January 1942 the XP-51 and

P-40F were flight-tested by Kelsey and his subordinates. Kelsey's and Wolfe's offices were both subordinated to that of Echols and Wolfe was responsible for notifying Materiel of results of flight tests. Wolfe filed a report in which Maj. Kelsey opined that the Mustang's "*... stability was satisfactory. Its controllability was satisfactory except for lateral control. Its rolling rate was about one-half that of other pursuit types, such as the P-40. The relative high speed compared with the P-40F was obtained by simply flying side by side and opening both planes up to military power at 12,000 feet, at 16,000 feet, and at 21,000 feet. At 12,000 feet the P-51 pulled away from the P-40F with an estimated margin of approximately 10 mph. (XP-51) take-off is sluggish and the landing gear retraction is slow so that initial climb is not fast.*" At about 500 mph in a dive "*...there was an unpleasant shudder*" caused by a "*...tendency of the wheel fairing doors to open. In general the P-51 should be superior to the P-40E (and) superior to the P-40F up to about 15,000 feet and inferior above except for diving in which it is superior at all altitudes.*" [2]

In March 1942 Wolfe asked Kelsey to elaborate on the spot check of the XP-51. Kelsey replied: "*... the comment on combat between the P-40 and the Mustang is probably correct. The conclusion is that the Mustang is able to engage or break off combat at will, due to its higher speed. The XP-51 was flown against the P-40F at Wright Field and was faster at all altitudes below 16,000 feet.*" [3]

Despite Kelsey's comments, the P-40F was preferred as a fighter because it had high-altitude capability, and Echols attempted to stop Mustang production once RAF contracts were fulfilled later in 1942.

Throughout most of 1942, few officers approved of the P-51. The first American fighter pilots to get into combat were the "Eagles" and the "Flying Tigers." Both expatriate groups saw action in 1941. The three Eagle squadrons were transferred from the RAF to the USAAF in September 1942 and sometime in October of that year, Lt. Col. Chesley Peterson, who was later to command the 4th FG, was ordered to proceed from Britain to Wright Field to serve on a board of officers to select the best fighter for 1943.

Before Peterson left Britain, Tommy Hitchcock called him to talk about the P-51 and invited him to fly the Rolls-Royce

Merlin-Mustang. Sometime after 13 October Peterson flew it and liked it. Upon arriving back at Wright Field, Peterson flew P-51 serial number 42-37320 and stated it was his choice as the best new type. An authority on the "Eagles", Vern Haugland, has recorded that Saville, Maj. Gen. George Stratemeyer and Brig. Gen. V.E. Bertrandias told Peterson that the P-51 as a fighter was "...*not in the inventory*" and "...*not in the terms of reference*." Kuter was enthusiastic about the Mustang and got Peterson an appointment with Arnold who told Peterson "...*the P-51 is finished. The last one coming off the line will be a dive bomber*." [4]

Hitchcock arrived in America on a brief visit and had dinner with Peterson in Washington. After Peterson told Hitchcock about the coming end of the P-51 as a fighter type, Hitchcock probably met with Roosevelt. Peterson recalled: "...*two days later, President Roosevelt announced that a new version of the Mustang, with the Rolls-Royce engine, would be built*." [5] The date of Roosevelt's announcement was around 10 November 1942. On that date Roosevelt sent a note to Arnold:"*I am told by an American friend returning from England that the British are very keen about the P-51 and feel they could use Rolls-Royce engines in them. Do you know something about it? They tell me it is essentially similar in design to the Focke-Wulf Fw 190 A-3. Can you give me a tip?*" [6]

Roosevelt's query turned Wright Field's plans around. Within seconds of receiving Roosevelt's note, Arnold sent a memo to Echols asking him to fill in numbers of P-51s to be built, in the blanks in a rough draft of Arnold's proposed reply to Roosevelt.. Within hours Arnold received Echols' figures and responded to Roosevelt: "*The Royal Air Force is very keen about the P-51 and we have installed Rolls-Royce engines in two of them - one in England and one in the United States. Tests indicate that they will be highly satisfactory Pursuit planes for 1943. We think so much of them that we have already given orders for approximately 2,200. They are similar in design to the Focke-Wulf 190 but we believe them to be a very much better airplane on account of their ruggedness, superior armament, and equal, if not better performance.*" [7]

Echols changed the original draft of Arnold's proposed reply in order to show that no more Mustangs would go to the RAF. [8] In fact, many Mustangs later went to the British. Echols' figure of 2,200 Mustangs included 1,200 P-51As, 400 P-51Bs, 550 P-51A-1-NAs, and 57 takeovers totaling 2,207.

After learning that the Generals had turned down Peterson's choice and that Arnold told Peterson the Mustang would not be a fighter type, Hitchcock wrote a memo in October which criticized Materiel. Major Hitchcock took Major General Echols into account. In part the memo stated: "*The order (for RAF Mustangs) did not pass through Wright Field.*"

The British Air Fighting Development Unit report dated 5 May 1942, said the Mustang was "...*an excellent low and medium-altitude fighter and certainly is the best American fighter that has so far reached this country. The interesting qualities of the Mustang airframe were brought to the attention of General Arnold and Admiral Towers when they were in London on June last, by the American Ambassador, Air Chief Marshal Sir Charles Portal, Chief of the Air Staff, Air Chief Marshal Sir Sholto Douglas, Commander in Chief Fighter Command, and Air Marshal F.J. Linell, Ministry of Aircraft Production Research and Development. Robert Lovett, Assistant Secretary of War for Air, was also advised by letter dated June 5, 1942, of the importance which English and various American representatives attach to the Mustang airframe and the desirability of energetically pushing the Merlin development. Mr. (Phil) Legarra, North American representative, reported when he came back from the United States in the early part of September, that the Mustang had the lowest priority that could be granted to an airplane. Sired by the English out of an American mother, the Mustang has had no parent in the Army Air*

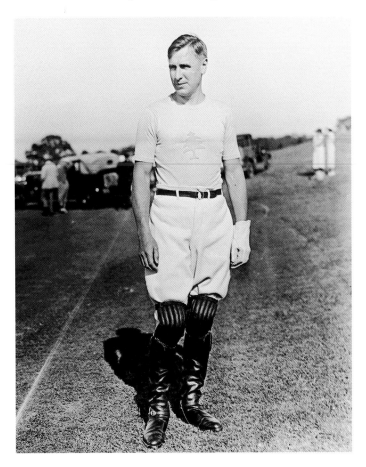

Tommy Hitchcock, Jr., was a great thorn in the side of General Echols over the issue of Echols' dislike of the Mustang. The greatest polo player in the world in the 1930s and a hero of the First World War, Hitchcock had flown fighters in one war and wanted to fly Mustangs in the second. He was from "high society" and was unafraid of Echols and the so-called "experts" in the Materiel Command.

Corps or at Wright Field to appreciate and push its good points. It does not fully satisfy important people on both sides of the Atlantic who seem more interested in pointing with pride to the development of a 100 percent national product than they are concerned with the very difficult problem of rapidly developing a fighter plane that will be superior to anything the Germans have. [9]

Disputing this, Kelsey had said the XP-51 had a sluggish take-off, thus the Mustang would not be an interceptor because it received judgement that it was too heavy. In September 1942, Col. (later, Lt. Gen.) Benjamin Chidlaw, Chief of the Experimental Engineering Branch, told the Assistant Chief of Staff commanding the War, Organization, and Movement (WO&M) Division that: *"...no other known airplane has the combined qualities of high-speed and low-speed handling characteristics as the P-51 airplane."* [10]

In a letter to Colonels Mervin Gross and Boatner, Chidlaw noted: *"...the AAF Representative stated that the climb characteristics of this aircraft were its most undesirable feature and that every effort had been made to eliminate weight."* [11]

In November, Chidlaw repeated his quote at a Joint Aircraft Committee's (JAC) sub-committee meeting in which representatives from the War Production Board (WPB), AAF, Navy, BAC, Royal Navy and NAA were present. Chidlaw commented: *"... the Army Air Forces' representative stated that the climb characteristics of this aircraft was its most undesirable feature and that every effort had been made to eliminate weight in an attempt to improve this characteristic."* [12]

Because America had not declared war until two years after Germany had invaded Poland, USAAF fighter types were developed slowly. In 1942, Echols promoted personally two

types, the XP-60 and XP-75. In November the AAF contracted with General Motors to design and develop two prototype XP-75 Eagles, and despite the fact that Curtiss had been told in January 1942 that the XP-60 series was cancelled, the AAF allowed the company to continue to experiment with it. One year after the US went to war, the USAAF was desperate to field a world-class interceptor. By November, fresh interest in the P-51B raised the Mustang into prominence like a Phoenix from the ashes. However, officers searching for interceptors thought the Mustang was too heavy. Echols told Brig. Gen. Franklin O. Carroll that he, Echols, had promised Saville that he: *"...would see to it that we did everything reasonable to keep the initial structure of the P-60 and P-75 light. As you know, in our endeavors to increase rate of climb, particularly with such an airplane as the P-51, the basic airplane is so heavy structurally that it seems to be an impossibility to ever get an airplane that will meet the modern ideas in regard to rate of climb."* [13]

Schmued's Lightweight Mustang

By October 1942, flight test comparisons of a captured Japanese Zero in the US revealed its light construction, high climb rate, long range, and outstanding maneuverability. Respect was afforded to Japanese designers who had previously been thought to be incompetent. The USAAF began considering stripping fighters of excess weight and equipment to convert them into interceptors, and Saville sent Arnold the first reports about it. The concept of the 400 mph, 4000 lb fighter emerged and Bell's XP-77 was completed but not ordered. A report dated 12 October 1942, had as its subject the *'Elimination of Weight in P-51A-1-NA Airplanes.'* NAA began a thorough search of items to remove from the Mustang. Edgar Schmued understood that stripping was less satisfactory in the long run because it would delay production. Schmued opted to design a model of the Mustang from the ground up, as a lightweight fighter and it was to be an improvement on the Merlin-Mustang, not the P-51A. Schmued visited Britain in February and April 1943 to discuss using lighter British-type landing gear and propellers. His visits had not been formally requested on the part of the USAAF and were monitored by USAAF officers, some of whom doubted reasons for an American, born in Germany, to be talking with British officials about a model of the Mustang for which the USAAF had not yet ordered prototypes. Schmued's concept created the first great change in fighter development since 1937 and was so successful that the XP-51F was ordered on 20 July 1943. It made its first flight on 14 February 1944, weighing 1,500 lb less than a standard P-51D.

The AAF was extremely interested in securing interceptors and NAA worked intensively to design a lightweight Mustang. Edgar Schmued created this XP-51F, the first true AAF fighter built from scratch as a lightweight fighter designed to climb as high as the German Bf 109G.

Brigadier General B.W. Chidlaw, though mostly interested in single-engined interceptors, continually described the P-51B as being too heavy.

Control of Plants - Part III

The peak of America's production came in 1944, but in 1942 production was increasing so rapidly that President Roosevelt requested an astronomical figure of 125,000 aircraft to be produced in 1943. He made the request late in 1942, when industry was already producing to full capacity and the monthly rate of production would carry over into 1943, preventing achievement of the President's goal. Roosevelt's request was immediately rejected by his closest associates and by the AAF. He became disappointed with Military's control of plants. After the war, statistics revealed that 85,898 aircraft were built in 1943 alone, in itself a world-class feat by any measure. More were produced in 1944 while other countries produced far less. But in 1942, Roosevelt created the Aircraft Board under the direction of C.E. Wilson. Donald Nelson, Chairman of the WPB, told Wilson that a Navy officer and Echols would be members of the Aircraft Board. Nelson's letter angered Arnold, who reacted against creation of the Aircraft Board saying that although the Board might *"...facilitate the production of military aircraft – we all recognize the fact that an evil now exists – a lesser production rate. The method proposed does not accomplish that, but on the contrary definitely substitutes another evil, namely the breaking-up of a going concern, the Army Air Forces Materiel Command."* [14]

When Echols learned that much of his command was to be ruled by civilian authority, he offered to resign. In the event, Arnold decided to retain him. However, the Army was so alarmed about the situation that it prepared a *'Digest of War Department's Views on Proposed Transfer of Military Procurement to Civilian Control'* which listed precedents dating back to 1917. The Digest said it would be a *"grave mistake"* to shift the *"...procurement of munitions from military to civilian control"* because it *"divides responsibility and authority."* The timing of the shift *"...would require a complete disruption of the organization of the Army."*

Eleventh-Hour Criticisms

The AAF did not stop believing that the P-38 was the best in its inventory and best in the world, until 1944. After June 1943, when the P-51B was being mass-produced, Col. Chidlaw, who had earlier viewed the Mustang as being too heavy, stated: *"...at first glance from a comparison of dollars-man-hours, fuel used, materials, versus performance, it might seem uneconomical to go on building P-38s as against P-51s on a strictly fighter basis. On the other hand, from a fighter-bomber-torpedo-photographic-reconnaissance general utility standpoint, (the P-38) comes close to being the best all-around airplane we have."* [15]

Eglin Field's test-pilot reports specifically mentioned that the P-51A had the longest range of any AAF fighter. That news drew sarcasm from Chidlaw. He commented: *"...the information as presented has no particular significance except as it might influence the decision as to fighter types to be used in places like China, Attu, etc., where the problem of supplying fuel, oil, ammunition, and other supplies is critical."* [16]

Chidlaw thought it would have been better if the P-51 were based where long, boring, unimportant flights were the norm and fuel-economizing P-51s found a place worthy of their "restricted" capabilities.

In 1943 Arnold made a tour of Far East facilities and met with very senior officers, but he also met with Col. Homer Sanders, who led the P-40-equipped 51st FG in Karachi. Sanders had won the Silver Star for aerial combat on 25 October, and Arnold honored him with a meeting. Sanders, in a letter sent to his friend Col. (later, General) Mark Bradley, a test pilot at Wright Field, said: *"... it was in February when Gen. Arnold came through Assam on his way to China and when I told him 'we do all right, we make the Japs pay 25 for 1 of us, but the airplane we have just does not have the range for us to perform our mission.' He answered 'What airplane do you want?' and I told him the P-51 Mustang. Whereupon he replied 'Why build last year's airplane today?'"* [17]

Colonel Mark Bradley about to fly a P-47. Bradley succeeded Colonel Ben Kelsey as Chief of Fighter Projects at Wright Field in 1943 and made the central modification to the P-51B which allowed it to fly as far as Berlin. That fuselage tank idea saved the European bombing campaign from defeat by the Luftwaffe.

An F-5, 'Dim View', serves as a noisy backdrop for, from left, an unidentified Major General, Col. Homer L. Sanders, and Col. James G. Hall. At the time of this photograph, Sanders was succeeding Hall as CO of the 7th Photo Group.

A Last-Ditch Discreditation

After the P-51B had been put into production, criticism continued. On 6 July 1943, a flight-test report of a P-51B was sent by Col. Mervin E. Gross to Echols. The report quoted the ravings of an anonymous officer but Gross sent it anyway. Gross said: *"... an officer in this division"* flew a P-51B and listed *"...the following unsatisfactory"* comments. The propeller *"...discharges a fine spray of oil"* and the engine had *"...a very pronounced beat not unlike a twin-engined airplane with engines unsynchronized. The airplane seems to shrink and expand in unison with the beats. This unpleasant phenomenon appears to be more pronounced at high altitude. The climb indicator and altimeter momentarily react in reverse to the application of control. It is desirable to be able to exhaust one main tank at a time"* when operating the fuel system. [18]

Colonel M.E. Gross was handed General Arnold's order to acquire an escort fighter from Lieutenant General Barney Giles. Gross established the performance minimums necessary for an escort to fly as far as a B-17 and B-24, but opened the door – on Echols' advice – for the XP-75. Until Gross set new range minimums, the AAF had neglected to experiment with escort possibilities other than the XP-58.

Whoever wrote such absurdity was neither a test pilot nor a fighter pilot. Probably he was someone ordered to resurrect the XP-60 by casting a cloud over the Mustang. He was too late. Gross told Echols the P-51B was slower than the XP-60E, adding that *"...the decision not to build the P-60 type should be restudied in the light of increasing fuel capacity to produce a high-speed offensive fighter powered by a two-stage air-cooled engine."* Echols reminded Gross that the P-60 series *"...had been definitely canceled."*

The fighter development program contained lingering problems and was managed in some departments by a few officers with towering egos. These drawbacks revealed themselves in the months during 1943 when bomber and crew losses threatened to exceed replacements. Arnold, alarmed by mission reports filed by bomber crews over Germany, decided that the time had come to put an escort into combat.

Chapter 10

"Into the hands of the wolves"

The Need for Escort Increased

Following the first B-17 mission in July 1942, the tempo of bombing operations over France from Britain increased only slightly; the Eighth AF would become a fearsome armada only much later. A reduced Eighth AF continued operations as the Allies invaded North Africa in November, using many former Eighth AF units. During the second half of 1942, a few deceiving trends surfaced. Bomber gunners were credited with shooting down two enemy aircraft on 21 August and by the end of the year nearly 200 victories were credited to bomber gunners. On the 20 December mission to Romilly-sur-Seine, gunners were credited with the very high and somewhat unverifiable number of 53 victories, yet very few bombers were shot down over Europe in the latter half of 1942. Two B-17s were lost on 6 September with a total of 31 bombers being lost by the end of the year. These statistics justified the belief in the four-engined, daylight, self-defending bomber and went hand-in-hand with decisions which left just one fighter group in Eighth Fighter Command (VIII FC).

Light bomber losses, coupled with a large number of enemy kills claimed by the gunners, contributed to a wave of good feeling. This allowed combat operations by the Eighth AF to continue throughout the latter half of 1942 which eased officers into overconfidence. On 11 January 1943, 16 days before the first USAAF bomber mission to Germany (Wilhelmshaven), Eaker wrote to Arnold: "*The bubble of the invincibility of the GAF has been, I think, completely pricked.*" The 18 March mission to Vegesack was hailed in glowing terms because, for a loss of two bombers, 52 enemy fighters were claimed destroyed or damaged.

Upbeat statistics lulled desk staff back in the US into complacency over escort development. The ground support type was the most-wanted new fighter, not the escort. Hitler's forces were fighting in North Africa and Russia and the *Führer* was not bothered by Eighth AF pinprick raids to France. In late 1942, Germany was far more concerned with winning its stand-or-die offensive at Stalingrad. A few raids by B-17s did not constitute a dangerous threat to Germany and they were not as seriously opposed, as happened later in 1943.

Eaker was not alone in sensing that victory from aerial bombardment would be possible either in 1943 or 1944 at the latest. Some thought a land invasion would not even be necessary – Germany would be beaten by air power. Bomber crews were the knife-edge of the air effort and desk officers were content to let fighter pilots fly their assigned sweeps which had little effect. Fighter pilots were not held in high regard. As far back as 1933, when Capt. Chennault's air defense claims had been overruled by Army judges sympathetic to Westover's bombers in his military exercise, fighter pilots were believed to be less important than bomber crews who constituted the primary mission of the Air Corps. Excessive optimism carried the bomber mission on a collision course with the *Luftwaffe*.

Because the Air Corps had set extremely high standards for pilot recruitment in the budget for the 1930s, some men who could not get into the service to fly fighters, signed contracts to fly and fight in foreign uniform. Three RAF Eagle Squadrons were subsequently formed of Americans who flew fighters but these units were criticized by Air Corps officers based in the London Embassy. General Arnold later visited Britain, met the Eagles and said in his last published book that some were prima donnas. After the Eagles were inducted into the USAAF as the 4th Fighter Group in late September 1942 and began flying escort for bombers in their Spitfires, they were told to serve the bomber war and keep their high-spirited fervor to themselves.

By November 1942, at the time of the invasion of North Africa, all fighter groups in Britain except the 4th FG had been ordered into the North African air war. Flying its Spitfire Vs with American markings, the 4th FG did its best to escort

North Weald, November 1941: American fighter pilots of No 71 Eagle Squadron, RAF, pose with Congressman J.B. Snyder, Chairman of the Military Affairs Committee and General Ralph Royce, Air Attaché. Of note is the American flag sewn with the symbol of the Eagles.

what the real combat radius of the Thunderbolt was). The P-47 carried 305 US gallons of fuel internally and a Spitfire carried only 85, yet the fuel-guzzling R-2800 engine consumed 300 gallons per hour which limited combat radius of the P-47 to between 170 and 200 miles – barely more than the Spitfire. Instead of acceding to Eaker's request for more drop tanks, Materiel did nothing. Overlooked was the statistic that VIII FC operations in the last half of 1942 registered only 10.5 victories. There appeared to be no urgency for drop tanks for fighters since bomber gunners were racking up all the kills.

The drop tank Eaker requested was either the 75-gallon or a 200-gallon, bulbous-shaped, non-pressurized, drag-producing ferry tank which was not being mass-produced. Without pressurization, fuel could not be forced upward out of any drop tank and a P-47 could not use its drop tank fuel above an altitude of 22,000 ft. It would have been normal for a fighter group climbing above 22,000 ft to drop the tanks whether or not fuel was in them. Carrying the 200-gallon drop tank in flight caused turbulence around the tail.

Between 5-16 February 1943, the RAF and AAF conducted tactical trials at Duxford using the P-47, P-38F, Spitfire IXs and XIIs, Hawker Typhoon, and a Rolls-Royce Mustang X. USAAF pilots flew the Mustang and liked it. General Eaker however believed wholeheartedly in the P-38. Eaker, ever the quiet General, had lost his P-38s to the Twelfth AF in late 1942 but it was not until 15 February 1943 – the

Taken at Debden, this photograph shows 4th Fighter Group pilots at rest on a Jeep. Captain Don Gentile is nearest the camera reading a book. Lieutenant Ervin L. "Dusty" Miller, without cap, is standing directly behind him.

bombers, but they could reach no farther than perhaps 40 miles inland from the French coastline before pilots turned back for home bases with just enough fuel remaining to get them there. Many *Luftwaffe* fighter pilots had flown in combat on many fronts, yet VIII FC fighter pilots seemed unable to score victories. It must have appeared to desk officers in the US and Britain that there was nothing to be alarmed about because B-17 gunners were doing all the necessary damage while so few bombers were being shot down. So it was that neither General Arnold or his desk officers saw need to criticize fighter pilots openly in the first half of 1943.

P-38s were pulled out of the ETO and Spaatz was reassigned to the Mediterranean in December 1942. Eaker was given command of the Eighth AF. The first P-47Ds were assigned to VIII FC and in October 1942 Eaker – who had test-flown a P-47 and praised it – asked Materiel for drop tanks (he may have known

Left to right: Colonel Edward W. Anderson, CO of the 4th FG, Lord Trenchard, Brigadier General Frank Hunter, Major General Ira Eaker, Group Captain Nixon, and Brigadier General Newton Longfellow.

Above: Taken by Roy Evans, this close-up of a P-47 carrying a 200-gallon ferry tank illustrates the drag potential produced by such an unwieldy bulge below the belly. Evans came to the 359th Fighter Group from the 4th Fighter Group as an ace and an Eagle who began flying for the RAF in May 1941.

Above: Lieutenant Colonel Don Blakeslee of the 4th FG goes over last-minute checks on his P-47D prior to engine start.

Above: Later a Lieutenant Colonel, Oscar Coen sits in the spacious cockpit of a P-47D, possibly his own — QP✪E — of the 4th Fighter Group.

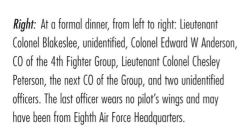

Right: At a formal dinner, from left to right: Lieutenant Colonel Blakeslee, unidentified, Colonel Edward W Anderson, CO of the 4th Fighter Group, Lieutenant Colonel Chesley Peterson, the next CO of the Group, and two unidentified officers. The last officer wears no pilot's wings and may have been from Eighth Air Force Headquarters.

Left to right: Colonel Edward W. Anderson, CO of the 4th Fighter Group, Brigadier General Frank Hunter, Commanding General of VIII Fighter Command, and Assistant Secretary of War for Air, Robert Lovett. The men are standing on top of the control tower at RAF Debden during the departure of P-47s.

Colonel Edward W. Anderson, CO of the 4th Fighter Group, Brigadier General Hunter, and an unidentified crewman point out the P-47D's armament to a curious Duchess of Kent.

penultimate day of the trials – that he told Arnold: "*…we are just getting up off the floor from the loss of our P-38 fighters.*" Spaatz had taken them with him to the MTO.

After the 4th FG converted to P-47s, it flew the first Thunderbolt combat mission on 10 March 1943, but teething troubles plagued the aircraft and caused a lull in operations. By early April, elements of two more fighter units were combat-operational and pilots of the 56th and 78th Fighter Groups flew their new P-47s into the base of the 4th FG at Debden, on 8 April for the first large mission on the 10th. On the 15th during the raid to St. Omer, three enemy aircraft were shot down by P-47s but three of the latter were lost due to engine failures. Arnold sent an angry letter to Echols demanding that he bring it "*… to the attention of the Pratt & Whitney company and (have) some drastic measures taken to remedy such a terrible situation.*"

Two days after the first, big P-47 mission, the bombers suffered a disaster from lack of escort. As part of a force of 117 B-17s, the 306th BG dispatched 22 over Bremen and lost 10, a 45 percent loss rate – almost half the force. Bomber losses totalled 16 but the gunners claimed 63 victories. P-47 Thunderbolts could not fly as far as Bremen and were confined to "sweeps" over Holland.

The 17 April mission was the turning point in the academic debate over whether or not to furnish escort; days after the P-47s made their appearance, they were simply unable to escort bombers to Bremen.

VIII FC was commanded by Brig. Gen. Frank O'Driscoll Hunter, a former First World War fighter pilot who had a distinctive moustache, loved parties, but was not admired by the black Americans he once commanded.[1] Hunter fully understood fighters and asked Eaker to expand VIII FC:

"*… the fighter mission will continue to be the support of day bombardment both at high and intermediate altitudes but the size of an adequate force is determined not by the number of bombers to be protected but by the strength of the opposition to be expected, the range at which we must operate, and the relative performance of our fighters and those of the enemy.*" Hunter asked for "*…20 fighter groups*" to gain air superiority and said "*… it is not believed that the P-47 is a suitable airplane for close escort but that it can be more effectively employed either in general support or as high cover to close escort fighters. A medium-altitude fighter of sufficient range is required and it is believed that the most suitable one in the picture at present, is the P-51 equipped with a Merlin 65 engine. There is no need in this theater for a high-performance short range fighter until invasion of the continent is attempted. It is not economical to use our fighters at their extreme range until they can be concentrated in sufficient numbers to neutralize the enemy fighter force by sheer weight of numerical superiority.*" [2]

Hunter showed a certain grasp of what was required, but he was to be the victim of character assassination in June when failure of the P-47 to escort was blamed on him instead of its short range.

Less than a month after the 306th BG suffered its 45 percent loss rate, 136 bombers took off to bomb Kiel. During the mission, the 44th BG lost five of its 17 bombers and a total of eight heavies did not return. Gunners claimed 62 enemy fighters.[3] The P-47s were again sent on sweeps over Holland and downed three enemy aircraft, but lost four of their own.

Above: A line-up of P-47s of the 368th Fighter Squadron, 359th Fighter Group, photographed on 28 January 1944 and all bearing nicknames taken from the 'Lil' Abner' comic strip. All have drop tanks and are painted in the standard camouflage and understated personal markings of the early period.

Above: The 359th Fighter Group exchanged P-47s for P-51s in April 1944 and in May, this photograph commemorated the changeover. S/Sgt. Marshall L. Binder hands paperwork to Lieutenant Harold L. Hollis. The large number of mission symbols painted on the P-47 indicates the great effort expended by the 359th Fighter Group.

On 17 May an entire unescorted flight of ten Martin B-26 Marauders was lost on a mission to Ijmuiden in Holland. Three days earlier, the same group had attacked the same target and none was lost. The next B-26 mission was not flown until 16 July. Later, all B-26s were given to the Ninth AF.

Four out of 18 B-17s from the 91st BG were shot down on 21 May during a raid on Wilhelmshaven, while P-47s flew sweeps over Holland, losing three, but not scoring. The 91st BG's loss rate was nearly 25 percent. Even a 10 percent loss rate made it virtually impossible for replacements to arrive in time to maintain unit strength.

Development of the XB-40 "destroyer" conversion (see Chapter 3) had proceeded to the point that a handful of YB-40s – the service test version fitted with additional machine guns – were flown to Britain. Eight machines were operated for the first time in combat on 29 May. Losses were relatively light on the missions to nearby targets in France and P-47s escorted also. YB-40s escorted on 22, 25, 26, 28, and 29 June and 4, 10, 14, 17, 26, and 29 July.[4] On 16 August, one YB-40 escorted and after that date the type was withdrawn from service.

It was theorized that since a YB-40 could carry the same fuel load as a B-17F, it should fly as far. Installing extra guns and ammunition added weight, and planners wanted the YB-40 to carry bombs! Pilots used extra power to keep in formation and thus used extra fuel; either that or the other bombers had to slow down to retain their 'escorts'.

By mid-1943 the YB-40 was finished, the XP-58 was still being tested, and the P-38 was not demanded by the Army for use in Britain because it had no troops there. It was the P-47 or nothing. Yet it was not until a significant number of bombers had been shot down that officers became

Above: One of the last P-47s to operate in the 359th Fighter Group, this 368th Fighter Squadron P-47D has a natural metal finish and green nose band.

concerned about the situation. They simply relied on the unverifiable statistics of credits given by bomber gunners. Kills were claimed when, after firing at a German fighter, they saw a burst of black smoke escape from the engine. The fact was that smoke appeared when the German pilot suddenly added power to evade bullets. Several gunners may have all been shooting at the same enemy fighter and all made claims. Post-war investigations could throw doubt upon – but not revise effectively – credits given to bomber gunners.

Statisticians thought bomber gunners were reducing the size of the *Luftwaffe*, yet bomber loss rates began to mount in 1943. Charges of non-support voiced by bomb group commanders about lack of escort by P-47s soon caused friction and even fights in bars. P-47 pilots were sent on many sweeps over Holland but they did not have the range to fly to Germany. After barely two months of operating with short-range P-47s, AAF headquarters became angry about the lack of escort. Perversely, one of Arnold's subordinates found fault with P-47 pilots and saint-like characters in bomber gunners, and Arnold believed him. Arnold was now extremely concerned about bomber and bomber-crew losses and a memo that reached his desk criticizing the lack of escort was taken by him to be the truth.

In 1943, while a Colonel on General Arnold's Advisory Council, Major General Emmett O'Donnell attempted to force a turnaround in the manner in which fighter escort was employed.

O'Donnell's Memo

Until 1962, when General Charles Gabriel, a career fighter pilot, became Chief of Staff of the USAF, all Chiefs were bomber men. Arnold was a bomber man and his staff was manned by bomber men. They respected bomber crews and by April 1943, there was more than just a tinge of disrespect for fighter pilots. Fighter pilots were often thought of as grandstanders, prima donnas, glory boys, fortune hunters, and soldiers-of-fortune. Desk officers believed that Brig. Gen. Hunter preferred to send P-47s on ineffectual sweeps rather than to drone along on straight-ahead bomber escort missions.

On Arnold's Advisory Council was Col. Emmett O'Donnell, a former bomber pilot. On 12 June 1943, O'Donnell issued a memo to Arnold which resulted in a dressing-down for Eaker, relief of Hunter, and severe criticism of P-47 pilots. Even today in reading, the worst part about O'Donnell's memo is that it is evident he was ignorant of fuel usage by a P-47 in a combat situation. This is a verbatim record of O'Donnell's memo:

" *1. Scrutiny of combat reports from (the) UK reveals that fighters are not escorting our heavy bombardment to the full extent of their capabilities. They have been in very little combat,* *have few operational losses, and have knocked down very few enemy aircraft.*

2. In talking with several pilots who have recently returned from (the) UK, I found that the maximum combat radius of the P-47 airplane is generally acknowledged to be only 160 or 170 miles.

3. This airplane has large internal tankage with a 300-gallon capacity. In addition, provision is made for an external 200-gallon tank. This quantity of gasoline should give a combat radius of action of at least 300 miles, and possibly up to 400. This takes into consideration formation flying, 20 minutes' combat, suitable reserves, and cruising at 75 percent sea-level power, which is maximum cruise condition.

4. It is reported customary for fighters in the UK to climb to ceiling on their belly tanks and then to drop the tanks, even though about 80 gallons of gas remain unused. Pilots are naturally anxious to burn the gas out of the auxiliary tank behind the pilot seat before getting into combat, in order to obtain a more favorable position of the center of gravity. While these practices will give the pilots a slightly better chance in combat, they are not essential and considerably reduce the distance over which close escort can be rendered to bombardment. The bombers are sustaining heavy losses and shooting down most of the enemy fighters accounted for in that theater themselves. Fighters to date have given them no real support.

5. It appears to me that the Fighter Command in the UK must be made aware of the fact that it is not fully executing its mission. If the P-47 airplane does not actually have the ability to escort on fairly deep penetrations, we have been badly fooled and our planning has been extremely faulty. We have a lot of eggs in that basket. It will be the only American fighter-type airplane in the UK until December 1943, when one Group of P-38s will make its appearance. If the P-47 does have the capabilities which are attributed to it, an investigation is warranted to determine why it is not being so employed. The large number of fighters which we have allocated to the UK are not paying their way if their participation in the bomber

A pair of 368th Fighter Squadron P-47 Thunderbolts take off for Germany in May 1944. CV✪Y (*nearest*), was flown by Lieutenant Arlen R. Baldridge and CV✪X was flown by Lieutenant Gaston M. Randolph.

This 351st Fighter Squadron, 353rd Fighter Group P-47 carries the 200-gallon ferry tank which caused vibration to the stabilizer in flight. Serialed 41-6528, this P-47C has, in common with most others, the turbo exhaust gate under the star-and-bar fuselage insignia.

offensive comprises escort across the Channel only. This in effect simply ensures the bombers' safe delivery into the hands of the wolves.

6 *Recommend that the attached wire, or something akin to it, be sent to General Eaker."* [5]

A P-47D of the 78th Fighter Group with its pilot and crew. The drop tank appears to be one of the 108-gallon paper tanks. The emblem beneath the cockpit depicts Superman.

No one had demanded that Republic make a long-range escort fighter of its P-47 and the AAF was extremely pleased to get it as it was. There seems to have been no pre-introduction flight test of combat range capability with a P-47 or presumably the report would have been in O'Donnell's hands. The P-47C and D carried 305 gallons internally and on that amount could fly 835 miles in still air on cruise power on a ferry flight. Combat radius is not half of range. The P-47 could not fly from Britain out to a distance of 417 miles in a combat situation.

Test pilots at Eglin Field should have been tasked to calculate the combat range of the P-47, but Materiel distrusted non-engineering testing and resisted sending new aircraft to the AFPGC. When aircraft were sent late, reports of results of tests from Eglin came late. Materiel refused to provide test aircraft until late in 1942. However, there was one logical, but short-sighted idea which governed all thinking: no one believed that a single-engine, single-seat fighter could possibly have long range. It was thought impossible that the fuel to carry it to Berlin and back could be crammed into a small aircraft and still have it carry offensive weapons. Efficient aerodynamics was not then an accepted science. Had someone demanded long range in a single-engine, single-seat fighter, Fairchild's directorate might have written specifications for such an aircraft, yet it would have been extremely difficult to design. NAA achieved the impossible in its P-51 in terms of long range in a small fighter. However, in 1942 and 1943, the Mustang was still not considered formally and officially to be a fighter or an escort.

Lovett's Letter

The Assistant Secretary of War for Air, Robert Lovett, had made his own inspection trip to Britain, during which he visited all the UK-based fighter groups. Few of the fighter pilots he spoke with knew that Lovett was a decorated veteran of the First World War. He was a tall, trim, patrician man who came from a wealthy family, had a place in high financial circles, and who on sight did not appear to be a combat veteran. He was, in fact, a pioneer of air combat.[7] During the First World War he and some friends formed the Yale unit of the Naval Reserve Flying Corps and although this was a millionaires' club, the men learned how to fly. Lovett quit Yale in his Junior year, volunteered in 1917 for war service, served in the Royal Naval Air Service, and researched ways to destroy enemy submarines while they were docked. He led attacks on submarines and his success and bravery assured him promotions in rank and responsibility, and won him the Navy Cross.

P-47D 'Roger the Lodger' of the 78th Fighter Group is refueled.

Following the First World War, Lovett gravitated to Wall Street but his expertise with Germans caught up with him. While on a trip to Italy in 1940 for his financial corporation, he heard Germans boasting about how the war they had just started was going to be worse for Britain than it had been in 1914. Lovett wanted to help America re-arm and prepare. By December 1940 Lovett was invited to be Assistant Secretary of War for Air in the War Department. The AAF was fortunate to have a man of Lovett's background, patriotism, experience, and intelligence.

When Lovett returned from his visit to Britain, he wrote a letter to Arnold dated 18 June 1943, which, coming from the highest civilian official supervising the AAF, amounted to a direct order:

"By the time I arrived in England the majority of the engine difficulties of the P-47 had been licked and the planes were operating in very substantial numbers on sweeps over enemy-occupied territory. I visited all the fighter groups and talked with a large proportion of the fighter pilots. As a result of the engagements they have had with the enemy the pilots proved to their own satisfaction that the P-47 is faster than the Focke-Wulf at altitude and in the dive. Its radius of turn and rate of roll are as good as the Focke-Wulf's and enable it to follow the flight path of the Focke-Wulf in diving turns. The great majority of the pilots are sincerely pleased with the plane and its performance and state that while it is inferior to the Focke-Wulf 190 in rate of climb, angle of climb, search vision, and simplicity of control, they regard themselves as having an edge on the Fw 190 in fire power and in any combat where they start with an initial height advantage. General operation procedure calls for the use of the P-47 at altitudes

Major Harold Comstock in UN✪V and six other P-47s of the 63rd Fighter Squadron, 56th Fighter Group fly in tight formation somewhere over Britain. The lone "razorback" has been relegated to a rear position. After relaxation of regulations within the AAF regarding camouflage and markings, pilots and crew members experimented with a variety of finishes, evident here.

between 25,000 and 30,000 feet where the Fw 190 is definitely not very happy. Up to the time I left they had only one or two brushes with the Me 109G. The majority of the experienced pilots feel that the 109G has a definite edge on them in all the important fighter characteristics and they will, therefore, have to adjust their tactics accordingly. There are several things which they feel can and should be done promptly to improve their chances. They want to emphasize the changes which can be quickly made or installed in the field in England. The principal items are listed below, the first four being urgent necessities:

a. Larger propellers, perhaps of paddle airscrew type, to improve climb and general performance.

b. Water injection boost to give them more emergency power.

c. Belly tanks with adequate pump to operate at altitudes of 38,000 feet or over.

d. Improved rear visibility by use of bulged canopy similar to the Fw 190 or British Typhoon.

e. Paint inside of cockpit black to reduce reflection on canopy.

f. Provide automatic boost controls, particularly mixture control.

g. Improve rudder control – now too stiff.

h. Lighten up plane where possible.

i. Can maneuver flaps similar to Grumman F6F be used?

On the general subject of use of fighters out of Britain, it is increasingly apparent that fighter escort will have to be provided for B-17s on as many missions as possible in order particularly to get them through the first wave of the German fighter defense, which is now put up in depth so that the B-17s are forced to run the gauntlet both in to the target and out from it. The P-47s can serve as top cover if satisfactory belly tanks are developed for them. The ideal plane, however, now in production is the P-38 for long escort duty. Its two engines are a definite advantage and, strangely enough, its ease of recognition is a definite protection to both B-17s and the escorting fighters themselves. It has been used in over-water escort duty on operations with a radius of slightly over 400 miles. However, the moment it drops its wing tanks it must turn back. High hopes are felt for the P-51 with wing tanks. The Eighth Air Force needs from three to five groups of P-38s and some P-51s as escort fighters in order to meet the increasing opposition it is facing and will face on an ascending scale during the balance of this year." [6]

Lovett probably got his information about P-38Fs – built in the Lockheed factory to carry factory-built drop tanks – from veterans in North Africa. Though he requested P-51s and drop tanks in June, they had been given no consideration. Tens of thousands would have been needed and desk officers thought it wasteful if fighter pilots dropped them on every mission. The correct usage is that drop tanks are dropped in *combat*, but desk officers were more often career administrators and not combat-experienced fighter pilots

Lieutenant Wayne O'Connor poses for the camera on his P-47 with his pet dog. From the 63rd Fighter Squadron, 56th Fighter Group, this P-47C had the s/n 41-6216.

Arnold Reacts

General Arnold had O'Donnell's and Lovett's letters on his desk in mid-June and although both men had noted urgent problems with short range in the P-47, Arnold's anger thundered down upon innocent men instead. He criticized personally his old friend and book-writing associate, Ira Eaker, in a manner better suited to dressing down a private airman. His messages to Eaker humiliated a very loyal, hard-working, senior officer who had asked Echols during the previous October for more drop tanks. Arnold seethed:

"Of grave concern to me is the employment of your fighters. I cannot comprehend what value is derived from the frequently reported so-called offensive fighter sweeps in which the enemy is rarely sighted. Except as a means of consuming gasoline I can see no purpose in this practice. Meanwhile your bombardment goes out and returns unescorted or inadequately escorted to a distance which is definitely short of the P-47 capabilities... Bombardment is bearing full brunt of enemy fighter attack and to date have had no real support from American fighters. Apparently Germans know that our escort will leave bombers shortly after reaching the mainland and consequently withhold their attack until the departure of fighters. The P-47 was originally allocated to your theater because its characteristics were supposed to be such that it could escort bombardment on fairly deep penetrations. What is the reason for the short escort? I hesitate to ascribe it to the range characteristic of the P-47. This airplane has large internal tankage which should enable it to provide escort in large formations up to a distance of at least three hundred miles. I realize of course that there is a reluctance on the part of fighters to enter combat with internal auxiliary fuel full or partially full. I realize also

A bubbletop and "razorback" duo of P-47s of the 62nd Fighter Squadron, 56th Fighter Group take off. Note the belly-mounted drop tanks and non-standard camouflage on the rear machine.

the speed differential between the bombardment and fighter-type aircraft. I know too that the two hundred gallon auxiliary tanks, though useable are not entirely satisfactory at bombers' flight level. However, I cannot help but compare the excellent results accomplished with the P-38, an airplane with small internal tankage and the meagre results accomplished by your fighter command equipped with our best high-altitude escort fighters. I understand it is a practice in your theater to climb to altitude on the belly tank thus consuming about one hundred twenty gallons of gas and then dropping the tank with remaining eighty gallons of gas even though no combat is imminent. I consider this practice, if true, to be not only unnecessary but also inconsistent with the purpose for which the airplane was built. I understand further that it is a universal practice to cruise at high power while escorting in order to have speed up for combat if encountered. By throttling back and obtaining increased range should not our fighters have ample time to accelerate before actually engaging in combat? German pilots are known to avoid clashes with our fighters and go direct for the bombers. This practice should afford our fighters an advantage. I feel that a vigorous escort can successfully be accomplished if the fighters are less cautious. Higher fighter combat losses than those now reported may result from this policy but will be more than offset by reduced bomber losses. Desire you give this subject your personal attention and forward me your comments as soon as possible." [8]

The ferry tank was not mass-produced and dropping it caused a shortage. The story of availability of drop tanks in the first half of 1943 is one of access to records of individual fighter groups and is beyond the scope of this study. However, the history of the 4th FG states that it received 200-gallon unpressurized belly tanks on 16 July, one month after O'Donnell's memo. [9] Yet some groups must have employed drop tanks earlier for there to have been so much criticism of their use. The P-47 could carry the ferry tank but its underside was so close to the ground that the ugly addition nearly scraped the turf on take-off.

The other main fighter escort type, the P-38, was a complex design and its manufacturer was committed to building many other types of aircraft, thus P-38 production was slow. Lockheed was producing P-38s throughout 1942 and Republic began production of P-47s in May. Naturally there were more P-38s than P-47s produced in 1942 – 1,264 to 524. [10] But in 1943, production problems with the P-38 were revealed when only 2,213 rolled out compared to 4,426 P-47s.

Germany had been defeated at Stalingrad and in North Africa by mid-1943 and returned several veteran *Jagdgeschwader* to Europe to face the growing aerial threat emanating from Britain. RAF Bomber Command and the Eighth AF constituted a second front, just as deadly as the first front – the ground war in Russia. The growing number of AAF bombers was reaching targets in Germany. It was the bomber, not the fighters, which constituted a greater threat, though Germany's daytime air defenses were much stronger than in 1942. The *Luftwaffe* had been using head-on attacks to avoid most of the defensive machine gun fire coming at them from dozens of bombers in formation. AAF bomber loss rates became nearly intolerable. Lovett suggested making escort available, but there was none.

A line-up of Fw 190 A-6s of Sturmstaffel 1. This unit was formed to combat the Allied daylight bomber offensive and adopted a tactic of head-on attack which proved highly sucessful as the bombers had no defense against this maneuver.

Chapter 11

"You have got to get a fighter that can protect our bombers..."

Thoughts turn to the P-75

The 10.5 victories scored by fighter pilots in the ETO during the second half of 1942 was a trend which continued through into the first half of 1943. This is the record: 14 January, 2; 22 January, 4; 15 April, 3; 14 May, 5; 16 May, 3; 18 May, 2; 21 May, 1; 12 June, 1; 13 June, 3; 22 June, 7; 24 June, 7; 26 June, 4; and 29 June, 2.[1] By July 1943, VIII FC had been in combat for a year and had little to show for it, but in that month, the number of victories began to increase greatly. After April 1943, bombers and their crews – ten men to each B-17 and B-24 – were being lost at a prohibitive rate.

General Arnold wasted no time after digesting Lovett's letter and four days later, on 22 June 1943, gave an order which, by December, finally resulted in using the P-51B as an escort fighter. After a widespread reorganization of the AAF on March 29, Materiel lost some of its grip upon its responsibility for almost every aspect by which an aircraft proceeded from being a design entered in a competition, to mass-production. The Office of Operations, Commitments and Requirements (OC&R) now helped to control selection. Sent to Maj. Gen. Barney M. Giles who commanded OC&R, Arnold's order read:

"…*attached are Mr Lovett's comments on the P-47 situation in England. This brings to my mind very clearly the absolute necessity for building a fighter airplane that can go in and come out with the bombers. Moreover, this fighter has got to go into Germany. Perhaps we can modify some existing type to do the job. The P-38 has been doing a fine job from North Africa in escorting our B-17s 400 miles or more. Whether this airplane can furnish the same close escort against the (German Air Force) on the Western Front is debatable. Our fighter people in the UK claim that they can't stay with the bombers because (the bombers) are too slow and because (the fighters) must have top speed by the time they hit the coast. The P-38 is notable for its poor acceleration so perhaps it too will not be able to furnish close escort and be able to meet the FWs and 109s. About six months remains before deep daylight penetration of Germany begins. Within this next six months you have got to get a fighter that can protect our bombers. Whether you use an existing type or have to start from scratch is your problem. Get to work on this right away because by January 1944, I want fighter escort for all of our bombers from the UK into Germany*."[2]

Several phrases in Arnold's order were not followed as stated and it appears that the General changed his mind on some issues; for example, deep penetrations began earlier than six months.

Furthermore, the suggestion to create an escort from scratch if necessary prompted Echols to lead the AAF into a dead-end, wild-goose chase again with one more wasteful experimental fighter, the XP-75. However, Arnold stated that getting an escort was an "*absolute necessity*" and Giles later looked back on the emergence of the P-51B escort as the crowning achievement of his brilliant career.

Giles passed Arnold's order to Col. Gross in the reorganized and less powerful Air Defense Office (Saville had been given a new assignment). Giles requested that "…*you initiate a Routing and Record Sheet to MM&D calling for information as to which of our types of fighter aircraft now in production is most suitable for accompanying bombardment. Also which of our present types will lend itself more readily to modification for such a mission*." Giles wanted a reply in "…*the next 3 or 4 days*." [3]

MM&D stood for Materiel, Maintenance and Distribution, which was Echols' new and less powerful command following reorganization.

The GM/Fisher XP-75 Eagle

In most works on aviation and Second World War history, if the XP-75 is mentioned at all, it is usually as a footnote. In fact from July 1943 for more than a year, Echols promoted the XP-75 to be the supreme escort fighter and it was destined for mass-production. The XP-75 had its modest beginning in February 1942 when, in answer to a Request for Proposal (RFP), the huge General Motors corporation offered to produce aircraft for the war effort. GM had never designed an aircraft and later in the war, its Eastern Aircraft Division built Navy types designed by the Grumman Corporation when Grumman's production lines were filled to capacity. Seven months after the RFP, in September 1942, Echols negotiated with GM when Materiel thought the company could produce a single-engined interceptor. In 1942, the search for a single-engined interceptor was greater than that for an escort. GM responded with a design designated "XP-75". In signing a contract with GM, Echols let himself be guided by optimistic engineering promises, preference for big business rather than science, and resentment toward NAA. GM took a very long seven months to create a mock-up of its design.

The mock-up appeared at the exact moment that the USAAF had been driven to its knees in desperation to field an escort fighter type. Arnold's order of June 1943 to acquire an escort fighter had opened a loophole for Echols when Arnold said "… *start from scratch*." Yet Echols' actions of July 1943 – agreeing with GM that the XP-75 could be made into an escort type – went beyond all bounds of sound engineering principles. Because Echols believed in big companies, he put another unnecessary, distracting, expensive and, for him, typical roadblock in the path of destiny for the unique P-51B.

Briefly, the XP-75 was a mid-engined design with a cockpit placed far forward on the fuselage. It was powered by the experimental in-line Allison V-3420 (not ready in 1942), and was to have a ceiling of 38,000 ft with a 5,600 fpm climb rate. First flight came on 17 November 1943; according to reports, engineers had set the center of gravity incorrectly and the XP-75 had disturbing flight characteristics. Russel Thaw, company test pilot, said its "...*stability in yaw (was) questionable.*" The vertical and horizontal stabilizers were enlarged and redesigned. On 25 November, Echols wrote: "...*these airplanes are to be in production, fully service tested – all bugs out of (the) airplane and engine – and in service in overseas theaters by mid-summer 1944.*"

The 12,000 lb XP-75 grew to 16,007 lbs and its final weight was 19,420 lb, making it much larger than a 9,000 lb P-51B. Four of the ten guns fired through the arc of the moving, contra-rotating propeller. As an escort it was predicted to have a 3,112-mile range while carrying two 75-gallon drop tanks.

The designer of the GM XP-75 had come from Curtiss. Donovan Berlin had found success with his P-36, P-40 and C-46, a twin-engined transport. His other aircraft designs were often dismal failures. Donovan Berlin's Curtiss XP-42, XP-46, XP-53, XP-55, XP-60, XP-62, and XP-71 were only indifferent prototypes. It was said he quit Curtiss in late 1942 to go to work for GM because his P-40 was not allowed to be re-engined with Packard's two-stage V-1650-3. In fact, on 17 January 1942 a memo stated that installation of the Merlin 61 in the P-40 was "...*out of the question without major change in airframe design, principally due to balance requirements.*" Berlin would not concede that his ability to design fighters was at an end.

In September 1942, when Berlin, GM's new Manager of Aircraft Development, offered Echols the XP-75, he was at the end of his career. Unable to come up with a war-winning design, Berlin offered the XP-75 as an aircraft to be made by utilizing parts of other aircraft which were already in production! The XP-75 was consequently to have the tail of the Douglas A-24, Vought F4U landing gear, and the wings of the P-40! It was an indescribably bad creation but Materiel – turning a blind eye to the P-51B – let GM proceed. The cost of two XP-75 interceptors ordered in October 1942, a wind tunnel model and some engineering data, came to $428,271.

Between 1 and 3 May 1943, the mock-up of the XP-75 was inspected at GM's Detroit headquarters and afterward, a change from the wings of the P-40E to the wings of the P-51 was ordered. GM's Fisher Body Division plant in Cleveland, Ohio was to produce the XP-75. [4]

The XP-75 mock-up and prototype had been under construction for nine months and no one showed much interest in it until July 1943. On 3 July, just a few days after Arnold's and Giles' letters were sent, Gross told Echols:

"*In order to provide continuous fighter cover for bombardment aircraft operating from the United Kingdom into Germany under the current fighter-bombardment airplane ratio, it is necessary that the duration of presently available fighters be increased or that a new type of long-duration fighter be developed. It has been assumed in the past that a radius of action expressed in miles provides an intelligent basis for the determination of fuel capacity requirements. This assumption is erroneous. Duration of the bombardment mission is the controlling factor. In the case of present operations, fighter aircraft will require a duration of approximately six hours plus thirty minutes reserve. To absolutely insure this duration will be attained requires that all fuel be carried internally. This requirement is highly impracticable and would impose a severe limitation on the combatability of the fighter airplane. Study and flight test of available fighter airplanes indicate the following duration can be expected under the conditions listed:*"

a. *Warm-up and take-off;*

b. *Climb to 25,000 at maximum continuous power;*

c. *Fifteen minutes operation at military power;*

d. *Five minutes operation at war emergency power;*

e. *Thirty minutes fuel remaining at minimum cruise for landing. The P-51B with 184 gallons of inside (sic) fuel and 150 gallons of outside fuel will remain in the air for approximately four hours and forty-five minutes consuming an average of 64 gallons per hour. The P-38J with 300 gallons of inside fuel and 300 gallons of outside fuel will remain in the air for approximately four hours consuming an average of 144 gallons of fuel per hour. The P-47D with 305 gallons of inside fuel and 165 gallons of outside fuel will remain in the air approximately three hours consuming an average of 140 gallons per hour. The foregoing items are based on retaining external tanks until dry, at which time they are dropped. Preliminary investigation by this Division indicates the following:*

i. *No available fighter airplane can remain in the air for six hours under conditions outlined in paragraph 3. (The study and test - author)*

ii. *Available fighter airplanes most nearly approaching the desired range in order of ability are the P-51B, P-38J, P-47D.*

iii. *The P-38 type is best able to accommodate additional internal fuel. External fuel capacity must be 75 to 85 percent of internal capacity. Full consideration should be given to leak-proofing external tanks. It is requested that your comments reach this office by 09.00 July 5.*" [5]

Right: The XP-75 was part of a special Request for Proposal (RFP) of 1942 put to the huge General Motors corporation to compete in the process, even though GM had never designed a fighter. The result was the XP-75 Eagle, made up of the tail of an A-24, the landing gear of the F4U, and the wings of the P-40. The XP-75 had its engine aft of the cockpit. The photograph shows the stubs of four machine guns mounted behind the spinner; six more were to be mounted in the wings.

Left: This side view of the XP-75 reveals the unusual cockpit which came to an abrupt end at the rear.

Right: The centrally mounted V-3420 Allison engine and the forward nose weapons compartment of the XP-75 are illustrated here. Nose armament required an interruptor gear.

Above: This view of the XP-75 shows the strange canopy, fixed A-24-type tailwheel, and the F4U landing gear not covered by gear doors.

Left: A contract with General Motors in late 1942 to provide an interceptor made from parts of the F4U, A-24, and P-51 resulted in the Fisher XP-75 interceptor in 1943. The mid-mounted engine, its position indicated by the exhaust stacks, afforded four .50 caliber machine guns in the nose and more in the wings, but forced the cockpit too far forward. Urgent demand for a long-range escort meant that the XP-75 was in competition with the P-51B by 1943.

Right: This is the final configuration of the XP-75, having squared P-51-type wingtips and vertical and horizontal stabilizers. The vertical stabilizer area was increased and a bubble canopy was installed. Otherwise, the aircraft was unchanged and its unsatisfactory flying qualities persisted.

In the middle of the 1943 escort crisis, General Arnold voiced concern over the development of the "liquid-cooled" B-17 or XB-38 – as shown here – a modified B-17 powered by four V-1710s. This was not the first instance that senior American generals considered using bombers as fighter escorts.

Gross had defined the escort mission but external tanks were not being mass-produced in July 1943, as they were later in the year. There were some 75-gallon drop tanks created for the P-39 and P-40 which were mounted infrequently on other fighters until larger drop tanks became available. On 2 July, Giles told Materiel to "...*produce a fighter aircraft well armed and having a range approximately 2,000 to 2,500 miles for (the) purpose of accompanying B-17s and B-24s on missions into Germany.*" [6]

On 5 July, Echols, Giles, Chidlaw, and Berlin met in Washington and it was decided that the fuel capacity of the XP-75 should be increased. GM was given Gross' new internal and external fuel requirements. Within three days GM doubled the planned internal fuel capacity of the XP-75 and identified it as an escort fighter. Original fuel capacity was to have been 276 gallons but now GM and Echols said it would carry 539 gallons. The idea that a single-engined fighter could carry so much fuel swayed minds. [7]

On 6 July, Echols directed the Materiel Center to have an "...*order be prepared for 2,500 planes.*" [8] GM proposed to mount ten .50 caliber machine guns in the XP-75 Eagle, of which four were to fire through the arc of the moving propeller. The P-51B carried four.

Echols had ordered thousands of XP-75s before the first one was rolled out, but he had done that with the XP-60. Nobody – not even General Arnold – questioned Echols' way of doing business. Echols and Arnold believed in large companies whose claim lay in great productive capacity. GM was not on Arnold's 1939 list of manufacturers considered suitable for experimentation with fighter design, but in 1943 the list was ignored because of world war. While the XP-75 project was being mismanaged, Giles, a leader in the shooting

war, acted with distinction, advising Arnold that "...*a critical period has developed*" and "...*a minimum ratio of one fighter group to two heavy bomb groups for escort must be established in the UK at the earliest possible date. The P-47D-5, P-38, and the P-51B-1 are the best available answer.*" [9]

Giles did not mention the XP-75.

On 7 July, new requirements were written for the XP-75 and six more handmade Eagles were put into the contract for escort prototypes which was signed on 16 July. A total of 2,500 airplanes and spare parts were to cost $325 million and a further $97 million was to be allocated for materials and equipment for production.

General Arnold suffered through a series of heart attacks during the war and while under great stress in mid-1943, he may temporarily have lost touch with reality. After a meeting with his Chief of Air Staff, Lt. Gen. George Stratemeyer told Giles that Arnold wanted the AAF "...*to explore from all angles what we should do in order to develop a destroyer type aircraft to protect our heavy bombardment formations.*" Incredibly, Stratemeyer said Arnold "...*referred to the liquid-cooled B-17*" and further testing of the YB-40 and XB-41! The "liquid-cooled" B-17 was the XB-38, a B-17 powered by four V-1710s and not produced. Arnold told Stratemeyer that he wanted "...*every effort be made to increase the gas capacity on present types and to develop an accompanying fighter for heavy bombardment.*" [10] Improving existing types was part of Echols' job.

Echols' and GM's teamwork to produce an escort made up of existing parts joined together was more than experimental and patriotic and good for big business – it was foolish. It was like a mad scientist joining male and female parts and presenting the result as a socially acceptable human. The era of the piston-engined fighter was drawing to an end and designers were already creating jet fighters. A successful aircraft functions through careful design, not by riveting diverse airframe sections together because one part is a functioning tail, another is a wing, and a third is the landing gear. On 9 July Arnold, well aware of the order for 2,500 XP-75s, said that it "...*depends upon the performance of the first machine.*" On another document he said it depended "...*on performance of the first article.*" [11] Both statements meant the same thing: that the very first XP-75 had to be capable. But that is not what happened. Several XP-75s continued in flight testing after the P-51B had already impressed Eglin's test pilots.

Within days, GM raised the price. Col. R.C. Wilson, also in Air Defense, told Echols that GM was "...*requesting (an) increase in cost of approximately 3 times the original cost and (was) stating the project is only 20 percent complete.*" [12]

Stratemeyer wrote to Giles telling him that Arnold was concerned that newer German fighters might outperform the P-47 and had asked Stratemeyer what "...*we are planning to* meet this challenge." Stratemeyer told Giles that he had informed Arnold: "...we are all thinking about the P-75 and are in hope that it will be the airplane that we should put into production. If that is true then we should be planning to stop production of the P-47 and put in the P-75." [13]

Thus it was that the Number Two man in the AAF and his associates were all "thinking about" the XP-75. In their exchange of letters, Giles advised Stratemeyer that Arnold's concern about the supposedly better fighters Germany might produce, was a needless concern. Objectives "...will be met and exceeded by models of American fighter airplanes now in existence and there is currently no need to go to an entirely new model whose performance is completely based on optimistic estimates." [14] Col. Millard Libby, in Stratemeyer's office, saw Giles' letter and after showing it to Stratemeyer, wrote to Giles telling him that "...General Stratemeyer observes that no mention was made of the P-75 airplane, consequently he desires to discuss this paper with you personally some time when you can get in to see him." [15] Stratemeyer had intended to change Giles' mind and make him support the XP-75 project. Shortly afterward, Stratemeyer was reassigned and Giles got Stratemeyer's job as Chief of Air Staff. Arnold had changed personnel but did not stop the XP-75.

Col. Mark Bradley was the first USAAF test pilot to fly the XP-75. On 20 January 1944, Col. Ernest Warburton, Chief of the Flight Section of Engineering, flew the XP-75 and his report concluded: "...stability and control forces on this plane were unsuitable for a fighter. (The) airplane felt as if it were going to stall or go into a spin when making turns. None of the controls particularly inspired confidence in (the) pilot." [17]

In April an XP-75 crashed, killing the civilian test pilot. By May, officers expressed caution about continuing with the project. Congressman Albert Engel requested information about the XP-75 from Under Secretary of War Robert P. "Judge" Patterson. [18] Despite the fact that the P-51B had forced a turning point in the European air war during February 1944, and "Big Week", Echols responded to Engel saying "...production would commence in July." Following the D-Day landings in June, Gross flew the aircraft in July and said "...it flies less like a fighter than any other airplane we have."

The Aircraft Production Board met again on 31 July 1944 and Chairman Donald Wilson "...questioned the effort which was being put forth to produce P-75s." Anyone of importance was behind the XP-75 100 percent except for Giles and Mark Bradley.

The range of the new Republic P-47N was predicted to be better than that of the XP-75 but Echols refused to cancel the XP-75 until tests of the P-47N were in his hands. The P-47N carried 570 gallons of fuel and had a radius-of-action of "1,100 miles." OC&R recommended in August that the XP-75 be canceled.

In September 1944, Echols criticized others for its problems. One officer stated: "...the Requirements people have been given the brush-off by the Mat. Div. (Wash.) (sic) since (the) spring of 1944 regarding production of the P-75, and Gen. Echols didn't want to drop the project until a fair test had been given." [19]

The XP-75 project was canceled in October 1944 – at about the time Germany was operating its first jet fighters in combat. Eight Eagles had been ordered as escort prototypes, six were built, and five more were partially built. Official cancelation of 2,470 P-75As indicates that 30 Eagles were in some stage of production.

Colonel Bradley's Tank

Col. Mark E. Bradley had replaced Kelsey as the AAF's foremost fighter test pilot. In March 1943, Bradley was in Britain solving problems with the new P-47 and while there, was advanced to the rank of Colonel. When he returned to Wright Field, Bradley, by now Chief of Fighter Projects, found himself reluctantly attached to the XP-75 project. He knew the XP-75 would not be ready in time to meet Arnold's six-month date from the end of June. But increasing fuel capacity in current fighters provided him with a great challenge. The P-51B already had longer range on internal fuel than the P-38 and P-47.

On 10 July, after Echols had contracted for the 2,500-plus P-75s, Bradley was in the office with his boss, Col. Orval Cook, discussing Bradley's plan to put a fuselage tank in the P-51B. Cook listened, then telephoned his aide to call Echols. When the connection was made, Cook handed the phone to Bradley and both officers discussed the XP-75 and P-51B. The transcript made of that conversation survives:

Col. Cook: General, do you have time to have a few words with Colonel Bradley on what he thinks of the P-75?

Gen. Echols: Yes.

Col. Cook: Very well, sir. I'll put him on the telephone.

Col. Bradley: General, Colonel Cook put me on the spot a little bit. I told him that I would like to talk to you about it and he called you up. The thing that worries me, General, is that I think that they've (GM) lost entirely all the idea of the airplane's fighting ability, just to get range, and when they load that airplane down to the point that they're talking about I know Berlin's figures look pretty good – but I'm convinced from a pilot's point of view they are going to get reports back which are worse than what we just heard over in (the) UK.

Gen. E: You know what the problem is, don't you?

Col. B: Yes, sir, but I just don't think it's going to be feasible sir to take an airplane that's going to be loaded down like that, and fly at those speeds. They are going to be too vulnerable. The other fighter is going to come in and attack the fighter and he is not going to fool with the others.

Gen. E: Well, they're not going to be any more vulnerable than these P-51s and other things when they load them up.

Col. B: Well, I think the P-51 won't be any more vulnerable. I mean that the P-51, being a smaller airplane, might be a little bit better, but not much. Any of them that you load up are going to be as bad, but the P-51 I'm convinced would do just as much as this thing would.

Gen. E: How do you mean?

Col. B: I think you can put just as much range into it, sir. I think that by using a 75 gallon belly tank for the take-off and climb-up to the enemy coast, which is incidentally where they are going to drop tanks, in spite of everybody's corrections, I think, and then by putting another 85 gallons in the rear, which looks pretty feasible…

Gen. E: You know what they want with these things, don't you?

Colonel Mark Bradley (left) talks to senior officers after a raid over Germany in 1945. Bradley flew a few combat missions while assigned a desk job toward the end of the war in the ETO before becoming Chief of Staff of the Fifth Air Force in 1945. Bradley's obvious capabilities gained him the rank of four-star General in the 1960s.

Col. B: Yes, sir, I know, but I don't think this other one is going to do any better than the P-51 will. We can put in the P-51 half of the internal gas, which is in this airplane that they are talking about, and since it uses half of the gasoline, and is faster I would be willing to bet a good part of a month's pay that it would go just as far.

Gen E: We don't want it to go so fast. We want it to play around near the bombers. What they're trying to get is something that will actually go and fly right over, or right under the bombers.

Col. B: Yes, sir.

Gen. E: That's my information from the Navy.

Col. B: Yes, sir, I know that, but they can't get the fighters that they've got over there to do that for short-range missions.

Gen. E: I know they can't get them to do it, because they haven't been able to do it, but what they want to do is place something right out in front of the bombers and hold them there.

Col. B: Yes, sir. If they would go out there, and do that with what they've got for short-range missions and are successful, then I'd say that this had some chance, but I know that over there they don't think that is feasible. They don't think that they can do that. The fighters will come in and attack them rather than the bombers, and they will be easier picking than the bombers.

Gen. E: They'll fly right out in front of the bombers, fly right in formation.

Col. B: Well, they would probably come down on the side. You know the top of the bombers couldn't be – there would have to be a little space, and I don't think, just from knowing what is going on over there, the pilots' minds in the combat outfits, I don't think their attitude will change any from one airplane to another. They can order them to do it, but I think –

Gen. E: It's too much… The whole point is that something has got to be done for protecting those bombers out over that project … beyond anything they can do yet. We've got to do something. The attitude of some of the people up here is that something has got to be done.

Col. B: Well, disregarding that – I think that's none of my business – I think that I'm going to have 85 gallons put in a P-51 and I think that we can go further at any speed.

Gen. E: If you think maybe it can, go ahead with it. I don't know how you're going further. How far are you going?

Col. B: I think that gallon for gallon, I've got just as much, and having less drag, I think I'll go a little further.

Gen. E: Well, go ahead and try it, and it's ultra-critical; in fact the whole result of the war may depend upon it. Every time this is proposed lots of people find a lot of things wrong with it. We've got to get an answer some way or other.

Col. B: Yes, sir, I think we can give you a lot better answer in something like that, than this other thing.

Gen. E: Let's go ahead and get the answer to it. I've been hammering away at it for two or three years, and every time I've tried to get anything, something is wrong with it.[20]

In this conversation, General Echols showed a deep concern over the European air war. Bradley's fuselage fuel tank gave the P-51B phenomenal range and saved the AAF's daylight bombing campaign in North West Europe from defeat.

Mark Bradley was born on 10 December 1907, in Clemson, South Carolina. His father, a Professor at the university, "...could not afford to send me anywhere else" and young Bradley wrote to Senators and Congressmen for an appointment to the Military Academy. Once accepted he was asked in his first year for preferences for duty upon graduation and chose the Air Service. After graduation in 1930 he was assigned to the 1st Pursuit Group and flew P-12s at Selfridge Field.[21]

Military personnel formed part of President Roosevelt's Civilian Conservation Corps (CCC) and Bradley pulled CCC duty while married officers were allowed to remain in their base assignments. During his next tour, he met his wife-to-be and attended Engineering Maintenance School. Married, the couple moved to Hawaii where Bradley joined the 6th Pursuit Group.

In 1937, he was assigned to another school and upon graduation was given more options and requested Flight Test at Wright Field. In January 1939, he was on a board of officers that selected the P-40 as the next fighter to be procured. In mid-1943, he became Chief of the Fighter Branch of the Production Test Division and remained there until January, 1945. Bradley was Deputy Commander of the First Tactical Air Force in the Air Service Command in Europe. In May 1945, he was Chief of Staff of the Fifth Air Force in the Philippines, then Commander of the 301st Wing on Okinawa. Shouldering ever-greater responsibilities, higher command, and advanced rank, he finally became Commanding General of the Air Force Logistics Command in July 1962 as a four-star General.

Bradley received approval to instal a range-improving fuselage tank in the P-51B and proceeded to make the Mustang unique in history, whereas Echols was far more interested in continued development of the XP-75 for production as an escort. In July 1943, the two escorts were compared by statisticians. Col. Samuel Brentnall, Chief of the Production Engineering Section, asked the Engineering Division to predict statistics in a theoretical comparison between the P-51B and XP-75. He wanted fuel-burn figures and percent of power required, for both fighters to fly at 302.5 mph at 25,000 ft.[22] Col. Paul Kemmer of the Aircraft Laboratory at Wright Field responded that the P-51B would burn 51 gallons per hour at 56 percent normal rated power and consume 141 gallons per hour at military power. The unbuilt XP-75 would burn 62 gallons per hour at 40 percent normal rated power and consume 244 gallons per hour at military power, or about 100 gallons per hour more than the P-51B.[23] The big Merlin was fuel-efficient.

The first group to operate P-51Bs – without modifications – was the 54th FG at Bartow, Florida in August 1943.

Bradley's tank was fitted into a P-51B and in mid-August, Bob Chilton, NAA's Mustang test pilot, flew the aircraft and reported the facts to his boss at NAA. They in turn advised Brentnall who told Arnold a "...*radius of 737 miles has been achieved.*" [24] That astoundingly long flight guaranteed a bright future for the P-51B. An efficient engine, a low-drag airframe, and a fuselage fuel tank combined to give the P-51B phenomenally long range. Its like would not be seen again.

Chilton's long test flight seemed interminable! He flew for hours, performed a simulated dogfight over lower California and Arizona, and then flew for several more hours. The hard parachute under him in the seat seemed like he "...*had a spike on both sides and that I was sitting on it! Gave up! The first flight was a pain in the ass! I stood up in the cockpit with my back against the canopy and massaged my rump a number of times.*" [25]

Long-Range Fighter Aircraft

Brentnall's message to Arnold ignited a campaign of self-congratulation within the AAF for success in developing the escort fighter, yet officers still held out hope for the XP-75 which made its first flight in November. The P-47D was still the only escort type available in Europe since P-38s were not to enter combat in the ETO until mid-October, 1943. On the last day of August 1943, Maj. Hill, an officer in Air Defense, sent a memo to all officers: "*Recent inaccurate statements by officers who were not fully informed on present capabilities and developments of long-range fighter aircraft have emphasized*

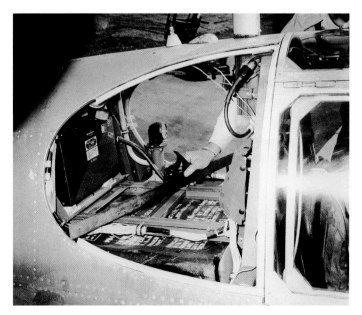

In July 1943, Colonel Mark Bradley convinced General Echols that a P-51B with a new fuselage fuel tank would fly as far as, or farther than, the XP-75 and would be available sooner from production. Here is the experimental tank and its primitive quantity gauge protruding up like a submarine's periscope.

During 1943 the AAF began a frantic search for a long-range fighter escort and NAA offered its XP-82 Twin Mustang, s/n 44-65168, coded PQ-168, which competed with the XP-75 and was to fly 12-hour missions to Japan. After the war, the XP-82 was redesignated F-82 and "Betty Jo" set a non-stop, unrefueled flight of over 4,000 miles.

the need for dissemination of up-to-date information on this subject within these Headquarters. The United States has in operation two long-range fighter aircraft – the P-51 and P-38. The combat radius of action of fighter aircraft used as offensive fighters is governed by the internal gasoline capacity. External fuel tanks can be used only after take-off and to the point of contact with the enemy. The combat radius of action of fighter aircraft used as escort for bomber [must have consideration that] fighters returning to base will be required to fly at their desired cruising speed for the length of time it takes the bombers they are escorting to return. A comparison of the present combat radius of action of the P-51B and P-38J follows."

The P-51B carried 180 gallons internally and the P-38J, 290. Two 75-gallon drop tanks would provide another 150 gallons. The P-38J would carry two 165-gallon tanks filled to 150 gallons to provide 300 total. Combat radius as an offensive fighter was 350 to 500 miles for the P-51B and 300 to 450 for the P-38. Combat radius as an escort was to be 250 to 350 miles for the P-51B and 200 to 300 for the P-38J. The P-51B and P-38J would cruise at 220 mph while protecting 180 mph bombers.

Hill continued: *"An 85-gallon self-sealing fuselage tank has been developed for the P-51B, and within 60 days will be ready for installation in modification centers. Similarly, self-sealing tanks with a capacity of 120 gallons have been developed for installation in the leading edge of the wing of the P-38J and are scheduled to be in production within 3 months. These increases in internal fuel capacity will affect combat radius of action as follows..."*

P-51B internal capacity would be 265 gallons and the P-38J's, 410 gallons. Maj. Hill then noted use of two 108-gallon British-type drop tanks on the P-51B and the same Lockheed tanks on the P-38J. With these tanks, the P-51B used as an offensive fighter would have a combat radius of 700 to 850 miles and as an escort, 500 to 600 miles. The P-38J used

offensively would have a radius of 550 to 700 miles and as an escort, 375 to 475 miles.

"Available information does not indicate any British, German or Italian aircraft that can be termed long-range fighters. The Japanese Zero, without armor or self-sealing tanks, has an estimated combat radius of action of approximately 600 miles. The XP-75, which is now being developed, will, it is believed, have an internal self-sealing fuel capacity of 511 gallons and a combat radius of action of about 1,000 miles as an offensive fighter, and 650 to 700 miles as an escort fighter. This combat radius of action is considered beyond the fatigue limit of a fighter pilot under combat conditions. It is desired that all officers should be more discreet in the future in their comments with respect to AAF equipment, and that no officer should criticize such equipment unless he is fully posted on its present capabilities and on recent developments affecting its operational characteristics." [26]

The British resin-impregnated, paper, 108-gallon drop tank was not available but its production for the USAAF was due to begin much later in 1943. A history of the 4th FG mentions first use of that drop tank in April 1944. The P-47 was not regarded as an escort even though it had been used as such since introduction. The XP-75 was mentioned as both. None of the three – P-51B, P-38J, and XP-75 – was flying in combat. The intent of the message was to correct impressions, stop gossip and keep people informed, but fighter pilots in the ETO had their own problems with language. VIII FC fighter pilots could not face bomber crews in a bar over a beer and avoid an argument or a fight over who was responsible for lack of escort. [27] Bomber crews often wondered where the Thunderbolts were, when *Luftwaffe* fighters closed in at high speed. Arnold saw the Air Defense memo and approved it, saying OC&R "must provide" long-range fighters for the UK. To accomplish that, OC&R reversed some of Saville's dispersals, finding many P-51Bs that were assigned to training and reconnaissance units. An amazing total of 183 Mustangs were obtained for the UK just by paperwork.

Officers who had criticized the *"British Project"* that was the P-51, now did an about-face and took it to their hearts like any good home-made product. The great P-51B would not be ready for use from Britain until December. Four months of preparations – as well as confusion over the mission of the Mustang – lay ahead.

Chapter 12

"Beehives"

Deeper Penetrations – Changing Tactics

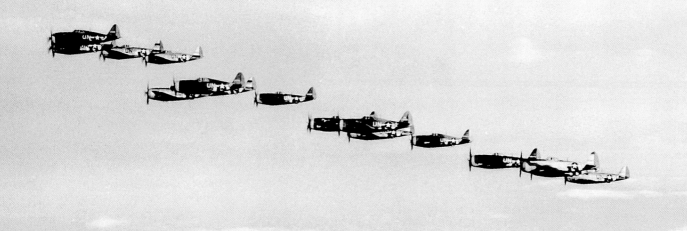

Gentral Arnold's 22 June order to Giles to acquire an escort within six months, because – as he said – deeper penetrations would begin, did not mean that long, unescorted bombing missions would be halted until escort became available. For example, Eaker sent bombers to Hüls in the first big attack on the Ruhr on the 22nd, which was farther than Thunderbolts were able to fly, and other raids went to Norway, Belgium, and France to targets also beyond the radius of P-47s. The AAF did not want to let up its offensive against the Third Reich if the weather permitted the despatch of bombers deep into Germany.

Hamburg

Much further from Britain than a P-47 could fly, the city of Hamburg was Europe's largest port and the second-largest city in Germany. It had been bombed several times but between the nights of 24/25 July and 2/3 August, RAF Bomber Command and the Eighth AF created so much destruction that the name Hamburg, afterward, ranked in a pantheon of the Second World War's most awful visitations upon urban centers along with Hiroshima, Nagasaki, Tokyo, Coventry, Rotterdam, Dresden, Shanghai, Nanking, and Leningrad.

The Eighth AF made two daylight raids on Hamburg on 25 and 26 July. Seventeen bombers and crews were lost, and gunners were credited with 11 victories. Bombers also visited Kiel and Hanover. What the RAF called the "Battle of Hamburg" was a one-sided form of punishment of civilians so devastating that it drew from the *Luftwaffe* their highest pitch of anger and it took its revenge in the air upon the Eighth AF over Schweinfurt in August.

On the third night, the RAF's bombs ignited a firestorm, the like of which had not been seen previously. Separate fires that continued to burn following the first raids, joined, forming a towering pyre which sucked oxygen inward to the center like a magnet draws iron filings, creating violent, tornado-like winds strong enough to drag people down streets into the firestorm. Everything over an area stretching more than a mile around Hamburg burned. Forty thousand people died and 1,200,000 fled the city.

Metallic strips of foil were dropped from RAF bombers filling German radar sets with confusing "snow" in order to evade *Luftwaffe* night fighters. It was later said that the chaff, called "Window," saved 130 RAF bombers. The usually frighteningly effective German night fighters were – in that battle – ineffective. In daylight, Eighth AF P-47s were unable to escort.

Success

More than a month after O'Donnell put Eaker's career in jeopardy with his memo, drop tanks arrived at the base of the 4th FG. On 28 July, drop tank-equipped P-47s penetrated German airspace for the first time, reaching a radius of 340 miles.[1] The bombers went to Kassel and Oschersleben and the Thunderbolts flew 30 miles further than they had on the previous mission. The 4th FG shot down nine enemy aircraft for a one-day record by a single group in the ETO. Over the city of Emmerich, the 4th FG dropped its tanks and waded into a formation of *Luftwaffe* fighters which had stayed, they thought, beyond the known arc of extreme radius of a P-47 without drop tanks. In one day, VIII FC claimed virtually the same number of kills it had shot down in the second half of 1942! The 56th and 78th Fighter Groups did not score that day, but nine kills seemed like a great success to the 4th FG and there was much celebrating at Debden.

The Best Day So Far

On 30 July, the *Luftwaffe* came out in force against 134 bombers sent to Kassel, firing air-to-air mortars at bombers for only the second time. In 1943, Germany's air defense was aided by two factors: knowledge that P-47s could not fly to Germany, and that the *Luftwaffe's* large, armored, cannon and rocket-carrying twin-engined aircraft would have B-17s and B-24s all to themselves without fear of encountering P-47s. Bf 110 heavy fighters were supplemented by single-engined Fw 190s and Bf 109Gs that were also heavily armed and armored. These bomber destroyers were relatively slow and less maneuverable than P-47s. The *Luftwaffe* waited beyond the point where it was normal for P-47s to turn around and fly home, but again, drop tank-equipped P-47s flew the extra 30

A crewman poses for a photograph with Lieutenant Wilfred A. Van Abel of the 63rd Fighter Squadron, 56th Fighter Group. A yellow ring surrounds the national insignia. The s/n of the P-47C was 41-6537.

miles to Bocholt, in Germany and the surprised *Luftwaffe* was caught again. The 78th FG set a new one-day record of 16 kills and Capt. Charles London got his fifth victory to become the first Ace in VIII FC. Total fighter victories amounted to 25, for seven losses. Twelve bombers were lost.

In other theaters of war, many Aces had already surpassed their fifth victory. ETO fighter pilots had operated for a full year before Capt. London achieved his fifth kill. For instance, Maj. Richard Bong, America's greatest Ace, operating in the South West Pacific Area, had 16 victories by the end of July, 1943.

A photographer in a B-26 shot this climbing formation of P-47s of the 56th Fighter Group en route to a target.

Changes to Fighters and Tactics

Once Brig. Gen. K.B. Wolfe supported the Merlin-Mustang as a special project, and following description of the P-51B, P-38J, and XP-75 as offensive fighters, Echols requested lowering the P-47 to Group III in the preference list in order to elevate the P-51B to Group II. When he asked the Joint Aircraft Committee to change priorities "*…because of the strategical importance of the P-51*," priority for the Packard Merlin was upgraded too, and Packard received more machine tools faster.[2] The P-51B was being produced at the rate of 189 per month to be increased to 250 by March 1944.

The CO of the 56th FG, Col. Hubert "Hub" Zemke, liked his P-47s, but he was irritated with the outdated way of forcing 400 mph fighters to stay beside 180 mph bombers. The fighter air war was being mismanaged by bomber theoreticians. Fighter pilots were not allowed to go after the enemy, who dived in to shoot, or lob mortars at bombers then were allowed to escape unthreatened. Policy required escorts to drive the enemy away and then return to the bombers' sides. Zemke changed tactics, and recalls that it "*…was no good for fighter escort. You can't just fly close to bombers at slow speeds and wait for the enemy. You kill the escort's initiative and flexibility. Once an enemy is seen, you've got to go out. He's got to be engaged and (his formation) broken up*" before it reached the bombers.[3]

Zemke, and probably other Fighter Group COs, changed tactics during that summer, perhaps in July, and avoided telling Hunter or his successor, Maj. Gen. William E. Kepner about it. The Generals would have forced him to obey policy even though fighter pilots had not been shooting down very many enemy fighters. Zemke wanted to bounce the enemy aircraft and pursue, to destroy them, and certainly not let them make attacks with impunity. Aerial victories increased dramatically in July and that fact was due not just to the use of drop tanks.

HUBERT "HUB" ZEMKE

Hubert "Hub" Zemke was born to parents who had emigrated from Germany yet German was spoken at home more so than English. After Americans fought Germans in the First World War, the Zemke family was ostracized and Hubert learned to fight bullies with his fists at school. At High School he excelled in boxing and football and won a scholarship to the University of Montana. He became Montana State middleweight boxing champion and coached the sport in the region.

A professor influenced Zemke to try for acceptance into the Air Corps, and after he was inducted into uniform, he was flight-trained and assigned to the 8th Pursuit Group. Zemke undertook test flights on the XP-37 and as a result of his skills he was given other special assignments. When the Second World War began, he and another officer were ordered to travel to Britain and Russia to assist those countries' pilots in learning to fly the P-40. When he came home his 8th PG was in Australia and Zemke was assigned to the newly-formed 56th FG. By the early winter of 1942 he was its Commanding Officer and was on his way back to Britain.

In August 1944, Zemke was asked by the new CG of VIII FC, Brig. Gen. Francis Griswold, to take command of the P-38-equipped 479th FG which soon transitioned to P-51Ds. Zemke became probably the only man to command groups operating all three front-line types: the P-38, P-47, and P-51. At the end of October 1944, Don Blakeslee and Zemke were ordered to assignments in the USA. Blakeslee went home in November. Zemke wanted to fly one last mission and in flight, his P-51D was damaged by violent weather and he parachuted into captivity. After repatriation he flew again for a while but retired from the Air Force and entered the University of Nevada where he finished his education.

Fighter Successes

Brig. Gen. Hunter was relieved of command in July 1943 but stayed on to assist his replacement, Kepner, while adjusting to his new appointment as Commanding General VIII FC. Showing support for Kepner, which bordered on hypocrisy, Giles sent a letter to Eaker praising Kepner, who was not officially CG of VIII FC until 29 August. Eaker replied to Giles saying: "…*you spoke about the two missions in which our fighters have escorted bombers on deep penetrations. This must not be credited to Bill Kepner, as you indicated. It is entirely due to the receipt of the first long-range tanks.*" Eaker had enough drop tanks "…*for two special missions*" but plans were being made for Britain to supply 108-gallon paper drop tanks. Eaker said their availability would, "*for the first time, permit long-range accompanying missions in force and with continuity of operations.*" Eaker supported Hunter saying: "*I am sorry that you were of the opinion that the failure of the fighters to accompany the bombers has been due to…*" Hunter's inattention. 'Jug' pilots "…*have been unable to accomplish it until recently for lack of droppable tanks.*" [4]

Kepner did his best to save the tattered reputation of the outgoing Hunter by saying he, Kepner, had been ordered to Britain on a simple, change-of-command, routine basis.

Col. Cass Hough of the Eighth AF's Air Technical Section and his staff had been working for months to develop a pump to pressurize the drop tank so that fuel would be forced upward into the P-47's fuel system. Until the pump was developed, fuel in the tanks could not be drawn on above 22,000 ft. On 12 August 1943, the first three P-47 groups were

Major General W.E. Kepner (left) and Major General Idwal I. Edwards in 1943 during a visit to the 55th Fighter Group at Nuthampstead.

joined by those of the newly initiated 353rd FG and most drop tanks used on the mission were pressurized by Hough's pump. Bombers went to Bochum, Gelsenkirchen, and Bonn; 25 bombers were lost, gunners claimed 29 enemy aircraft shot down, and P-47s accounted for four.

On 16 August 1943, 237 bombers went to Paris-Le Bourget airfield and the 4th FG was directed in the air by its brilliant tactician, Lt. Col. Don Blakeslee, who orbited and vectored his pilots like a football quarterback, changing plays at the line of scrimmage to adjust to defensive formations. The 4th FG downed 18 for a new one-day record. Three P-47s and only four bombers were lost. Gunners claimed 29 kills. One YB-40 participated, but after the mission the four-engined "escort" was shelved.

The tempo of the fighter air war increased dramatically once drop tanks were available and their pressurization pumps were operable. It must have been a wistful moment for Hunter, who was on his way out just as his former VIII FC was enjoying its greatest days to date.

From 14 August 1942 to the end of June 1943, fighter pilots were credited with 48 victories. In the month of July 1943 alone, 37 were credited. By mid-August, P-47s had totalled as many aerial victories in a month and a half as had been scored in a year up to 1 July. VIII FC now had over 100 victories.

Schweinfurt and Regensburg

On 17 August 1943, USAAF bombers attacked Schweinfurt's ball bearing production plant 400 miles from their bases in Britain, and Regensburg's Bf 109 assembly plant over 500 miles away. To avoid losing too many aircraft and crews – because P-47s could fly only half the distance – the plan had the Regensburg force continue southeast and fly across the Alps to land in Italy. The Schweinfurt force would return. P-47s were to escort the 4th Bomb Wing part way on its course for Italy, and would form in the central sector which the 1st BW would fly through, and then would protect the 1st BW on its way home. By dividing the times of bomb runs, planners hoped to confuse German air defenses.

Bad weather delayed take-off of the 1st BW by 90 minutes because crews were inexperienced in foul-weather departures.

The 129 bombers raiding Regensburg were attacked for an hour and a half and lost 24 aircraft and 240 crewmen before reaching sanctuary in Italy. The 230 bombers sent to hit Schweinfurt were attacked as soon as they passed Antwerp and the mauling lasted all the way to the target and on the return until they crossed the English Channel. A total of 36 bombers and 360 crew were lost on that half of the operation. Altogether 60 bombers were lost. It was one of the war's most serious and deadly air disasters. Bomber crews tried to do the impossible and suffered the unimaginable.

Above: Debden RAF Station looking towards the east end of the E-W runway from the tower. P-47s of the 336th Fighter Squadron, 4th Fighter Group, take off while aircraft of the 335th Fighter Squadron wait.

Above: Three room mates at Debden; from left to right: Captain Don Gentile, Major Carl H. "Spike" Miley, and Captain Ervin Miller, all of the 336th Fighter Squadron, 4th Fighter Group.

Above: Major Oscar Coen of the 4th Fighter Group talks with staff while seated in his P-47 (coded QP✪E). The Thunderbolt was a huge fighter aircraft for its time.

Left: Major Oscar Coen of the 4th Fighter Group flew P-47D QP✪E, s/n 41-6187. This was the scene at Debden in February 1944, just before the group transitioned to Mustangs. Note the sandbags forming a hardstand revetment.

Out of reach of P-47s, the bombers were met by swarms of enemy fighters. Machine gun bullets, cannon shells, air-to-air mortars, and bombs were fired and dropped on the American formations from above, tore bombers apart and tossed crews into the air. Later, reconnaissance photographs showed that Schweinfurt's factories were not destroyed and production was not halted.

It was said after the mission by an American survivor that huge claims credited to bomber gunners sustained the morale of other survivors! A total of 288 kills were credited. Later, AAF figures quoted 148 enemy aircraft shot down. Postwar records showed that 27 German fighters were destroyed.

Zemke's 56th FG downed 17 enemy aircraft and other groups won victories. Maj. Gen. Kepner phoned Zemke to congratulate him and asked what had brought about the great success of his group but Zemke "...wasn't inclined to talk tactics." Close escort policy had not been followed.[5]

Col. Curtis LeMay had led the 4th BW to Italy and on arrival it was realized that repair facilities were inadequate. His bomb wing returned to Britain on 24 August minus 60 bombers which could not be repaired. Thus, a total of 120 bombers were lost or became incapable of flying.

After the disaster over Germany, bombers were sent generally to targets in France but on September 6, the Eighth AF hit Stuttgart and various surrounding targets and lost 45 bombers. P-47s scored just a single victory that day. A total of 322 bombers were effective and the loss rate was 14 percent.

The Fifteenth Air Force was created in Italy and in mid-1944 was used to complement the Eighth AF in bombing Germany. Italy signed an Armistice agreement on 8 September 1943, but many Italian units joined forces with the Germans who fought on in the north of Italy to the end of the war. Subsequently, southern Italy, and especially air bases in and around the city of Foggia, became a second giant center for American strategic air forces.

A Necessity for More Fighter Groups

The fifth fighter group to enter VIII FC, the 352nd, flew its first mission on 9 September 1943. Kepner knew there was a growing number of replacement bombers, and he needed a greater number of long-range escorts. He visited all the commanders above group level in Bomber Command, Fighter Command, as well as B-26 medium bomber group commanders and he had talked to the Air Service Command and the RAF in an attempt to find ways to improve escort. Besides needing more fighter groups, Kepner devised a system of fighter escort "areas." These areas were to be strung along bomber routes which were to be filled with P-47s aloft, and the bombers were to fly through these protective areas on their way to and from targets. Kepner called these fighter areas "beehives."

He sent a letter to Giles stating: "... *we have expended all*

Major General W.E. Kepner during a visit to the 55th Fighter Group at Nuthampstead. Partially hidden behind Kepner is Lieutenant Colonel Jenkins and at center is Colonel Frank James, CO of the 55th Fighter Group. To the left is Major Milton Joel, CO of the 38th Fighter Squadron.

of our 200-gallon tanks and all that we have are some 75-gallon tanks. Since 300 miles is about the maximum you can use a P-47, it follows that some longer ranged fighter is necessary. One beehive of escort is used up in a distance of about 100 miles." Kepner required *"... 8 groups of P-47s and 10 groups of P-38s or P-51s, or a combination of both. Thus a Ramrod* (Ramrod = a bomber and escort mission: author) *of over 500 miles would require 18 groups."* If Eighth AF sent out four Ramrods at once, Kepner *"...would require 72 groups. Don't faint! Thirty-six groups would be as thin as we ought to go on fighter strength."* [6]

VIII FC had five groups and Kepner was asking for 18 or 72. He specifically asked for Mustangs. He emphasized to Giles that the ETO, with the most direct route to Germany and having the only air force operating from British bases strategically over Europe, was a backwater affair compared to other theaters where fighters were much more plentiful. P-38s had been operating in the MTO since November 1942, but they would not begin combat operations in the ETO until October 1943. The AAF was operating bombers to their greatest distances, over the most heavily defended territory, without enough fighters. The Army preferred to have P-38s and other types where its troops were in ground combat with the enemy. Until October 1943 there were no P-38s in the ETO and production was just then catching up with demand around the globe. Giles' immediate expression upon reading Kepner's letter is not known, but having sent Kepner to Britain and praised him prematurely, Giles could have understood the request for more fighter groups. The final number of groups attained in the Eighth and Ninth Air Forces was 33, but, for example, the 355th FG did not begin operations until late September 1943.

Bomber missions to Germany were resumed in late September – first to Hanover, then to Emden on the 27th on a Pathfinder (bombing through cloud using radar) mission. On 4 October 1943, 16 bombers were lost on missions to several German cities and P-47s downed 19 enemy aircraft. On 8 October, 30 bombers were lost on the Bremen and Vegesack raids and P-47s accounted for 12 enemy aircraft shot down. Twenty-eight bombers were lost on the 9th and another 30 on the 10th. Deep penetrations were not halted. Hamburg's destruction had caused a deep and dark change of attitude on the part of every German citizen. RAF targeting had long since changed from bombing military installations to damaging German morale.

Long-range escorts were not available and the British paper drop tanks were not acceptable. The grass-hugging belly of the P-47 barely allowed room to mount the 108-gallon tank under it, and P-47s were not yet manufactured with wing shackles. The P-47 was incapable of range-improvement prior to very late 1943. Two P-38 groups had arrived in Britain, one without its aircraft, and there were high hopes for combat

The 353rd Fighter Group joined VIII Fighter Command in the summer of 1943 and converted to P-51s in late 1944. This P-47 carried the early markings of the group before a colourful diamond pattern on the cowl was applied in April 1944.

introduction of Lightnings in October. Time was running out for the Eighth AF, and for Germany.

Second Schweinfurt

Halting ball bearing production would, the planners said, stop German vehicle production and with this aim, Schweinfurt was revisited on 14 October. A force of 320 bombers was dispatched but again weather affected take-offs, rendezvous, and return to bases. The plan this time was for two bomb divisions to fly near to each other and escorts were to protect both, to some extent. However, B-17s of the 1st BD flew a course widely separated from the 3rd BD allowing the *Luftwaffe* to attack a divided force. The eight-hour mission cost 60 bombers and their crews. Gunners claimed 186 enemy aircraft shot down and P-47s accounted for 13.

Second Schweinfurt was more than just another disaster – it was a final warning: deep penetrations required escort. Four days after the mission, Eaker told Arnold that he had scolded Sir Wilfrid Freeman saying "...*the failure to get the promised supply of 108-gallon tanks had cost us at least 50 bombers during the last month*." He told Arnold "...*we may get as many as 1,500 this month and 3,000 in November*." [7] Eaker's caustic remark to Freeman should have been aimed at Materiel. Britain did not have a monopoly on the process of forming resin-impregnated paper into the shape of a drop tank, and the USAAF refused to order production of such tanks in America.

Colonel Cecil Wells, probably seen on the left in this photograph, was CO of the 358th FG from 1 January 1943 to 20 September 1944. In the center is Colonel Westbrook and on the right Major Bartincek. "Martha Ann II" carried a new type of metal drop tank on its belly rack.

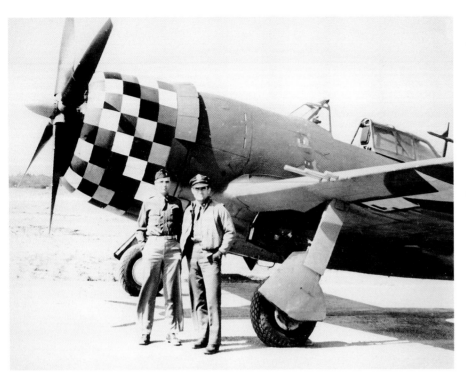

Just above the guns of this P-47D is a "Mighty Mouse" insignia. The aircraft – belonging to the 66th Fighter Wing – was decorated with nose colours representing all the groups in the Wing.

Pointblank, Overlord, and Argument

The mighty Eighth Air Force was being defeated. The official history of the AAF records: "...*the fact (was) that the Eighth Air Force had for the time being lost air superiority over Germany. After the early part of December the decision* (not to send deep penetrations: author) *was forced by weather.*" [8] Defeat and poor weather forced an agonizing reappraisal of the air war. Escort was the great need. Planning of the air war promised victory yet impressive titles could not defeat the *Luftwaffe*. Operation 'Overlord' – the invasion of northwestern France – was code-named in May 1943, and 'Pointblank' – the air offensive – in August. On 2 November, the Combined Operational Planning Committee endorsed Operation 'Argument' as a "...*coordinated and decisive blow at the industries*" supplying the *Luftwaffe*. 'Argument' depended upon having clear weather, but there was none. 'Pointblank' was initiated in August but without escorts it was ineffective. The official history says it best; the "... *problem of escort for*

deep penetrations into Germany was faced squarely only after lack of escort had seriously hampered the execution of 'Pointblank'." [9] Overlord could not occur if the *Luftwaffe* remained dominant. Lack of escort threatened to delay the invasion.

In November, Arnold offered to the Combined Chiefs of Staff his 'Air Plan for the Defeat of Germany' in which "...*fighter protection must be provided for our bombers whenever required. The defensive concept of our fighter commands and air defense units must be changed to the offensive.*" He asked the CCS for a directive setting forth "... *an overriding first priority*" for defeating the Luftwaffe and that bombers be allowed to concentrate upon German fighter aircraft factories rather than attack general sources of German military strength. He asked for authority to designate a commander for "...*a Strategic Air Force.*" [10]

Arnold received almost everything he wanted. On 27 December he issued a five-point message to the Commanding Generals of the Eighth and Fifteenth Air Forces. Point Five read: "...*my personal message to you – this is a must – is to Destroy the Enemy Air Force wherever you find them, in the air, on the ground and in the factories... Overlord – will not be possible unless the German Air Force is destroyed.*" [11]

General Arnold's message freed fighters from close escort. Fighter pilots now could chase an enemy to destruction and strafe airfields to destroy *Luftwaffe* aircraft on the ground. The official history states: "... *the CBO (Combined Bombing Offensive) in its last phase became so completely a counter-air offensive that... Pointblank came to mean the attack*" [on the *Luftwaffe* itself]. [12]

By December 1943, P-38s and P-51Bs were operating in the ETO. Yet the final development which allowed long-range fighters to operate over all of Germany – the drop tank – was not ready in October, when P-38s became operational. And there was to be a major controversy over who controlled the P-51Bs.

Chapter 13

"A war-winning idea"

The Range Extension Program

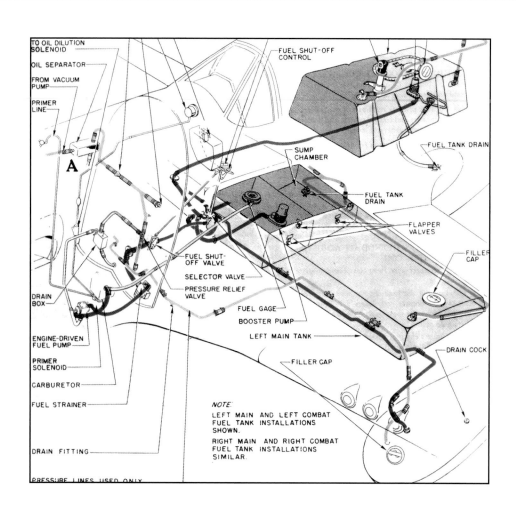

TO OIL DILUTION
SOLENOID

OIL SEPARATOR

FROM VACUUM
PUMP

PRIMER
LINE

A

FUEL SHUT-OFF
CONTROL

SUMP
CHAMBER

FUEL TANK DRAIN

FUEL TANK
DRAIN

FLAPPER
VALVES

FILLER
CAP

FUEL SHUT-
OFF VALVE

SELECTOR VALVE

PRESSURE RELIEF
VALVE

FUEL GAGE

BOOSTER PUMP

LEFT MAIN TANK

DRAIN
BOX

ENGINE-DRIVEN
FUEL PUMP

PRIMER
SOLENOID

CARBURETOR

FUEL STRAINER

DRAIN FITTING

FILLER CAP

DRAIN COCK

NOTE:
LEFT MAIN AND LEFT COMBAT
FUEL TANK INSTALLATIONS
SHOWN.

RIGHT MAIN AND RIGHT COMBAT
FUEL TANK INSTALLATIONS
SIMILAR.

PRESSURE LINES USED ONLY

Innovation sometimes works by quiet inspiration and at other times, out of urgent necessity. Within the USAAF, not all the improvements to fighters and tactics had come from the Materiel Command or from Col. Hough's group in Britain. Lt. Gen. George Kenney's Fifth AF operating in the South West Pacific Area included the 348th FG which – unique within the AAF – made its own drop tanks. Produced in Australia and starting in August 1943, the 200-gallon tanks gave the group's P-47s better range.[1] The tank became standard in the South West Pacific.

The innovation by the 348th FG brought anger from Arnold at Materiel for not developing drop tanks, Bradley's P-51 fuselage tank, and Lockheed's incorporation of extra wing leading-edge tanks in the P-38J, prompted Brig. Gen. Muir Fairchild, in September, to initiate a formal program to put more fuel in existing fighters. The Fighter Airplane Range Extension Program (FAREP) capped the effort to acquire long-range fighters. Back in April and May 1943, Fairchild had instructed Materiel to extend the ferrying range, and in September, he further extended combat radius.

General Arnold was in the midst of a personal health crisis as well as a global war that summer. In August, when he heard of the privately-made drop tanks used by the 348th FG, he told his staff: "...*there is no reason in God's world why General Kenney should have to develop his own belly tanks. If he can develop one over there in two months, we should be able to develop one here in the US in one month*."[2]

Arnold had not always appreciated the lowly drop tank. Originally bathtub-shaped in the 1920s, the ferry tank had been developed into a teardrop shape by the mid-1930s and then temporarily banned in 1939 from use in combat because it was considered a fire hazard.[3] By 1940-41, Capt. Kelsey had unilaterally persuaded Lockheed to instal factory-produced drop tanks on production P-38s without Arnold's knowledge. When Arnold learned about this he was furious for not being kept informed – but he agreed to it.

It was apparent from the July successes in VIII FC, that drop tanks changed the nature of the air war. In June Col. Gross had stated that the length of time it took a bomber to complete a mission was to be the basis for extending the duration of a fighter's flying time. Urgency after June 1943 demanded immediate changes to fuel capacity for fighters. Fairchild's FAREP became official in September 1943, and it formally

In 1942, Major General Muir Fairchild pushed to get Mustang fighters produced instead of just A-36 dive bombers. In late 1943, he originated the great Fighter Airplane Range Extension Program which made drop tanks a common piece of equipment.

ordered shackles, drop tanks, and internal tanks to be mass-produced and added to fighters already in production.

Prior to September, there were shackles under the bellies of P-47Ds but not under the wings. At the end of the year, the P-38J was nearing its debut fitted with new internal wing tanks. The mass-production of thousands of drop tanks was an entirely new and important program but no one in the AAF had pushed for mass-production. Although General Arnold had once been lukewarm on the issue, probably because Echols had made up his mind not to order drop tanks. The FAREP was the final act in the development of the long-range escort fighter. Hesitation to produce drop tanks may have been due to a scarcity of aluminum, but defeat of the Eighth AF would have been a disaster. Reserving aluminum just for aircraft would have been stupid. Extending range in single-engined fighters was difficult because there was so little internal room in which to instal additional tanks, and shackles and drop tanks were not urgent items prior to September. Many officers still believed the P-38 could fulfil escort needs even though they were not being produced fast enough by late 1943. Behind that notion were years of thinking that bombers were self-defending. Drop tanks were to make the difference between victory and defeat in the air war.

Wing Tanks and Shackles

The range of the P-47D was to be doubled. Shackles attached to their bellies enabled them to carry the 75-gallon drop tanks formerly produced for P-39s and P-40s. Shackles were also attached to outer-wing panels which permitted the carriage of British 108-gallon paper tanks, or bombs, when almost all P-47s were transferred to the 9th AF in 1944.

On 27 September 1943, P-47s reached Emden, more than doubling the radius-of-action to 375 miles. But Berlin lay further on. and although the British 108-gallon paper drop tank was used on the Emden mission, mass-production in Britain for the USAAF did not begin until mid-December. Although not all the P-47s had drop tanks, the day's score totalled 24 kills. This was one of the most satisfying fighter missions in the ETO for the whole of 1943. This was a milestone, and an occasion for celebration by Bomb Wing Commanders who were elated. The huge Thunderbolts had been in combat since April, and now, almost six months later, were paying their way and providing good news for folks back home.

Right: From the control tower balcony at Debden, England, officers watch Republic P-47 Thunderbolts take off for a rendezvous with Flying Fortresses on 25 September 1943. The officers are, left to right: Lieutenant Colonel Chelsey Peterson and Brigadier General Frederick L. Anderson, Jr. Mr. Donald Nelson, Chief of War Production, stands between the two officers. The Flying Fortresses – nearly 250 in all – were assigned to bomb port facilities and industrial areas in northern Germany. For the first time, relays of VIII Fighter Command P-47s with new 108-gallon paper drop tanks were able to provide escort all the way to the target and back, resulting in the downing of 18 German fighters.

Because of Fairchild's FAREP, P-47D outer-wing shackle kits were shipped in October, November, and December. The first P-47D built in production with wing-mounted shackles was due to roll out on 15 October, and a new additional 65-gallon internal tank was undergoing development for a later model of the P-47D.

In one of the first reports written of progress of Fairchild's FAREP, Brig. Gen. Chidlaw said three P-38Js were being flight-tested at the airfield of the new Army Air Forces School of Applied Tactics (AAFSAT) in Orlando, Florida. AAFSAT replaced the ACTS. New internal wing leading-edge tanks were to give P-38Js much better range, although AAFSAT

One of the great "weapons" that helped win the war was the British 108-gallon paper drop tank. Seen here is the last remaining example of the type, on display at the Air Force Museum. It was found in a shed in England in the 1980s and given as a gift to the US.

reported additional weight "...*reduces the climb rate by 540 feet/minute at all altitudes and adversely affects flying characteristics above 25,000 feet.*" (4)

The production change point was set for January 1944 when Lockheed would roll out the first P-38J built with new, internal wing tanks. Until then, kits would be installed to P-38Js already produced at modification centers. In September, kits were being shipped to Lockheed's European modification center at Langford Lodge in Northern Ireland for the incoming P-38Js of the 20th Fighter Group.

Fuselage Tank Kits

Col. Mark Bradley's fuselage tank experiment worked and months after Bob Chilton flew a 737-mile radius in a P-51B, Mustangs were being fitted with the tanks. However, problems surfaced and Lt. Col. L.T. Bradbury in the Production Branch told OC&R that the tanks "...*had to be returned, (and) the date for availability of three P-51B planes for AAFSAT has been set back to 1 October, 1943.*" (5)

Simultaneously with AAFSAT's testing, production P-51Bs were sent to modification centers to have kits installed, when it was discovered that the man-hours needed to instal a tank far exceeded estimates. Wright Field had estimated it would be a 350-hour job and NAA estimated 400 hours, but those on the job required from 800 to 1,100 hours.(6) The learning-curve would later reduce that number. An officer said "...*it is not believed*" that 339 P-51Bs scheduled to be ready by 1 January, would be modified in time.(7) Kits were shipped to Britain to be put into Mustangs stationed there. Two hundred and fifty kits were available in November and 100 per week after January 1944. It was anticipated that the first P-51B built with a tank during production would roll out on January 1, 1944.

The first P-51Bs shipped to Britain did not have the new fuselage fuel tanks installed, but modification soon enabled Mustangs to fly much further than the P-47 and P-38. In October 1943 another problem arose. The joining of dissimilar metals within the radiator caused corrosion in the cooling system. Following a determined search for a solution to the problem, an inhibitor known as NaMBT was added to the coolant to stop corrosion.

Men of the 361st Fighter Group pull out a British 108-gallon paper drop tank prior to a mission.

Drop Tank Problems

By late 1943, mass-production of drop tanks was hailed as a war-winning idea. Fighter pilots understood that combat was dangerous anyway and one more hazard of hanging dozens of gallons of flammable avgas beneath a fighter in a thin aluminum shell was a supportable, victory-producing burden on the men flying in the deadly air war. Lockheed drop tanks built for P-38Fs and Hs were not mass-produced until the end of 1943, and P-38 pilots often flew without one or both of them because they were so scarce. One source states that Arnold had supposedly ordered "*all-out*" development in February 1942, but "...*progress was slow.*" In fact, it was glacial! In October 1942, Eaker had asked for more drop tanks for incoming P-47s but did not get any. The official history states: "*In January, 1943, the Eighth Air Force, which in the preceding October had inquired whether jettisonable tanks* could be made available for its use, gave some consideration to local manufacture of tanks for the P-47." [8] The AAF was willing to let Britain produce paper tanks but did not demand them from its own country.

Eaker wrote to Echols on 18 May 1943 addressing him as "Dear Oliver" and enclosing some battle damage photos intended to rouse Echols to a combative posture: "… it seems to me that the P-47 situation has worked out all right, with one exception. That concerns the early supply of auxiliary tanks to extend the range of our fighters sufficiently to accompany our bombers to their targets and on their return. I would appreciate it, however, if you would figure out how to get us the (tanks) which will maintain pressure at altitude, and get them here in quantity to extend range." [9]

No matter how many times Eaker addressed the problem of supply of drop tanks and no matter how nicely he put it, Echols ignored him. Echols would not let it be assumed that he took orders from Commanding Generals in Theaters of War. Eaker was naturally an extremely soft-spoken man with a bottomless reserve of integrity and a manner so quiet it made other people edgy. Neither Eaker's dire straits nor his kind personality had any effect upon Echols.

When Echols failed to act, Col. Cass Hough and his staff in Britain devised the pressurization system. One or more of the British 108-gallon paper drop tanks, each with its pressurization pump, were sent to Materiel. In August 1943, Echols told the Deputy Chief of Air Staff General Hall that the "…8th AF tested an approved paper and fabricated tank which is pressurized from the vacuum pump. The Materiel Command is in agreement that this is the most satisfactory solution." [10] British – not US – production for the AAF was to start on 18 December 1943.

Mass-Production of Drop Tanks

After the FAREP was ordered, things began to happen fast. In September the AAF supplied the first real drop tanks. The bulbous, drag-producing ferry tank for the P-47D was replaced. NAA conducted a long-range flight test with two 75-gallon drop tanks on a P-51B. Although the older, drag-producing tanks worked, NAA designed its own aerodynamically shaped, low-drag tank which was later installed on F-86s. Materiel was procuring 400 75-gallon drop tanks and 500 85-gallon fuselage tank kits for Mustangs. The official history states: "…about ten thousand 75-gallon tanks reached England in October; by 12 October the British had been able to supply a total of 450 paper tanks." [11]

The FAREP ordered tens of thousands of tanks as production got under way. One of Chidlaw's reports of

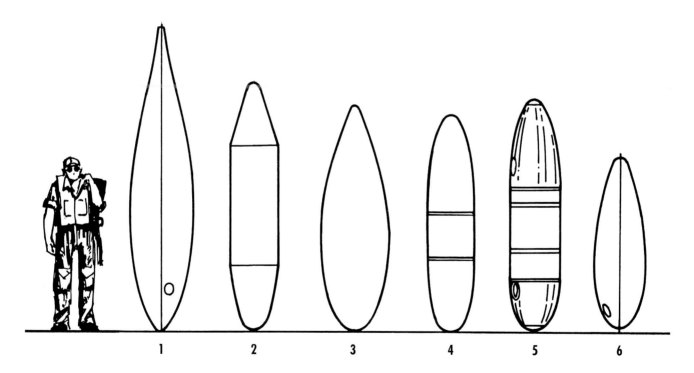

1. 150 gal. P-38 drop tank, metal. The tank was actually a 165-gallon tank capable of carrying only 150 gallons. It was manufactured by Lockheed.

2. 150 gal. metal drop tank for the P-47.

3. 150 gal. metal drop tank for the P-47. This tank had a flat top and undersides because the belly of the P-47 was too near the ground to carry a bulbous-shaped tank.

4. 150 gal. paper tank.

5. 108 gal. paper drop tank. British manufacture.

6. 75 gal. metal drop tank. This tank was originally made for use on P-39s and P-40s.

progress of the FAREP said eight varieties of US-designed and produced metal drop tanks were to be considered for mass-production. Long after Echols had dragged his feet over the issue, MM&D ruefully reported in October, with tongue-in-cheek, that the British 108-gallon paper tank was to be duplicated in America in metal and that "...*a current sample of this tank is expected to have passed its tests successfully.*" [12]

Initially, 9,000 Lockheed 165-gallon (150-gallon capacity, unpressurized) tanks were to be produced in October and 14,325 were anticipated in November, to be followed by 30,000 per month after that. Chidlaw said future needs of drop tanks for P-38s, P-47s, and P-51s were to be based upon "...*20 missions per month per group of 50 airplanes.*" That formula meant a single fighter group needed 1,000 tanks per month. Thirty-three groups would require 33,000 every 30 days. Planned for 1944 were "...*300,000 each 150-gallon tanks of 1,000 per day. 570,000 each 108-gallon tanks at the rate of 600 per day. 3,000 each 150-gallon tanks in addition to the 4,000 now on order (are required) at the rate of 20 tanks per day.*" [13]

These astronomical figures indicated the complete change of heart about drop tanks.

The Plus Sign

Once P-38s and P-51s were modified with new internal tanks, it was necessary to provide a visual clue identifying modified fighters. Mechanics and fuelers of long-range fighters parked next to non-modified ones would be aided by a tell-tale symbol. In November, the Headquarters of the Aircraft Distribution Office located at Patterson Field – adjacent to Wright – issued a statement stating: "...*all P-38 and P-51 type airplanes being processed through (the) Mod. Center on the long range tank installation program are to have a white cross, 6 inches high and 6 inches wide painted on the nose of each airplane below the serial number.*" [14]

Camouflaged P-38s and P-51s had a white "+" sign, and bare-metal airplanes had a black one. P-47s modified with shackles provided an apparent visual identification so no plus sign was applied to Thunderbolts.

Charles Lindbergh

After April 1944, the US government authorized Charles Lindbergh to apply his expertise toward improving aviation technology by visiting combat units in the Pacific theater of war, as a civilian and once the most famous aviator in the world. He had fallen into disfavor over certain political remarks and visits to Hitler's Germany in the late 1930s. In May and June, he flew F4Us in combat with the Marines and since the Corsair's R-2800 engine also powered the P-47, Lindbergh visited the base of the AAF's 35th FG in June. He instructed ways to nearly triple the radius-of-action of a P-47. Officers put his ideas to paper and transmitted them to other units. At the end of June, Lindbergh travelled to the base of the AAF's 475th FG and flew P-38s through the month of August. It was noticed in July that Lindbergh's P-38 returned to base with more fuel than other airplanes. Lindbergh was asked to explain and he taught that the range of a fighter could be increased by reducing rpm and staying below 1,000 ft. This way, the radius-of-action of P-38s was greatly improved. Word of his improvements went up the chain of command through Lt. Gen. Kenney, and eventually General MacArthur summoned Lindbergh. When MacArthur heard of the previously unknown advantage of a fighter flying farther into enemy territory, Lindbergh was given wide latitude in traveling to island bases to help combat units reach the distant enemy.

The radius-of-action of the P-47 was increased nearly three times by leaning the mixture, using 1,400 rpm and 36 inches of manifold pressure and by staying below 1,000 ft. Because distances between Allied and Japanese forces were often very great, there was no problem with a unit flying at a very slow speed to reach the battle area and then reverting to high speed and high rpm on return. By employing Lindbergh's methods and by carrying huge drop tanks, P-47s were later flown from Morotai Island 700 or 800 miles, one-way into battles during the recapture of the Philippine Islands, and the same number of miles on return.

Range extension in the piston-engined combat fighter was improved near the very end of its useful existence, during a world war, and just prior to the jet age.

Chapter 14

"Opportunity, once lost, may not recur..."

P-51Bs for the ETO

When "Hap" Arnold became Chief in 1938, he had the rank of a Major General. In 1941, he was promoted to Lieutenant General although until March 1943, he was at some disadvantage in dealing with British Air Chief Marshals and the most senior US Generals. Although the AAF was subordinate to the Army, in March 1943, Arnold was given four stars – then the highest rank permitted. Later in the war, a special five-star rank was accorded to a few select US Generals and Admirals, and Arnold was included in that since-deleted lofty rank. As no General can command in a vacuum, General Arnold needed to hear the advice from one particular USAAF officer who did not acquiesce to every Army wish to control fighters. In July 1943, Lt. Gen. Eisenhower was fighting the Sicilian campaign – codenamed "Husky" – and telegramed Arnold asking for two long-range fighter groups, either "*P-38s or P-51s*" for the forthcoming attack on Italy. Arnold asked Brig. Gen. (later, General) Laurence Kuter, now on Arnold's staff "*…where the groups are to come from*" and Kuter told him: "*UK bomber offensive operations are of (the) highest priority. There are now in UK only four medium-range fighter groups (P-47). These cannot provide adequate cover for the twenty heavy bomber and four medium bomber groups which will be in UK by July 31, 1943. Consideration of the relative urgency of various projects indicates that the need for reserve long-range fighter airplanes (P-38) in Australia and South Pacific and North Africa is of lower order than the need for long-range fighter airplanes in United Kingdom. Recommendations. The 20th Fighter Group (P-38) be diverted to United Kingdom immediately in lieu of remaining committed to North Africa. Reserve P-38 airplanes now earmarked to be shipped to Australia be diverted to United Kingdom to provide equipment for the 20th Fighter Group. The P-51B airplanes earmarked for July delivery to United Kingdom and the unit they will equip be not diverted to North Africa. The Air Force position be stated as opposing the provision of two additional long-range fighter groups for Post Husky operations from North Africa. The three long range fighter groups (P-38) now in North Africa be diverted to United Kingdom immediately upon completion of Husky.*"

Kuter listed 60 P-51Bs "*…for replacement of P-47s in a fighter group now in United Kingdom. These will be ready to leave the east coast by July 15th.*" [1]

Kuter and Arnold stood up to Eisenhower as the USAAF acknowledged the importance of the escort fighter in the European air war. In August, Arnold told Spaatz that he wanted bombers "*from Mediterranean bases*" to hit German fighter factories. Eventually the Fifteenth AF did attack Germany from Italy. Spaatz wanted P-51s for the air war over Italy and Arnold commented: "*It was originally planned to equip the P-40 Groups with P-51Bs when the Packard-powered P-40 was discontinued. However, due to the urgent need in UK for a balanced fighter force*

Lieutenant General Arnold (center), seen here visiting the Packard plant on 1 August 1942, was not permitted to hold equal rank with more senior officers until 1943. However, once he became a four-star General, Arnold applied considerable and successful pressure upon Charles Portal to get Mustangs for Eaker's Eighth Air Force.

including airplanes with greater range than the P-47, it was decided to send all available P-51s to England and therefore the only airplane available for re-equipping your P-40 groups is the P-47." [2]

Throughout all of 1942 and half of 1943 there had been a tug-of-war – as well as a real war – between the RAF and AAF over which country should be allowed to do what with the new Merlin-Mustang. In early 1943, Arnold had raised priority for reconnaissance temporarily above fighters.[3] A plan to exchange Mosquitos for Mustang airframes had been taken all the way to Arnold's desk. Part of the reason for getting Mosquitos was slow production of P-38s and increased demand for F-5s. Mosquitos were expected to fill a gap in delayed production of F-5s. The USAAF actually obtained very few Mosquitos. This tug-of-war ceased abruptly when the AAF found in the P-51B the long-range fighter it had needed all along but had denigrated forcefully. Now in September 1943, Arnold, equal in rank with Air Chief Marshal Sir Charles Portal, wrote to ask the RAF to reduce allocations for Mustang IIIs – P-51Bs. Arnold advised: *"The total planned production of the two suitable types, the P-38 and P-51, is not sufficient to fulfil requirements. The total P-38 production is already allocated to the Army Air Forces. There are 1,200 P-51 airplanes allocated to the Royal Air Force in the remainder of 1943 and the first half of 1944, which are urgently needed to fulfil requirements which cannot be met by the number presently allocated to the Army Air Forces."*

To emphasize his need, Arnold quoted one of Portal's own statements back to him: *"If we do not now strain every nerve to bring enough force to bear to win this battle during the next few months, but are content to see the 8th Bomber Command hampered by lack of reinforcements just as success is within its grasp, we may well miss the opportunity to win a decisive victory against the German Air Force which will have incalculable effects on all future operations and on the length of the war. And the opportunity, once lost, may not recur."*

Portal's statement was probably made in 1942 or early 1943 and argued for getting more bombers into the Eighth AF, not fighters. Now in September, Arnold wanted Mustangs, and in his letter, told Portal: *"Our most effective and expeditious way of reinforcing the 8th Bomber Command is to provide it with adequate fighter protection, thus reducing attrition. In view of the urgent need at this critical time for increased bomber escort, I am asking that you give early consideration to the following proposals: That you place Royal Air Force Squadrons, now equipped and to be equipped with P-51 airplanes, under the operational control of the Commanding General, 8th Air Force, for use as bomber escort units, until the launching of the Overlord Operation. That you release to the Army Air Forces sufficient*

P-51s to equip Army Air Forces Fighter Squadrons to the extent of General Eaker's needs for bomber escort and accept P-47s in return therefore." [4]

The first Schweinfurt disaster had occurred in the month prior to Arnold's message and the second lay just ahead. After the 14 October carnage over Germany, Arnold became frustrated over the impossibility of the escort situation and sent a letter to Portal criticizing the RAF. Portal replied ten days after Schweinfurt Two, quoting Arnold who had said the RAF was a force of "thousands" idled and not supporting the Eighth AF as fully as possible. In part, Portal remarked: *"With regard to your statement as to our failure to employ our forces in adequate numbers against the German Air Force in being, I do not know the extent to which your statement is based on precise figures, but I would like you to be aware of some facts in regard to the operation of the various forces engaged. During the last three months 73 percent of the total effort of Fighter Command has been in offensive operations; 64 percent of the total effort was on offensive operations against the G.A.F.; 76 percent of the offensive effort was for the protection of bombers. It will interest you to know that nearly one out of every three fighter aircraft of Fighter Command that left the ground for operations did so in order to provide protection for the Eighth Air Force. The difficulty is to persuade the Germans to come up and fight. It is rarely that the German fighters can be engaged at a point nearer than forty miles inland from the enemy coast. The recent attacks on G.A.F. airfields have made the enemy move back his fighters to the extreme limit of range of our Spitfires even when they are fitted with drop tanks. With present drop tanks, we have an operational radius of action of 175 miles. Your comparison of the ranges of the P.47 and the Spitfire, as these aircraft were originally designed, is not correct. The latter is a much smaller aircraft designed as an interceptor fighter; the P.47, developed later as a general purpose fighter, is a much larger aircraft which, as you well know, is not very good for some of the essential tasks in which the Spitfire excels. It was possible to increase considerably the main tankage of the P.47 without much difficulty, principally because its size permitted. The P.51, in the design of which we had so large a share, is pre-eminently suitable for long-range penetration. Unfortunately there was a great deal of prejudice in the early stages in accepting the virtues of this aircraft and getting it into production. Admittedly, we have fallen far short of what we hoped to accomplish. So far as the Eighth Air Force is concerned, we have been unable to carry out the plan mainly because the aircraft strength of this force has been only 70 percent of that planned, and because the crew strength has been only 70 percent of establishment. In effect, the Eighth Air Force has had approximately only 50 percent of the operational strength provided for in Phase I of the Combined*

Plan. The great tactical advantage, including the element of surprise which your heavy bombers had at the start of their operations in this theater, have therefore been largely thrown away by the slow rate of build-up which you have achieved. We have already decided to re-organize Fighter Command and to relieve the Air Commander in Chief, AEAF of detailed responsibility for the defense of this country. This will enable him to give his undivided attention to the prosecution of the offensive in POINTBLANK and OVERLORD." [5]

No American statistics are available to show how many Spitfires escorted US bombers or how often, but there was considerable escorting done even though the Spitfire had short range. After the war, Arnold wrote a book in which he revealed that during the height of the war he ordered Wright Field to shoe-horn fuel tanks as small as 10-gallon capacity into every conceivable space in a Spitfire IX owned by the US and once done, he had a test pilot fly it across the Atlantic to Britain. That slap-in-the-face experiment was *"…our attempt to get the British to put extra legs on the Spitfire."* [6]

Portal agreed in October to give incoming Mustang IIIs to the AAF. Arnold thanked him, saying: *"…yesterday I decided to stop any long-range P-38s and P-51s from going to Tactical Recon. Units or to any Theater other than (the) UK during October, November, and December."* [7]

Many of these British-marked Mustangs were hastily repainted and given to the first AAF groups formed in the UK.

Left: In an effort to persuade the RAF to develop a long-range escort comparable to the P-51, General Arnold authorized the installation of internal tanks on two Spitfires at Wright Field in 1944. In May, Lt. Col. (later, Brig. Gen.) Gustav Lundquist, Chief Experimental Fighter Test Pilot of the Flight Test Section at Wright Field, flew this airplane back to Britain using a B-25 as a navigational pathfinder. Stops were made at Goose Bay, Baffin Island, Bluie West 8 in Greenland, Iceland, and Prestwick in Scotland before the flight arrived at Boscombe Down, England in June. Though two Spitfires were modified, one had engine failure at Wright Field but during a delay in Greenland, managed to catch up. Sgt. Petta painted the fetching figure in Greenland; 'Tolly' was Lundquist's wife's name.

Spitfire IX MK210, minus the girlie nose art, almost ready for its trans-Atlantic flight in May 1944 after having fuel tanks fitted into every crevice by Wright Field.

Chapter 15

"All incoming P-51s should go to the Ninth..."

Eaker's Gift

One of the mysteries of the European air war surrounds Eaker's gift of P-51Bs to the Ninth AF in October 1943. There can be only one explanation for this because Eaker preferred the P-38. It had long range and its firepower was heavier than that of the P-47 and P-51. Up to 15 October 1943, he found no use for Lightnings in all the time he was CG of the Eighth AF. Prior to that – when he commanded Eighth Bomber Command in 1942 – he had not been able to take the measure of P-38s when they were part of the Eighth AF. In 1942, before the P-38 could demonstrate either its capabilities or faults, they had all been ordered into the 12th AF. A year later in mid-October 1943 – when P-38s became operational again in the Eighth AF – Eaker was asked by the incoming CG of the re-established Ninth AF (in Britain) for some aircraft, and Eaker agreed to give him all the P-51Bs due to be delivered.

So far as is known, the aura of superiority surrounding the P-38 which begun at its roll-out in 1939 had never left Eaker's mind. Everyone in the USAAF had extremely – if not to say excessively – high regard for the P-38. It did have a fine record in the South West Pacific Area and in the MTO. However, now that Eaker was to receive the P-38, he was optimistic about its capabilities and adamant about keeping them.

A month after Arnold had practically demanded of Portal that the RAF provide the Eighth AF with Mustang IIIs, Eaker gave them away! If any action by Eaker can be said to have been the straw that broke the camel's back – causing him to be reassigned to command the Mediterranean Allied Air Force – his giveaway was probably that straw. Eaker had misunderstood Arnold's intentions and he simply did not grasp the superior qualities of the P-51B.

Even in October, some officers in the AAF still regarded the P-51B as a tactical, ground support fighter. In all the time leading up to October 1943, Arnold's subordinates had grudgingly found a place for the Mustang in the AAF but only as a tactical weapon. Directorates had siphoned off all Mustangs to be produced in 1943 and the first half of 1944 for ground support and reconnaissance and as late as in mid-1943 were lobbying hard to retain them. Yet, because he was a

Commanding General of an Air Force, Eaker was able to decide which types of aircraft were necessary to his mission, and he decided to give P-51Bs to the Ninth AF. General Arnold honored that decision.

The Ninth AF was transferred from North Africa to Britain in late 1943 and the 67th Tactical Reconnaissance Group was ordered to join IX FC. The 67th TRG employed Spitfires and was due to receive F-6 Mustangs at the end of 1943 or in early 1944. The tactical, ground support reputation of the Mustang preceded it to the ETO, but Eaker still preferred the P-38 over the P-51B.

Maj. Gen. Lewis Brereton, CG of Ninth AF, had to leave Britain and travel to Washington to receive assistance in organizing and equipping his air force. On 7 October 1943, he was in the capital, probably in the newly-finished Pentagon, in

Major General Ira Eaker, Commanding General (CG) of the Eighth AF, decorating members of the 13th Photograph Squadron, 7th Photo-Recon Group. Eaker was unimpressed by the coming availability of the P-51B and preferred the P-38 and P-47 for escort work. He gave all the incoming Mustangs to Major General Brereton, CG of the Ninth AF.

a meeting with General Arnold's staff. He needed tactical fighters and set down a brief statement recommending that "...*the Ninth be assigned only the P-51 and P-47 initially*." [1]

Brereton returned to Britain and met with Eaker in late October and the two agreed "...*that all incoming P-51s should go to the Ninth to simplify maintenance and repair*." [2]

Kepner, who had a higher regard for the Mustang, protested.

Simplification of maintenance and repair had been addressed by Maj. Gen. Hugh Knerr, who wore two hats as Deputy Commanding General for Administration of the United States Strategic Air Force (USSTAF) and Commanding General of the Air Service Command (ASC) in Britain. In April 1943, when Knerr was a Colonel, he had accompanied Maj. Gen. Follett Bradley (no relation to Col. Mark Bradley) to Britain to help build up bomber strength in the Eighth AF. After Knerr became a Brigadier General, he suggested in August, a plan to control supply and maintenance for the two numbered air forces. By October, Brereton and Eaker wanted to "...*simplify maintenance and repair*" by putting all P-51Bs into one air force – the Ninth.

When the Ninth AF was in North Africa it had P-40Fs powered by Packard V-1650-1s engines. There had been a plan to replace these with P-51Bs because both were powered by Packard Merlins. Issues such as maintenance, parts supply, and training of mechanics affected logistics. When the Ninth AF was reformed in Britain, it had no P-40Fs but as a tactical air force, the lingering idea that the "tactical" P-51B was to be available to the Ninth AF must have influenced its staff officers to suggest to Brereton to request it from Eaker and from Washington.

Although Arnold left it up to Eaker to choose, Arnold did not have Spaatz – senior to Eaker in the field – to rely upon for advice since Spaatz was in the MTO and may not have been aware of Eaker's gift. Spaatz reversed Eaker's gift in January 1944, but whether or not he appreciated the potential of the P-51B in October 1943, is unknown. In November, after Eaker gave Mustangs away, Giles told Brig. Gen. A.B. McDaniel, Commanding General of the 3rd Reconnaissance Command: "...*it has become necessary to support the heavy bomber operations over Germany with long-range fighters, which means full utilization of P-38J and P-51B production; hence, the cut to the Reconnaissance Program. As a matter of fact, recommendations have been sent higher that all production of the P-38J and P-51B until March be diverted to supporting the heavy bomber operations*." [3]

Fighters were once again higher priority than reconnaissance. There is no explanation as to why Giles and Arnold did not specify to which air force Mustangs should be supplied except that it was Eaker's choice.

Lieutenant General Lewis Brereton was Commanding General of the Ninth AF.

After Giles' November statement and before late December, Arnold agreed with Eaker's choices of equipment. Giles sent a memo in late-December to Lovett which stated that from 31 December 1943 to 31 June 1944, no assignment of P-51s was to be made to the Eighth AF. The Ninth AF was to be assigned eight Mustang groups. As Arnold's Chief of Staff, Giles – who replaced Stratemeyer – would not have drafted a message for Lovett without Arnold knowing about it. [4]

Arnold and others influenced Eaker about the needs of the Eighth Strategic Air Force, because on 31 December Eaker commented: "...*the primary tactical role of all US Fighter units in (the) U.K. until further notice will be support and protection of Heavy Bombers engaged in Pointblank*." [5] All incoming P-51Bs remained assigned to the Ninth AF.

Could it be true that Eaker was unaware the P-51B had the longest range of any fighter; of Arnold's plan to use P-51Bs as escorts; was not told of the FAREP; that Arnold had gone to great lengths with Portal to get Mustang IIIs from the RAF? Why did it take Eaker an additional two months, to December, to appreciate the P-51B as an escort for his bombers?

For several months after Eaker's October meeting with Brereton, the P-51B was a tactical fighter in a tactical air force. Only days before that meeting the P-38s began combat operations in VIII FC.

Right: Pioneers in more than one sense, this trio of 354th Fighter Group pilots; from left to right: Maj George R Bicknell, Lt Col Wallace P Mace, and Maj Owen M Seaman, all of whom were at Pearl Harbor the day the Japanese attacked. Behind the pilots is 'Peg O'My Heart' a frequently photographed P-51B.

Below: Lt John T Godfrey, ace of the 4th Fighter Group, clowns with his dog "Lucky" at Debden, 10 April 1944.

Bottom: A formidable combination of the P-51 Mustang with drop tanks helped doom the Luftwaffe fighter force in the West, the 354th Fighter Group leading the process. In this 18 January 1944 picture are, left to right: Lieutenants Franklyn E Hendrickson, William E Pitcher, and Edward E Phillips.

Chapter 16

"Morale is high. The mechanics are going wild!"

Disappointment with the P-38

Second Schweinfurt, the final warning, drove VIII FC to order the P-38H-equipped 55th FG into combat the day after the disaster, on 15 October. Lt. Col. Harry Dayhuff, an experienced and decorated pilot, was not a member of the 55th FG, but led the group on its first sweep over the Continent. Flying not far inland the newcomers were, at 28,000 ft, flying at 390 mph on a familiarization flight. The aim was to view landmarks, as well as getting over their first-mission jitters.

In his diary, Lt. Col. Jack Jenkins, Deputy Group Commander, recorded that the first few missions were flown without drop tanks.[1] Only two months previously, the 55th FG had been in America and Lt. Col. Frank B. James, Group CO, was notified that his unit was ordered into combat and an advance echelon, including Maj. Jenkins, was sent ahead to Britain to prepare for the group's arrival. When Frank James became a Colonel, Jenkins was promoted to Lieutenant Colonel. In September the men as well as aircraft arrived and training began. In October two officers from VIII FC told James that Washington was applying pressure to get P-38s into combat. The AAF arranged for a big newsreel, newspaper, and photo session to publicize P-38s being on strength in the UK. The order to begin combat operations

Colonel Frank B. James, CO of the 55th Fighter Group in its early days. This photograph was taken at Nuthampstead in 1943.

helped the 55th FG set a record for being combat-operational within one month after arrival. Besides meeting ordinary requirements within those 30 days, such as housing the men, checking aircraft and engines, learning protocol, adjusting to English food and lack of indoor heating, the 55th FG had to adjust to the ETO. Pilots learned to navigate across the confusing, crazy-quilt countryside, and to fly in bad weather and poor visibility almost constantly; make hairy instrument approaches, and to know how to cope if they went down in the Channel or were shot down over Europe. It was an extremely busy month.

Little occurred during the 55th FG's mission to Duren on 20 October. On 24 October, 72 Ninth AF B-26s raided St. Andre airfield 45 miles west of Paris. P-47Ds flew high cover and 48 P-38Hs flew close escort carrying what probably was a single 75-gallon drop tank each. Jenkins, on his ninth mission, fired at a yellow-nosed Fw 190 and "...*at the instant I was diving and firing*" four Bf 109s went on the tail of another P-38 while other Lightning pilots drove the enemy off. ETO P-38s had fired their first shots of the war four years after the rollout of the XP-38.

Ever since the first flight of the big 'twin' in 1939, many fighter pilots wanted to get their hands on the fast, beautiful and steady P-38. The arrival of P-38s sent a long-withheld wave of hope through the Eighth AF. The ETO had become the AAF's proving ground for strategic bombardment but it was in the Mediterranean – where P-38s were present – that the Twelfth AF had proved the efficacy of protecting bombers with long-range Lightnings. Now that P-38s were available in the UK, bomber crews began to breath sighs of relief in anticipation of being escorted to and from distant targets. However, one group alone could not protect the entire Eighth Bomber Command.

The ETO P-38s first made a name for themselves on 3 November 1943 when 539 bombers were escorted to Wilhelmshaven and the 55th FG scored its first victories – and suffered its first losses. Only seven bombers were lost and that low number had to be attributed to protection from escorting P-38s. Top-

From left to right: Major Dallas 'Spider' Webb, Colonel Jim Stone, CO of the 78th Fighter Group, Lieutenant Colonel Harry Dayhuff, Deputy CO of the 78th Fighter Group, and Lieutenant Colonel Jack Jenkins. The photograph was taken at Duxford in the fall of 1943.

scoring unit was the 353rd FG with its P-47s claiming five from a total of 14 kills, and the 55th's three victories brought hearty congratulations from Kepner and Maj. Gen. Idwal Edwards, Deputy Commander of the Eighth AF. Jack Jenkins led the mission on 3 November, taking 48 Lightnings on a two-drop-tank escort and shot down an Fw 190. He later saw the bombers being stalked again and attacked a Bf 109. After the group got back to RAF Nuthampstead he wrote in his diary: "*…all our boys are home safely. We claim six destroyed and several damaged. Morale is sky high. The mechanics are going wild! We got our first Jerries before Sadie Hawkins Day, November 6th.*"

Sadie was a cartoon character in newspaper comic strips and she was so popular that her "day" was an annual event among some pilots. Maj. Gen. Kepner reviewed the mission and wrote a letter of praise to the CG of the IV FC back in the US to which the 55th FG had once belonged. Kepner said: "*…your Seattle group of P-38s acquitted themselves admirably since leaving McChord Field.*" 2nd Lt. Robert L. Buttke "*…got his ship into a flutter*" but downed his second victim, and Jenkins' victory was praised. A "flutter" was Kepner's term for an encounter with compressibility.[2]

Engine Failures

Except for two groups of P-38s which were in the ETO for a few months in mid-1942 before departing for North Africa, the first Lightning group which came to Britain and which remained with the Eighth AF was the famed 7th Photo Group with its F-5s. The 7th PG was not formed until July 1943, but the 13th Photo Squadron – which eventually was one of four photo squadrons in the 7th PG – arrived and flew its first combat mission in March 1943. F-5s flew photo missions above 24,000 ft starting in May 1943, but explosions of Allison V-1710 engines began to reduce effectiveness of the unit. According to former pilots, the problem was hot supercharger air entering ineffective wing leading-edge intercoolers after which it was sent to the carburetor causing overheating and explosions which could cause an engine to blow up. The USAAF restricted F-5 operations to a 300-mile radius on 15 July 1943,[3] and the 7th PG had to live with the restriction, though later in the year, the unit acquired some British Spitfire PR XIs for one squadron. The Spitfire PR XI often flew to 42,000 ft with no problems and was the first photo aircraft in the 7th PG to fly to Berlin following the USAAF's first bombing mission to that city in March, 1944. F-5s remained in three of the four squadrons in the 7th PG and the restriction was lifted later in the war. The F-5 remained as the USAAF's primary photo aircraft despite problems.

Little was done to correct the situation with Lightnings before the 55th Fighter Group began combat operations in October 1943, yet following realization that the P-47 had short range, all hopes for escort of bombers were placed squarely upon the men of the 55th FG.

The weather had already turned cold when the 55th FG was ordered to be ready. P-38s flew with bombers often at altitudes above 30,000 ft where the air was much colder than on the ground – often reaching –50 deg C. However, disappointment in the P-38 in the ETO, raised its ugly head on the 5 November mission, in and out of Munster. Engine and turbo failures began to occur. No one seemed to know why and the 55th FG continued to operate as normally as possible despite these problems. It was not until the rash of failures became so widespread through the long winter and into the first few months of 1944, that it was acknowledged that the Allison V-1710 engine and General Electric turbo did not perform well when operated for hours in cold air at high altitude.

P-38 fighter groups in other theaters were seldom required to climb above 30,000 ft and stay there for hours as was ordered for ETO P-38s. Those other groups did not have as many failures as occurred in P-38 units over Europe. Histories written about the European air war seldom explain the problems with the V-1710 and turbos and simply state that transfer of P-38s to the tactical Ninth AF in 1944 was nothing more than a high-level decision. In fact it was an admission that the P-38 flew best below 20,000 ft and was much less suitable as an escort in the Eighth AF. One month after the 5 November mission, P-51B fighter pilots began to write a new page of success in the history of fighter escort. After April 1944, the P-38 had slipped from prominence in the ETO as an escort.

The truth about engine failures has been dismissed, as if the sordid record of failed engines and turbos was incorrect and that the poor showing by P-38s in the Eighth AF was, instead, evidence of lack of aggressiveness on the part of Group Commanders. Nothing is further from the truth. Real mechanical breakdown became so widespread that the Commanding General of the Eighth AF eventually asked Spaatz personally for a batch of special fuels to operate just his P-38s. Matters became so insurmountable that Lockheed sent Tony LeVier – its test pilot most familiar with the V-1710 – to Britain and he reported that, ultimately, 2,000 V-1710s failed in the ETO alone.[4]

The 55th FG did score five kills on the 5 November 1943 mission and lost no aircraft. Besides the bombers sent to Munster, others went to Gelsenkirchen with a total loss of 11 aircraft, a small percentage of the force of 436 reaching the targets. Enemy fighters shot down 18 and the 56th FG scored its 100th victory, the first group in the ETO to reach that mark. A few 20th FG pilots of flying P-38Hs operated alongside the 55th FG.

The Bremen Mission

After 5 November 1943, pilots and ground crewmen prepared for the next mission and tried to let the unexplained failures be resolved by experts in the days ahead. The much desired appearance of P-38s sparked enthusiastic plans at AJAX to employ the AAF's longest-ranging fighter to the most distant targets at that time. Bremen was at the radius-of-action limit of a P-38H.

From the time P-38s crossed the French coastline on 13 November, until returning to Britain, the 55th FG fought its way all along the bomber route – using extra fuel – in and out of North West Europe. Kepner had wanted 20 minutes of loiter time over the target but fuel usage made the order difficult to carry out. The way AJAX handled the escort part of the mission prevented the 55th FG from performing well. That and unexpectedly strong winds led to accidents and loss of morale.

Two factors – less-than-full fuel tanks and a jet stream – caused fuel starvation in the case of some of the seven losses which the 55th FG suffered that day. In the post-mission analysis, Kepner was not one to criticize himself for asking too much of his P-38s. He had sent fighters to their maximum radii and still demanded additional loiter time. When the mission did not meet his expectations, Kepner became very unhappy.

A P-38H had a theoretical range radius of 520 miles but in combat it was not much more than 300 miles. Planning missions to 400 miles was simply asking for losses due to fuel starvation. Bremen was about as far as a P-38H could fly and fight. Kepner was determined and needed to show bomb group commanders that escort, now that P-38s were on

The briefing room of the 55th Fighter Group at Nuthampstead 1943-44. A quotation painted near the ceiling read: "We have two scores we are aiming at – first the number of bombers we bring back safely, and second, the number of German fighters we destroy. W.E. Kepner, Major General."

strength, would not be as infrequent as it had been, nor as limited, when only short-range P-47s were available. The Bremen mission was an all-out fighter escort support mission for the 55th FG.

Jenkins recalled: *"...during the briefing, the weather officer informed me that there was a hell of a wind blowing at high altitudes from about 300 degrees."* Rain and stormy

A P-38H of the 343rd Fighter Squadron, 55th Fighter Group, s/n 42-66718, landing at Wormingford.

conditions delayed take-offs. After half the group got airborne, AJAX brought them back because the bombers were late getting off. Those P-38s that had flown briefly, landed, and refueled. Within 30 minutes however, AJAX ordered another departure, before the group had a chance to refuel all its aircraft! Jenkins led 48 P-38s and had to use extra speed and fuel to meet the bombers on time. They averaged 450 mph ground speed on the way in. "*We sighted the bombers as they were 20 miles northwest of Bremen – under attack by over 50 enemy aircraft. We swung into position and started slugging. There were dozens of Me 109s, Fw 190s, Do 217s, Ju 88s, Me 110s, and Me 210s. We didn't know it at the time we rendezvoused with the bombers but there were dozens of Huns above us.*" Jenkins estimated there were 300 enemy fighters observed "*…during our brief stay over enemy territory.*" The group was outnumbered six to one and it shot down seven but lost seven. After the combat ended, the P-38s started toward home.

On the way back, Jenkins was near Ijmuiden, Holland when he was hit by *flak* in his left engine and had to feather the propeller, cut the battery and lean the mixture on his good engine. The crossfeed was "*…shot out and I couldn't use the gas in my left main tanks.*"

One of the greatest worries for ETO crews was to have to cross the icy North Sea and the English Channel. Flying a shot-up aircraft over water made for concern. The water was so cold and rescue so uncertain that to ditch was to invite death as certainly as it was to let an enemy fighter get on your tail. A water-soaked pilot would become numb from cold in minutes. If he failed to get into his raft, he would lose consciousness and drown. Jenkins spent a tension-filled hour and a half heading southwest over the North Sea on one engine and when he realized his ground speed was slower than usual, descended to "*get below the headwinds.*" That day, the extremely strong headwinds Jenkins encountered were actually a phenomena unknown until the 1960s, when winds of over 100 knots were identified as a jet stream. Just as he passed over Debden he ran out of fuel and "*…crash-landed the ship there, because a damaged hydraulic line prevented me from lowering my gear.*"

Seven kills and seven losses indicated success as much as it did poor planning. The Bremen mission had been the longest to that date and a congratulatory report said P-38s "*…were responsible for holding bomber losses in the target area to a supportable level, and it could reasonably be hoped that a larger force could do the job still more efficiently and with relatively less cost to the escort itself.*"[5]

On that November mission, only 143 bombers, from a force of 272 despatched, reached Bremen because of weather. Sixteen were lost to enemy action. Three Bomb Groups were almost completely ineffective. In one that sent 18 bombers out – none reached Bremen; 520,000 leaflets were dropped over the city. Total fighter victories stood at ten and two P-38s crash-landed on the way back.

Turbo Failures

As if engine failures were not bothersome enough, on 29 November, 17 P-38s aborted another Bremen mission because of turbo failures. The remaining 38 were attacked by 80 enemy fighters. Cold, upper air affected the turbo superchargers. Oil in the turbo regulating servo congealed, altering the relationship between throttle position and manifold pressure. When the servo froze, manifold pressure on the engine served by that turbo would increase to 70 inches HG – a setting that would overboost the engine - and retarding the throttle one-quarter inch dropped pressure to 20 inches HG – a setting which could not sustain normal combat airspeed. A P-38 so affected would fish-tail around the sky and become a sitting duck in combat. The 17 aborts caused many telephones to ring across Britain, but correcting the turbo problem was nearly impossible. One company in America produced them and it would be months at the earliest before a fix came through. The 55th FG downed two but the seven losses hurt unit strength. Of 360 bombers sent to Bremen, only 154 reached the target because of bad weather. P-47s downed 13 enemy aircraft.

Colonel Jack Jenkins of the 55th FG poses with his ground crew in front of his P-38H s/n 42-67074 CG-T named "Texas Ranger".

Since the day it was first rolled out, a lesser but more personal problem with P-38s was cold cockpits. The ineffective heating system was reported through all the service years of the P-38, but it was never improved and the war ended before a fix was made. Pilots got so cold at high altitude that occasionally they had to be helped out of their cockpits by a crew chief after arrival.

All AAF aircraft were tested in sub-zero climatic conditions at Ladd Field in Alaska at the Cold Weather Test Detachment, and P-38s were operated in Alaska on combat alert during the war. There had been at least minimal cold-weather testing and operations, at some point before introduction to combat in the ETO. However, there may *not* have been a steady series of cold-weather tests of five-hour flights flown above 30,000 ft which was normal conditions for the 55th FG in 1943. Yet there was no denying what was happening. Operations over North West Europe were affecting the engines and turbos, while in other theaters, there were few complaints. Two months after the Lightning was in the theater that needed it most, it began to disappoint a lot of people. Troubles were encountered immediately instead of after a moderate period of action.

As had happened with Hunter and his P-47s, senior officers criticized the men and not the machines. By November 1943, VIII FC was operating short-range P-47s and troubled P-38s. It seemed as though the escort problem would never be solved. Kepner became more critical of P-38 pilots than Arnold had of P-47 operations, because it was generally agreed that the P-38 was the USAAF's true long-range fighter and since only ETO pilots complained about it, they thought the problem lay with the pilots and ground crews.

After a few 20th FG pilots had flown a mission as part of the 55th FG on November 5, the rest of the group arrived and began training. The initial cadre had arrived in August, ahead of the 55th FG, but the group was not up to unit strength and in a major gamble, the AAF decided to re-equip the group with the first P-38Js to be used in combat. P-38Hs of the 20th FG were assigned to North Africa. Maj. John C. Wilkins, Executive Officer of the 20th FG, had led the AAF's first P-38J mission on 3 November, but the entire group was not available until December. Although the group was commanded by Col. Barton M. Russell, VIII FC wanted a combat-experienced leader to take the 20th FG on its first full mission. Lt. Col. Jenkins was honored

From left to right: (unknown), Sgt. G. Lucky, 1st Lieutenant R. Rebout, and Crew Chief S/Sgt. Jim Lane. They stand in front of a 20th Fighter Group P-38J, "Betsy VI" which has the inscription "Pride O' Pershing Square" painted on the port engine scoop and "Pride of Piccadilly" on the starboard.

"California Cutie" was flown by Lieutenant Richard O. Loehnert of the 55th Fighter Squadron, 20th Fighter Group. Note the varied mission-flown markings, and especially the white cross which denoted the longer-ranging version of the P-38J. The Lockheed unpressurized 165-gallon (150-gallon capacity) drop tanks can be seen on the aircraft and on the grass.

with that assignment and he arrived at Kingscliffe on 27 December 1943 and led the entire group on the mission of the 28th. On the 30th he led a one-drop-tank mission over Holland.

Range Dispute

The P-38J was almost the second-to-last model in the long evolution of the big twin and the P-38L is regarded as the best of the line. When the 20th FG got its P-38Js, AJAX rightly believed it had the zenith of America's fighter designs in its hands, the ultimate fighter, the greatest of the great, the longest-ranging escort in use. Kepner expected wonderful results from the J-model. On the last day of 1943, Jenkins led the 20th FG and its new P-38Js on a two-tank mission to Bordeaux, 400 miles from Kingscliffe. Again, Kepner sent his pilots as far as a Lightning could fly and wanted loiter time as well.

The trip down south was uneventful, but Jenkins was surprised to see his own 55th FG orbiting Bordeaux. Jenkins and the 20th FG pilots rendezvoused with the bombers over the French city and Jenkins dropped his tanks to fire at an Fw 190. The group then flew north to attack a German-held airfield. "*By this time some of the boys were talking about gasoline shortage so we reformed the gang and started a long journey home.*"

They reduced RPM to 1,800 and pulled back the manifold pressure to 23 inches HG to conserve fuel. Jenkins was well aware that they could not fly as far as their base at Kingscliffe.

"*I took my section into Ford RAF Station with the gas gauge hitting the empty peg. We refueled and started on home. The weather kept getting worse. We got down to tree-top level and it began to rain. In all my career I have never had a bunch of boys in such a rough bit of weather. I rolled down a window, put my head out and prayed that those kids would stick on my wing. I was actually afraid to glance over to see. Once I did look and they were stuck in tighter than a cork. I found that I was surprised as well as happy about that! I passed over an airdrome and without further contemplation kicked it around and landed the flight. It was an RAF Station and after going through the usual red tape we got a truck to carry us home.*"

Incredibly, the 20th FG had been aloft for five hours and 48 minutes. As Tactical Commander, Jenkins filed a report saying that although a P-38J "*...can travel this great distance with ease it cannot be expected to fight an aggressive battle and return home safely. Had this group been bounced by half a dozen E/A on the return flight it would have lost almost half its force due to petrol shortage. A short sweep of the target area is about all that can be expected of the P-38 at that distance.*" [6]

Jenkins' report angered the Commanding Officer of the 67th Fighter Wing; it was New Year's Eve and there was a party. The report was duly sent upstairs to land on Kepner's desk.

The pilots' room of the 79th Fighter Squadron, 20th FG at Kingscliffe. On the right is Ed Steiner, the S2 Intelligence Officer.

From left to right, back row: Major Dallas Webb, Lieutenant Colonel Arthur C. Agan, Colonel Jack Jenkins, and Colonel Frank James. On the left center are Major General Kepner and Major General Edwards. The identities of the two men in the foreground are unknown. All are in the 55th FG pilots' briefing room at Nuthampstead in 1944.

P-38 Fuel Usage

Four days later Lt. Col. Jenkins led 20th FG P-38Js to Kiel on a two-tank mission and the 55th FG sent 51 P-38Hs to the same city. After returning to Kingscliffe, his tour with the 20th FG ended. Upon his return to Nuthampstead he was met by Col. (later, Brig. Gen.) Edward Anderson, Commander of the 67th Fighter Wing. Anderson and Kepner had reviewed Jenkins' report of the 31 December mission and were unhappy with his characterization of range of a P-38J. Anderson wanted a written explanation to give to Kepner. Dated 6 January 1944, Jenkins' description of P-38J fuel usage was as follows:

"Naturally, it is impossible to set up a definite range data chart for a P-38 Group. Colonel Russell, Colonel James and myself have discussed the various situations many times and have corrected our figures as the pilots gained experience.

"First, we will discuss gasoline consumption on an average, 2-belly-tank mission considering zero wind conditions. The belly tanks carry 150 gallons and the P-38J has approximately 300 gallons internal gasoline. Considering roughly 40 gallons for take-off and landing (using internal fuel tanks) (sic), this leaves 260 gallons internal gasoline. Now, after engaging the enemy and dropping the external tanks, we fight at Military Power around the target vicinity for 20 minutes. Our two engines burn a total of 320 gallons per hour at Military Power. A 20 minute fight would require 107 gallons.

"On the return trip we must consider a bounce from the Hun or, our giving protection to our single-engine stragglers. For this I have figured the return trip at a satisfactory cruising power of 2,200 rpm at 30 inches HG using 120 gallons per hour for both engines.

"Now, figuring that we have 260 gallons internally to use from and that we have 153 gallons left to get to an English Coastal Airdrome with a cruising consumption of 120 gallons per hour, we find we have one hour and 16 minutes to reach an airdrome after breaking off combat. If our combat ends over the target and we fly at 22,000 feet on the return trip indicating 210 mph, we find that we can fly only about 350 miles. However, if the combat is a running fight toward the UK then the mileage gained in combat is in our favor.

"From actual tests it has been found that our groups can climb and fly approximately 450 miles before running the drop tanks dry. Therefore a P-38 can fly farther on its external tanks than it can on its internal tanks.

"The P-38 is extremely loggy at 30,000 feet with and combat at those altitudes with tanks is almost impossible.

"Let's consider three long range missions to enemy territory: To Kiel, to Bremen and to Bordeaux.

a.	*From the English coast to Kiel we have about 390 miles. The greater part being over water and can be flown without much danger of interception. Occasionally, the group can keep its external tanks on the Kiel mission until they run dry. On extra long missions of this sort where bombing is done through overcasts, the bombers sometimes fly at 30,000 feet. As stated before, carrying belly tanks to this altitude is difficult. On the trip out from Kiel, a flight feels quite safe from interception. It is believed that a P-38 group should not be expected to remain in the Kiel area more than 20 minutes.*

b.	*From the English coast to Bremen is 300 miles. At this target we always fight every foot of the way through the target. We always have to drop our tanks and almost without fail some wingman in the rear flight will run low on gas after 20 minutes in the target area. There is always a stiff headwind on the return flight and on several occasions pilots have limped in to a coastal airdrome with tanks dry. It is believed that a*

Lightning Group should not be expected to remain in the area of a target as far inland as Bremen more than 25 minutes.

c. *The distance from Bordeaux to the South Coast of England is 400 miles, 50 miles farther than our maximum calculated range. It would be impossible to complete one of these Bordeaux missions if we met one-fourth of the opposition that we met at Bremen. The Bordeaux missions are usually lower, thus affording us more maneuverability with our tanks. We stayed in the Bordeaux area 15 minutes on December 31st and withdrew along the bomber route. Some of the pilots dropped their tanks soon after arrival at the target and found it necessary to cut down their power to minimum cruise in order to reach England. The group crossed about 325 miles of France on withdrawal and it is the opinion of the undersigned that had it been bounced by five or six aggressive enemy airplanes we would have lost half our force due to fuel shortage.*

"In summarizing this discussion of range, it is the opinion of the experienced pilots in the Lightning groups that with favorable or, at least not too unfavorable winds, we can successfully execute a target cover mission to coastal targets, such as Kiel and Bordeaux, 400 miles away from the English coast. However, we take a dim view on doing target support at a greater distance than our maximum calculated range of 350 miles if the target is well inland and enemy air superiority is certain." [7]

Jenkins' figures agreed with those sent by the Air Defense office to all officers in August 1943. However, Kepner disagreed and called Jenkins, James, and Russell into his office on 19 January 1944. Jenkins, afterward, said they *"..had a hell of a hot session"* with Kepner and *"his 'long-haired' boys with their slide rules and although they had never flown a combat mission, proceeded to tell Frank, Barney, and particularly me just how far we could fly. The General wants to push us to the very limit of endurance. I suppose he is right but we would rather fight the Hun than face a swim in the English Channel due to lack of fuel."*

On 24 January 1944, P-38J-5s and P-38J-10s were flown - the former carrying 300 gallons internally and the latter, 410 (a P-38H carried only 230). Added to these figures was fuel in drop tanks. The official history states that when P-38s carried two 75-gallon drops, radius was 520 miles. In February 1944, with two 108-gallon drops, radius was 585 miles.[8]

On 3 February, AJAX sent Kelsey, Hough, Tony LeVier, and some Lockheed representatives to Nuthampstead to check on engine failures.

On 8 February 1944, 1st. Lt. James M. Morris of the 20th FG shot down two Fw 190s and two Bf 109s in his P-38 to become the first AAF pilot in the ETO to get that many in a day. That, added to a victory over a Bf 109 on 11 February made him the first P-38 Ace in the ETO. He also shared a kill of an He 111 on 5 February and claimed an Me 410 on 7 July, but was then himself shot down and captured.

By that date there were already several P-38 Aces in the other Theaters. The P-38 had been the most-desired fighter operating in the MTO, and was still the best in the South West Pacific Area. At the end of the war America's greatest Ace, Maj. Richard Bong – who served in the South-West Pacific Area – had flown only P-38s and had 40 victories. 1st Lt. Morris' feat in the ETO was an occasion for rejoicing and celebration because the Eighth AF had been starved of Lightnings.

P-38 Problems Addressed

The 55th FG was not alone among P-38 users to suffer from engine and turbo failures. It was standard procedure in the ETO for escorts to fly at the levels bombers were ordered to reach, and yet the P-38H and J performed better at 15,000 to 20,000 ft while bombers often climbed to 30,000 ft or higher. When AJAX sent specialists to Nuthampstead in February 1944, to investigate the reason for engine failures, the 55th FG was made to feel it was being singled out for blame for those failures – until failures in other groups pointed a finger at the troubled V-1710 and turbo.

The 20th FG unit history states that the P-38 *"...was not equal to the*

Colonel Jack Jenkins' P-38H (s/n 42-67074) at Nuthampstead awaiting take-off and carrying no drop tanks.

Captain James Morris, 77th Fighter Squadron, and Colonel Barton Russell, CO of the 20th Fighter Group at Kingscliffe on 8 February 1944. Morris was the first P-38 Ace in the ETO.

extreme cold and moisture conditions that prevailed at operating altitudes (of) 20,000 – 30,000 feet (over) northern Europe." A P-38 *"...could not pursue the enemy to altitudes over 28 to 30,000 feet"* and in diving a P-38, *"...the enemy could not be followed down from those altitudes only under ideal conditions of surprise and altitude advantage."* The P-38 was *"...equal to any German fighter at altitudes below 15,000 feet. No satisfactory answer was found – until the weather itself had substantially improved."* [9]

During Big Week in February 1944, the Fifteenth AF based in southern Italy flew one of its first bombing missions over Germany and among the fighter groups escorting was the 82nd FG operating P-38Fs and Gs. The unit history states that their P-38s over Germany suffered a *"...major maintenance problem: the synchronization of the superchargers. One engine might run away, and the pilot would often fish-tail around with one throttle full forward and one almost full back."* [10]

On 1 March, Maj. Gen. James "Jimmy" Doolittle, who took command of the Eighth AF in January, 1944, sent a letter to General Spaatz commanding the US Strategic Air Forces, in which he advised:

1. *There have been 76 known Allison V-1710-89 and -91 engine failures in our P-38J aircraft during the few months they have been operating in this theater. It is not known how many more engine failures have occurred over enemy territory and prohibited the aircraft from getting home, but the high loss rate of this type of aircraft indicates that there have been many. The engine failures have been occurring with increasing frequency and the situation is now critical. The pilot's first indication of failure has, almost invariably, been a thrown connecting rod. This is often accompanied by engine fire in the air. Inspection of failed engines, torn down in the depots, shows that detonation, stuck or broken piston rings and scored cylinders have been present in varying degree. Detonation has been so bad in some cases as to burn off large portions of the piston head. Detonation has been most prevalent in cylinders four and six of the right bank, which cylinders have the poorest distribution and get the leanest mixture. Many engines which had not failed showed on overhaul that failure was imminent and would undoubtedly have occurred had the engine been operated longer.*

2. *Very little trouble was experienced with the V-1710-89 and -91 engines in the earlier P-38Hs operating with the same engine, fuels, and pilots under identical operating conditions. This indicates that a difference in the engine installation in the P-38J and P-38H is probably the cause. The only important difference in installation is the incorporation of a supercharger intercooler of greatly increased capacity. This has caused P-38J carburetor air temperatures to be from 35 degrees C to 50 C lower than in the P-38H operating under the same conditions.*

3. *The trouble has been diagnosed as resulting from the abnormally low mixture temperatures (as low as -20 degrees C), augmented by the admittedly bad distribution characteristics of the V-1710 engine. The trouble cannot be entirely corrected until better induction system manifolding is provided for the V-1710-89 and -91 engines and a method of controlling mixture temperature is provided.*

4. *As a temporary expedient, the fixed grill of the intercooler has been permanently sealed off so that with the intercooler shutters in the closed position there is no flow through the intercooler. This in itself has raised the mixture temperature 10 degrees C to 15 degrees C., but is not enough to cope with the temperatures experienced in daily operations in this theater.*

5. *Operating instructions have been issued to change power settings in order to make the turbo do more*

work and heat up the fuel/air mixture. This is accomplished by operating at lower RPM and higher manifold pressure when cruising. The standardized settings assure a mixture temperature of 10 degrees C or higher.

6. Compression in each cylinder is checked after every mission and the engine is changed if weak compression indicates stuck or weak rings. Engines are also changed if excessive oil in the exhaust indicates bad rings.

7. A combination of blanketing the intercooler, increasing boost, and careful inspection has tended to reduce failures but does not constitute the final solution. Failure of engines which may have been damaged prior to the time these remedial steps were taken makes analysis still more difficult.

8. New double venturi manifolds have been ordered from the factory for these engines and when they arrive should improve distribution and assist in the solution of our problem. New pistons and Keystone rings have been ordered and will, when they arrive, also help.

9. Pending the arrival of help from the United States, we must take every step possible to save pilots, aircraft, the morale of the excellent P-38 fighter groups, and confidence in American equipment. This can be accomplished if a fuel of higher lean mixture knock rating and preferably lower end point can be made promptly available for about one month's operation of these groups. It is fully realized that a serious inconvenience will result from the necessity of mixing up a small batch of special fuel, but it is felt that the situation is critical and any reasonable inconvenience should be accepted to save these groups and enable them to continue their long-range escorting of heavy bomber missions.

10. It is urgently recommended that a special batch of approximately 2,000,000 United States gallons of special aviation fuel be blended and delivered as follows: one-fourth to the 20th Fighter Group at Kingscliffe, one-fourth to the 55th Fighter Group at Nuthampstead, one-fourth to the 364th Fighter Group at Honington, and one-fourth to the 370th Fighter Group of the Ninth Air Force at Andover. (These last two groups will be operational in the next few days or by the time the fuel arrives.) (sic) The fuel should have an approximate knock rating of 110-130 instead of 100-130, and as flat a distillation range as specifications and available blending components will permit. In order not to introduce a possible additional complication at this time, this fuel should not contain more than the standard 4.6 ccs of lead per gallon. It is

presumed that as it is desirable to raise the lean mixture knock rating and the lead susceptibility, iso-paraffins rather than aromatics will be used as additives. This fuel will improve engine operation, reduce engine failures, save pilots, and boost the present sagging morale of P-38 pilots."[11]

Maj. Gen. Doolittle had a degree from the Massachusetts Institute of Technology and had worked for nearly a decade for the Shell Oil Company, promoting 100 octane fuel development and production. He knew more about fuel than any officer in the AAF.

Tony LeVier

Kepner's dispute with range of the P-38H and J resulted in him asking Brig. Gen. Knerr to ask General Arnold to direct Lockheed to send a test pilot to Britain. Knerr's letter said "...range of (the) P-38 in practice (is) only half of that previously feasible."[12]

Tony LeVier's reception in February by veteran pilots was less than cordial. They were subject to Kepner's investigation and were suspicious of a civilian expert in their midst who was not in the war, ate American food back home, stayed warm in California, and was not getting shot at. They were combat pilots and they thought he was there to find fault. LeVier was determined to give every waking moment his undivided attention to solving problems with Lockheed's great fighter.

Before he departed the US, he had been given a uniform devoid of insignia, a temporary rank of Major, and a battery of inoculations to ward off the evils of life in a foreign country. He arrived feeling sick from all the shots, but instead of going to bed and riding out the flu, he chose to get on a train to London, was driven to AJAX HQ, given flight gear, and sent to Nuthampstead. He was met by Ward Beman and other Lockheed specialists, was assigned Maj. Dallas W. "Spider" Webb's P-38 and took off, still suffering from flu and having missed a lot of sleep.[13]

LeVier conducted the flight as he would have done any test flight back home, taking readings every 5,000 ft, and planning to reach 30,000 ft. At 29,000 ft the right engine blew up, he feathered the prop, called for a radar steer, slipped into the overcast, landed and was taken to a hospital and kept there until he was well. Upon recovery, he was issued one of four new P-38Ls kept at Langford Lodge and ordered to fly to every P-38 base and talk about the Lightning and fly demonstrations!

He arrived at Kingscliffe at about the time the Group Commander was lost on a combat mission and morale was at its lowest. He was not invited to eat with the pilots. For a man who loved to fly aerobatics and who had mastered the P-38, the order to show it off to a crowd was like getting a

A.W. "Tony" LeVier next to a P-38 racer he owned after the war.

wonderful birthday gift. It was in Britain that Tony LeVier – the pre-war racing pilot – became a living legend.

LeVier and Lockheed were concerned about why the engines were detonating, as was Allison. LeVier's overseas duty was nearing an end around 25 May 1944, and he and Ward Beman "...*had spent almost a month trying to find a fix for the detonation problem and engine blow-ups. We had tried just about everything, including a new fuel nozzle.*" [14] LeVier and Beman were also aware of General Doolittle's belief that the fuel "...*was not acting like it should in Allison engines. Tests showed that the anti-knock tetra-ethyl lead was separating from the basic fuel in its path from the carburetor to the cylinders. This, in effect, caused the front cylinders to receive an over-abundance of lead which would foul the spark plugs at lower power and cause detonation, while the rear cylinders didn't get enough lead and would detonate at high powers.*"

LeVier and Beman eventually found a solution to the problem of detonation in V-1710s but by the end of May 1944, the P-38 was being replaced by P-51Bs. LeVier came home on 1 June and "Kelly" Johnson was so impressed by the test pilot's supreme flying ability and analytical mind that he assigned LeVier to test-fly the prototype of the XP-80A jet fighter on 10 June. Substantial problems with the P-38, the V-1710, and the turbo finally relegated the Lightning to use as a low-altitude tactical fighter. One of its final uses was as a level-flight bomber. The nose was modified to have a glazed bombardier's compartment and the variation was nicknamed the "Droop Snoot."

The November engine and turbo failures, Doolittle's January request for special fuels, and LeVier's and Beman's May discoveries revealed problems with the P-38 not experienced in other theaters. The result of insurmountable troubles was that three of the four P-38 groups in the Eighth AF converted to Mustangs. At the end of the war in the ETO, the only P-38 group in either VIII or IX FCs was the 474th FG. The last Eighth AF P-38 mission was flown on 3 October 1944.

Schweinfurt Two – the final warning in October 1943 – did not go unheeded. P-38s became operational in that month and pilots and ground crew struggled under very trying conditions to render escort. Eighth AF had lost air superiority – it had never really owned it – and during the darkest hour of the daylight bombing campaign, there appeared on the scene the fighter which had been ignored and, after it was produced as a fighter for the AAF, was siphoned off into reconnaissance and ground support directorates. It belonged to the Ninth Air Force, a wholly tactical organization.

Chapter 17

Who got the Mustangs?

In November 1943, when P-38s in the ETO were suffering from so many problems, members of the 354th Fighter Group arrived in England to join the Ninth Fighter Command (IX FC) of the Ninth Air Force. The men had not been told enroute they would be receiving Mustangs and after docking, they were sent to Greenham Common to check out in P-51As operated by the USAAF's 10th Reconnaissance Group. After a week the men took a train to Boxted RAF Station, their new home base. Awaiting them were rows of new Mustangs! Some had traces of British markings visible beneath the recently repainted AAF-style camouflage.[1]

The pilots of the 354th FG had flown the *obsolete tricycle-geared P-39s in the US and their introduction to the tailwheel-equipped Mustang was as challenging as was navigating around the non-geometrical English countryside. It was a culture shock. What was even more eye-opening was the first lecture given by Lt. Col. Donald J.M. Blakeslee. IX FC "borrowed" him from VIII FC because he had flown the Rolls-Royce Mustang and had been flying fighters in combat in the ETO since May 1941. Blakeslee wanted the P-51B for his 4th FG and jumped at the chance to indoctrinate the 354th FG and log some Mustang time. Blakeslee told the pilots about terrain, weather, the enemy, air discipline, and the expectations of his style of combat leadership. He left an impression. One thing he told them was never to break away from a German making a head-on attack. They were to make the enemy pilot break, shoot him down or run into him – but never, *never* veer. Blakeslee was as determined as any *Luftwaffe* ace to show who owned the sky, if it came down to a question of playing the game of "chicken." It was a tactic not taught back in the US and the men listened carefully.[2] On one of the first indoctrination flights the group returned to Boxted to land and a pilot cut in front of Blakeslee. He announced on the radio that the next man who did it would be shot down, and not by the enemy! The men had not been taught to expect that either. The pioneer Mustang group flew its first escort mission on 5 December 1943.

P-51Bs of IX FC escorted Eighth AF bombers because Eaker agreed to it. General Eaker was also Commanding General of a temporary organization known as the United States Army Air Forces in the United Kingdom (USAFUK), and had administrative control of the Ninth AF. Confusingly, the Ninth AF was also subordinate to the Allied Expeditionary Air Force (AEAF) commanded by a British Air Chief Marshal. All agreed – not without vehement objections – that Ninth AF Mustangs would escort Eighth AF bombers. In January 1944, General Arnold signed a memorandum of agreement with Air Chief Marshal C.L. Courtney which revised America's production. All Mustang IIIs to have been produced after 31 December 1943 "*are canceled*" and were to be assigned to the AAF as P-51Bs.[3] In fact, the RAF transferred 35 P-51Bs to the USAAF in the UK, and later received 34 B models and one P-51C as replacements. Ample Mustang IIIs and IXs were subsequently supplied to the British.

Although a well-known photograph, it is nevertheless significant, for few scenes can compare to one showing probably the first Mustang to be given to the first Mustang group — the 354th Fighter Group.

M/Sgt. Ralph Mathieson of Iowa, Crew Chief of the ground crew of the P-51 Mustang "Killer", warms up the engine at an air base somewhere in England. The insignia on the side of the aircraft shows that it has accounted for 9.5 enemy aircraft. It is possible that this machine was flown by Captain Bob Stevens, of the 355th Fighter Squadron, 354th Fighter Group, who flew several P-51Bs named "Killer." Stevens gained a total of 13 victories.

The 354th FG operated again on 11 December and lost a P-51B. On the 13th, the group flew 490 miles to Kiel, by far the longest escort mission to that date. On the 16th, the 354th FG claimed its first kill. It accounted for three more enemy aircraft on the 20th, but lost four of its own. It operated again on the 22nd.

The second Mustang group – the 357th – had six P-51Bs by Christmas Day, these being aircraft also recently painted in RAF markings, and flew their first combat mission on 11 February 1944. The third P-51B group – the 363rd FG – arrived at Christmas, received its P-51Bs in January, and flew its first mission on 24 February 1944.

All incoming P-51B groups belonged to the IX FC. As the first three Mustang groups arrived, the entire Allied command structure for the mid-1944 Invasion was being created. The Eighth AF had its Commanding General replaced, while the Ninth AF received much more attention as to how, and by whose orders, it would operate. Although P-51Bs escorted bombers, senior British and American officers commanding the Ninth AF and AEAF were

adamant about retaining control of aircraft assigned to them. The Ninth AF had all the Mustangs but was also subordinate to the AEAF which was commanded by a British officer. It was apparent long before January 1944 that the AEAF would exert firm authority over AAF Mustang operations. Changes had to be made.

Command Changes

The plan to equip and train the mighty Allied force planned to invade North West France on 1 May 1944 had been initiated in January 1943, and General Eisenhower was appointed to Allied Supreme Commander. He transferred his headquarters to England in January 1944. Later, the invasion date was changed to June because of the delayed availability of landing ships. It was Eisenhower's prerogative to name some of the senior officers to form his organization in England and one of the first to be called was Lt. Gen. Spaatz as head of the United States Strategic Air Forces in Europe (USSTAF) which replaced Eaker's USAFUK. USSTAF was established on 1 January 1944. Eisenhower had found Maj. Gen. James Doolittle to be an extremely capable air officer and brought him to England to command the Eighth AF. While that change drew outraged protest from Eaker, one of Eisenhower's appointments of a

In late 1943, General Arnold was successful in requesting that the RAF delay receiving Mustang IIIs so that the Eighth Air Force could have P-51Bs. This Mustang III – KH482 – of No. 126 Squadron had a fin fillet and a Malcolm hood and, according to records, was not on squadron strength until December 1944 or later.

Right: Aircraft at the NAA plant at what is now Los Angeles International Airport, looking west. At the left is the original terminal building for Mines Field, still standing in the 1990s.

Below: A scene at Mines Field. The barrage balloons protected against low-flying enemy intruders damaging or destroying these new P-51Bs. No enemy aircraft ever appeared over Los Angeles, but protection was ordered.

Above: Part of a few days' production by NAA at Mines Field. Clearly visible is the camouflage netting mounted over one area of the factory.

Right: P-51Bs under camouflage netting at the NAA factory on what is now Los Angeles International Airport.

British officer to high command caused an immediate rift among the already emotionally charged officers.

When Eisenhower appointed Air Chief Marshal Sir Arthur Tedder as his Deputy, Air Chief Marshal Sir Trafford Leigh-Mallory commanding the AEAF, protested at taking orders from Tedder by reason that he, Leigh-Mallory, as air officer for the Invasion, should have authority over all types of Allied aircraft. Leigh-Mallory was not disposed to ask Tedder, Spaatz, Eaker or the head of RAF Bomber Command, for permission to use aircraft in the British Isles. For several weeks this prospect caused an unpleasant rift during reorganization.

Leigh-Mallory had commanded RAF Fighter Command after November 1942 and was a xenophobic, contentious officer who, in his August 1943 appointment to command the AEAF, had traveled to America to discuss matters and found fault with every American senior officer there, as well as those he had met in England.[4] On 15 November 1943, a part of Fighter Command was renamed the Air Defence of Great Britain (ADGB) while the major element became the Second Tactical Air Force, informally known as 2.TAF which in turn became the AEAF. Leigh-Mallory was temporarily in command of the AEAF and ADGB but later commanded only the AEAF until reassignment.

Leigh-Mallory opposed Spaatz and refused to cooperate with USSTAF. The official history records his lack of cooperation "...*was the exception rather than the rule in Anglo-American relations in the European Theater.*" [5]

During the last few months of 1943, Arnold had given an offensive mission to long-range fighters. His messages were clear: the *Luftwaffe* had to be destroyed in the air and on the ground and "Argument" became a counter-air-force operation instead of being primarily a bombing campaign against industrial targets. *Luftwaffe* fighter factories and the fighters themselves had to be destroyed. Fighter group commanders were relaxing close-escort policy and chasing the enemy to destruction. Kill scores were climbing. Air superiority momentum was shifting to the AAF.

Leigh-Mallory considered himself a fighter expert and was unimpressed by AAF plans to use fighters to attack German fighters wherever met, during escort missions. "*One voice spoke out against this conviction that Eighth Air Force had to gain air superiority prior to Overlord. Sir Trafford Leigh-Mallory, Eisenhower's tactical air chief, believed air superiority would be gained on D-Day, over the beaches.*" [6] Leigh-Mallory anticipated that a great air battle would be fought over France to defeat the *Luftwaffe*. [7]

That view of a cataclysmic air battle not only lacked aggressiveness, but also echoed Leigh-Mallory's failed Big Wing theory. In 1940, when Britain's back was to the wall as a result of the *Luftwaffe's* aerial onslaught in the Battle of Britain, Air Vice Marshal Keith Park bravely and accurately

Air Chief Marshal Sir Trafford Leigh-Mallory held an extremely high position within the Allied command gearing up for D-Day, but he refused to co-operate with Spaatz or the USSTAF.

apportioned his Spitfires and Hurricanes into masterful defenses of London. Leigh-Mallory, then also an Air Vice Marshal, commanded the air defense sector north of London. Both Leigh-Mallory and Park were subordinate to Air Chief Marshal Sir Hugh Dowding. Leigh-Mallory objected to Park's air defense and to promote his Big Wing idea, went over Dowding's head to senior officials to take Park to task. A number of senior officials agreed with Leigh-Mallory. Dowding and Park were reassigned. Later, Leigh-Mallory was increased in rank and given Dowding's command.

Leigh-Mallory's blatantly selfish and false charges, supported by a small group of tired and worn officials who were more impressed by Leigh-Mallory's arrogance and dismayed by the worn impression of the older Dowding, allowed themselves to be swayed. Dowding – the hero of the Battle – was retired shortly after the Battle of Britain was won.

Leigh-Mallory's "Big Wing" – getting aloft entire wings of fighters – took too much time. It was a concoction which often, when called upon, failed to arrive in time over London and the South East to help the central fighter force defend the invasion-threatened and embattled country.[8] Leigh-Mallory was no fighter expert. Quite the contrary.

MAJOR GENERAL JAMES DOOLITTLE

Jimmy Doolittle was a boxer and held his arms slightly forward when he stood. He spoke quietly, almost in a whisper. He became a student at the University of California in 1916, enlisted in the Air Service in 1917, and soloed in a Curtiss Jenny. No one had flown across the US in less than a day and he did it, with fuel stops, in 21 hours and 19 minutes on 4 September 1922. In 1923 he entered MIT's school of engineering and following a series of flights performed to test the strength of airframes, for which he won a DFC, graduated with an Sc.D in Aeronautics in 1925. In the late 1920s he raced airplanes in the Schneider, Pulitzer, and Thompson races and won in all three. He became Chief of the Flight Test Section at Wright Field as a First Lieutenant!

The Curtiss-Wright company had universal influence within the Navy and Army and 1st. Lt. Doolittle was loaned to that company whenever it requested, for almost a decade, to make foreign tours to demonstrate Curtiss aircraft. He was chosen to test methods of blind flying using instruments for the Guggenheim Full Flight Laboratory in 1928. At the end of

1929, he and his family were pressed for money and Doolittle accepted a job with the Shell Oil Company and the Army put him on Reserve status as a Major, having skipped the rank of Captain.

He made more foreign tours for Shell and Curtiss, and flew more races and set world speed records. In 1931, he began to convince Shell to develop 100 octane gasoline and in 1936 a committee recommended that the Air Corps adopt it, starting in 1938. The Air Corps did adopt use of 100 octane fuel and had use of it throughout the war when enemy countries were forced to use lesser-grade fuels. In between, he served on the powerful Baker Board. In July 1940 he was reinstated into the Air Corps as a Major. His most famous feat, the B-25 raid on Tokyo in April 1942, gave

Left to right: Major Straff (25th Bomb Group Staff), Colonel Elliott Roosevelt, Lieutenant General James Doolittle, Lieutenant Colonel Gray (CO 25th Bomb Group), and Major Alvin Podwojski (25th Bomb Group Staff). Behind the officers is a Mosquito of the 25th BG. Colonel Roosevelt was a very capable officer who commanded some of the first AAF reconnaissance groups.

America some of the first news of heroism by its sons in the war and he was awarded the Medal of Honor. From the rank of Colonel he was jumped in rank to be Major General and chosen to command the 12th AF.

Giving Leigh-Mallory control of IX FC Mustangs was a mistake which had to be rectified. The issue of who was to command them now finally came to a head. Spaatz had learned the efficacy of using escort for bombers while in command in North Africa and became a convert to the superiority of the P-51B, probably after talking to Kepner. Spaatz agreed that bombers needed P-51B escorts, and that air superiority would be gained only by using fighters offensively, day by day, during escort missions.

He issued directives after 20 January 1944 which established his control of administrative and training matters of the Ninth AF and AEAF. [9] Brereton assumed that his Ninth AF would be built quickly, supplied directly from the US, would be as strong as the Eighth AF, and independent of it. Spaatz disagreed and ordered that "Pointblank" required equipping the Eighth AF first. Months later, in July, after the Invasion, Arnold reaffirmed Spaatz' administrative and logistical control of the Ninth AF and AEAF to the end of the war in Europe.

The matter which had escaped attention and which required top-level agreement to allow IX FC Mustangs to escort Eighth AF bombers, was plans to limit IX FC as a training command until the Invasion occurred. Eventually it was supposed to use all fighters which came under its control as fighter-bombers. Until the Invasion, the Ninth AF's mandate was to train fighter-bomber pilots for tasks relative to "Overlord." The official history emphasizes that the initial objective assigned to IX FC did not require it to use P-51Bs as escorts. *"The Ninth Air Force intended from the beginning that the IX Fighter Command should be primarily a training headquarters, preparing fighter groups for combat and aiding in the development of air support commands, of which there was to be one for each of the two US armies participating in Overlord."* [10]

"The IX Fighter Command retained control of fighter training down to D-Day. The unavoidable use of the fighters to support the strategic bombing campaign delayed their

training as fighter-bombers until the late winter and spring of 1944, when the Ninth was released from the major part of its commitment to Pointblank." [11]

"Until 10 March 1944 the Ninth Air Force had been primarily engaged in assisting the strategic air forces, to the restlessness of both Leigh-Mallory and Brereton, but on that date its bombers were freed for concentration on pre-invasion operations. The Eighth Air Force still had first call on the Ninth's fighters for escort tasks, a prerogative which it used more liberally than tactical air commanders liked." [12]

"Eaker's gift" of P-51Bs to Brereton caused problems which the transfer of P-47s and P-38s would not have done. Years of USAAF lack of support for the P-51 as a fighter aircraft had shown its face. Only a major change ordered by Spaatz in January 1944 reversed "Eaker's gift" and rescued the P-51B from the Ninth AF.

It was apparent to Spaatz that the bombing campaign was wedded to the invasion plan. The air plan and the ground plan were so intertwined that if the air plan failed, the ground plan could not succeed. Control of P-51Bs had to be removed from the AEAF and Ninth AF. What we now admire as having been, and will always be, the greatest amphibious landing on enemy soil in all history – D-Day – would have failed without – prior to D-Day – aerial bombing of Germany's armaments manufacturing capability, and the use of long-range fighters to shoot the *Luftwaffe* out of the sky.

On 3 December 1943, Air Chief Marshal Portal told the Combined Chiefs of Staff "…*that Pointblank was at that time a full three months behind schedule."* [13] The official history said "…*the success of Pointblank would determine the date of Overlord."* [14] Three months' delay would affect the Invasion. The only way to catch up was to employ long-range fighters offensively in air-to-air combats and in strafing.

Maj. Gen. James Doolittle understood the capabilities of the P-51B. It was a fast, high-altitude, long-range, and maneuverable fighter which was not to be flown as close-escort but to attack and destroy. On 18 December 1943, General Arnold appointed Doolittle as CG of the Eighth AF and Eaker was ordered to command the Mediterranean Allied Air Force (MAAF). Eaker felt shocked and betrayed, but he loyally assisted Doolittle in his indoctrination before flying to his new command.

There was no one quite like "Jimmy" Doolittle before or since. Doolittle and Kepner believed the P-51B would satisfy Arnold's demand for winning the air war. The best way to do the job was to put P-51Bs into the Eighth AF. The USSTAF was formed "…*partly to offset the AEAF"* and it coordinated operations of the Eighth and Fifteenth AFs, as a solution to control of the American strategic air forces. [15] Spaatz freed Mustangs from Leigh-Mallory's grasp. The official AF history states: "*By January 1944 the value of the P-51 as a long-*

range escort plane had become so apparent that the principles on which allocations had been made in the theater between the Eighth and Ninth Air Forces were completely revised. On 24 January British and American commanders came to an agreement which placed most of the P-51 units in the Eighth Air Force. Eventually, the Eighth would be equipped almost exclusively with the P-51s and the P-47s and P-38s being transferred to the Ninth Air Force." [16]

Four days later, the 357th FG was traded to the Eighth AF for the P-47-equipped 358th FG which became part of IX FC. During December 1943, the 359th FG joined other P-47 groups in VIII FC. Finally VIII FC began to receive its first Mustangs.

Good News and Bad News

From 24 January 1944, the P-51B was officially an escort fighter assigned to a strategic air force. On 16 December 1943, 1st Lt. Charles F. Gumm, Jr., of the 354th FG made the first Mustang kill in the ETO, when he downed a Bf 109. He had scored eight victories by 25 February and became the first P-51 Ace. Gumm was later killed in a training accident.

Col. Mark Bradley's fuselage fuel tank, placed behind the pilot's seat, forced the placement of the radios elsewhere inside the fuselage which gave the P-51B a slightly aft center of gravity. Eglin Field test pilots were unable to test a

The first man to shoot down five enemy aircraft in a Mustang was Lieutenant Charles Gumm of the 354th Fighter Group. Gumm was killed in a training accident after achieving eight victories.

P-51B-1-NA fitted with the tank until December and the report was issued on the 22nd. It stated: "*...the airplane is so unstable longitudinally that violent pullouts or tight turns must be executed with caution, as stick loads rapidly reverse.*" [17] Eglin suggested using fuel from the fuselage tank first before that in the drop tanks. But the capacity gauge on top of the tank was behind the pilot's head and even though the report stated it was "*unsatisfactory,*" other officers suggested the gauge to remain where it was.

However, Eglin's test pilots did have some good news! They reported that additional fuel "*...has no measurable effect*" upon top speed and with half a load in the new fuselage tank the turning radius "*...is about even with the P-38J and is smaller than the P-47D-15.*" Fuel in the tank gave an astoundingly large 45 percent increase in range and "*...allows the P-51B to engage in combat at greater distances from its base than any other contemporary fighter.*"

The first Mustang III squadrons became operational in the RAF during the first three months of 1944 and it was the British who discovered a very serious problem with the aircraft's engine mounting bolts. At Gravesend RAF Station two pilots were discussing matters while walking around rows of Mustang IIIs when they heard a sound similar to a pistol shot. Upon hearing the sound again they noticed it came from the nose of a Mustang. When they saw the cowl droop they opened it and found bits of engine mounting bolts that had snapped and were laying in the bottom of the cowl. [18]

The bad news traveled rapidly all the way back to the US and Maj. Gen. Walter Frank, CG of the entire Air Service Command, issued a Technical Order stating that the bolts should be magnafluxed and bolts which had no defects would be painted orange and re-installed. In March 1944, a P-51B crashed and it was discovered that some of the orange-painted bolts had sheared off, causing an engine explosion. Metallurgical analysis revealed that the nickel content necessary in the metal was absent. The problem was rectified and operations resumed.

Chapter 18

The Turning Point

In December 1943, the Eighth AF had welcomed with open arms its second P-38 group when the 20th FG began combat operations on the last day of the month. During December, the first P-51B group began operations and a second one was being formed. More P-47 groups arrived. VIII FC was growing and IX FC had its first fighters. Once the modifications were made to existing aircraft, and manufacturers rolled out fighters with extra tanks and shackles, bombers could be escorted to and from the most distant targets. Until he was hit with the bad news of change of command, Eaker could not have been more pleased. Doolittle was very pleased.

P-38 problems were being taken into account. However, Jack Jenkins and other fighter pilots' opinions about range and altitude capabilities were examined with scepticism and until new policy was created, there was only grudging inclination to accept the word of combat-experienced leaders. Yet they were on the cutting edge of all AAF wartime policy. Lightnings were required to climb to bomber altitudes.

Eaker, and then Doolittle, had two of the best long-range fighter aircraft in the world. Recently, the German air defenses had concentrated on destroying AAF bombers because they constituted a greater threat than fighters, but now, American long-range fighters forced the *Luftwaffe* to defend itself in the West. German fighters outnumbered the long-range fighters of VIII and IX Fighter Commands, but the numerical tide was turning. The fighter-versus-fighter air war was about to become more intense. For a period lasting approximately from 1 January to 1 July 1944, AAF long-range fighters carried the daylight air war to the farthest reaches of Germany. After D-Day, and when Allied bases in France were secured, Allied fighters *cruised* over the Reich.

High-Low Coordination

While Jenkins was away on temporary duty with the 20th FG, the 55th FG became embroiled in a big encounter on 5 January, claiming five enemy aircraft but losing four of its own. Only 70 P-38s drawn from both groups provided escort because in the 55th FG "...*fifty-one P-38s took off and over half had to come home with engine trouble.*" The Tactical Commander of the 55th FG's mission was Maj. Mark C. Shipman, whose report dated the 10th and addressed to the 65th Fighter Wing, helped change minds about the assigned altitudes at which P-38s operated later in 1944.

A veteran of the MTO, Shipman, a former butcher from Fresno, California had flown and used up three out of four P-38s all named "*Skylark.*" He was the first officer to state that the P-38 and P-51 complemented each other but that both types needed to arrive together over a target. By 5 January 1944, VIII and IX Fighter Commands were still not coordinating escort missions. Shipman praised the P-38 saying it performed well at 25,000 ft

or below. In his report he stated: "...*we crossed out (over the) English coast in the vicinity of The Wash at 09:55 and proceeded enroute out over the North Sea, remaining at all times approximately fifty miles out at sea along the Frisian Islands.*" [1]

He took his P-38s inland, saw other P-38s of the 20th FG near Hamburg at 20,000 ft, flew north, then saw that the bombers with whom they had to rendezvous were late and off course. At 11:35 hrs they saw "...*six-plus Me 210s*" but "...*about 10,000 feet above them or 7,500 feet above our altitude of 28,500 feet there was a gaggle of 25-plus contrails.*" Shipman took the P-38s up-sun, but the high-flying enemy aircraft dived on them so he set up a double Lufbery, "...*11 friendly fighters going in the one direction and the other 12 going around the circle.*" The diving Bf 109Gs were unable to break up the formation and the P-38s "...*were able to scrape the enemy fighters off each other's tails, so that by the time two complete orbits were made, the P-38 formation had been eliminated of enemy fighters.*" The P-38s downed six enemy aircraft and lost two of their own, according to the report. Shipman brought the group home.

Maj. Shipman wrote nearly two pages describing the mission itself, then a further four pages "...*to take up the mission from an analytical standpoint.*" These four pages were to affect high-low coordination.

"*It is beyond the realm of possibility for one group to give adequate cover to the bombers, when taking the present German tactics into consideration. Their tactics are to employ primarily a conjunction of twin-engined and single-engined fighters, with the twin-engined fighters being assigned to lob rockets from the rear of the bomber formation, and the single-engine fighters to protect the twin-engine fighters during their attacks.*"

Bf 109Gs generally enjoyed an altitude advantage but when they dived on P-38s, the American 'twins' "...*had dispersed them completely, (and) immediately after our departure from the area, the Mustangs were able to come in and destroy fifteen of the twin-engine ships with a loss of none to their own forces.*" Shipman did not want to take too much praise for his P-38 pilots who dispersed the Bf 109Gs because, he said "...*it is not beyond the realm of possibility that the enemy twin-engine pilots thought at first that the Mustangs were their own escort.*" By the time the Me 210 pilots realized the single-engined fighters entering their area were not Messerschmitts, it was too late. P-51Bs of the 354th FG were credited with 15 kills that day, awakening minds to what Mustangs could do in combat. Machine for machine, P-51Bs began to score more than P-38s or P-47s.

Shipman felt that 20 minutes of loiter time was too much and said the mission was a "*failure from our viewpoint*" because the bombers were late. "*On a mission as deep into enemy territory as this one we cannot hope to stay in the target area for a period of over fifteen minutes. True enough, we were in the area for an hour, but for at least thirty minutes of that time we were flying off of our belly tanks only.*" As soon as the encounter began and tanks were dropped, the P-38s had to turn around for home.

"*If it could be arranged for us to make a rendezvous with another fighter group, which could make this deep penetration with us (either the 20th Group or the 354th Group possibly making the rendezvous off the English coast), we could proceed to the target as a single unit. Upon reaching the target area one group could go after the fighter escort of the German single-engine ships, while the other group would be free to go down and engage and completely destroy the twin-engine ships.*"

However, in Shipman's view, VIII and IX FCs would have to cooperate in order to coordinate a rendezvous over a target and two groups of two different types of fighters might not be coordinated "*...close enough together to really work effectively as one unit.*" But they could fly in as a unit.

Shipman was confident about what a P-38 could do to any German fighter. On 5 January, he tried to invite P-51Bs into the action and "*made at least five*" radio calls to coordinate the fight "*but all efforts failed.*" P-38s "*...have superior fire power but cannot operate as effectively as the P-51s at extremely high altitudes. However, the P-38s are more easily recognized by the enemy twin-engine ships and (we) would, therefore, perhaps not be able to approach as close (to the enemy's twin-engine fighters) as the P-51s. On the other hand, the P-38s can mingle right in with the bomber formations, and due to their prominent recognition features not cause any confusion by way of identification for the bomber crews.*"

Lightnings that reached target area on bomber support missions performed admirably and demonstrated how well the big P-38 performed in a turning dogfight, using its devastating firepower. The P-38 was an excellent fighter but not as effective as the P-51B at high altitude, which also had better range.

Colonel James' Report

Jenkins, Shipman and others had tried to convince Kepner and Bomb Division commanders that the P-38 did not perform well above 25,000 ft. Col. Frank James stated it forcefully in his report as Tactical Commander of the 7 January mission, and since he was the Group Commander, his words had some effect. After James' report reached Fighter Wing and/or Kepner's desk, it was up to officers to decide what to do in order to coordinate the P-38s with P-51s.

"*Since a P-38 does not have satisfactory performance above 30,000 feet but is superior up to this altitude, it is the policy of this organization to stay at 30,000 feet and below*

and let the Bf 109s come down to us. I believe they have found by now that they never get back up." James wanted Fighter Wing to "*...send the P-51s in prior to the P-38s at 35,000 feet. The P-51 is more at home and has a higher performance at 35,000 feet than does a P-38. The Bf 109s have found it not conducive to good health to bounce the P-38 even from a superior altitude.*" [2]

Scores Began to Mount

On 11 January 1944, a P-51B pilot performed so bravely in combat that he was awarded the Medal of Honor. Maj. James H. Howard and his pilots were protecting a B-17 group when it was attacked. As the enemy dove through the formation, Howard ordered his pilots down onto the enemy. The Mustangs became separated and after initial attacks, Howard climbed back up to rejoin the bombers. He found them to be under attack from 30 enemy fighters. Howard was not aware he was alone and drove into the enemy, shooting down three and boring in on the others after his ammunition was expended. The enemy attack slackened and the fighters scattered.

Howard's courage was the brightest spot in a day of terrible disaster. Of the 551 bombers sent to targets, 60 were shot down. It was a severe loss and a day as black as those over Schweinfurt months earlier. The 1st Bomb Division went to Oschersleben and Halberstadt and lost 42 bombers. The 2nd and 3rd BDs went to Braunschweig, Osnabrück, Bielefeld, and other cities and lost 18.

Howard was with 221 fighters escorting the 1st BD. The P-47-equipped 56th FG claimed 10 enemy aircraft; however, Howard's 354th FG shot down 16. Escorts protecting the 2nd and 3rd BDs downed two enemy fighters. There were a total of 447 P-47s flying on 11 January and their kill record was 16. Forty-nine P-38s also escorted, but scored no kills. Forty-four P-51s downed 16 enemy aircraft. The total fighter victories amounted to 31, with the P-51Bs – representing eight per cent of the escort force – claiming 51 percent of the kills.

True enough, P-38s did not escort the 1st BD when most of the fighter victories were scored, P-51s did. Yet it was apparent that the P-51B achieved a better ratio of victories per sortie. There were ten times as many P-47s as there were P-51s but the "Jugs" downed only the same number.

The P-38 was quite capable of inflicting damage to the *Luftwaffe*. On the bomber escort mission of 29 January 1944, 89 Lightnings of the 20th FG claimed 12 enemy aircraft. The 55th FG downed one; 503 P-47s claimed 32; 40 P-51Bs were credited with five with 806 bombers reaching Frankfurt losing 29 of their force.

Between VIII and IX FCs, there were now 11 P-47 groups, two P-38 groups, and two P-51B groups – less than half the number both commands would grew to by 1945. There were not only more P-47s but the type had been operating longer

Left: This 354th Fighter Group P-51B had an unusual white starburst nose marking. Its serial number was 43-6976, the code FT✪D and the name "Rosey T." which identifies it as the mount of Haydon Holton of the 353rd Fighter Squadron.

Right: On 11 January 1944, Major James Howard of the 356th Fighter Squadron, 354th Fighter Group took on 30 German fighters alone and shot down three despite all but one of his guns failing. Here, one of his ground crew inspects damage on his P-51B "Ding Hao" on which the footrests had been moved forward and the seat moved back in order to accommodate Howard's 6 ft 2 in frame. For his valor, Howard was awarded the Medal of Honor.

Above: "My Toni" s/n 42-106749, coded GQ✪V, was Lt. Charles F. Gumm Jr.'s P-51B in the 354th Fighter Group. Gumm (second from left) was the world's first Mustang Ace but he was killed in an accident on 1 March 1944. Note the aircraft carries two 75-gallon drop tanks.

Above: 10 March 1944: Lt. Mailon Gillis and his Crew Chief inspect the guns on a P-51B, coded AJ✪N of the 356th Fighter Squadron, 354th Fighter Group.

Right: P-51B-5, GQ✪Z, was one of the first Mustangs assigned to the 355th Fighter Squadron, 354th Fighter Group in November-December 1943. Although the 354th Fighter Group was assigned to the tactical Ninth AF prior to D-Day, it generally flew bomber escort missions for the Eighth AF for which it was awarded a Distinguished Unit Citation. It continued to run up a big score of enemy aircraft while flying tactical missions from the Continent during the last year of the war. Its total by VE-Day was just over 640 (the figure of 701 usually attributed to it included claims that were not confirmed) and more than 40 of its pilots had become Aces. The 354th was known as the "Pioneer Mustang Group" since it was the first to fly the Merlin-engined P-51B in combat.

Left: "Mary Anne" was the mount of 356th Fighter Squadron ace Lt. Robert E. Goodnight, one of two Mustangs assigned to him, all coded AJ✪G. The aircraft is pictured here at the 354th Fighter Group's base at Boxted, England in February 1944. By mid-April, Goodnight had a total of 7.25 kills. The group moved on to Lashenden, Essex, in April, then to France shortly after D-Day.

Right: A Packard war workers' presentation Mustang "Sky-Clipper" (coded GQ-?) seen in service with the 355th Fighter Squadron, 354th Fighter Group (see also page 67). It was flown by Lt. Bruno Peters who was from Michigan. The Crew Chief was Laurence A. Wood, Assistant Crew Chief was S/Sgt. Joel O. Scruggs (seen standing next to the aircraft), Armorer was Sgt. W. Clifford, and Assistant Armorer was E.C. Cagley.

– ever since April, 1943. On 30 January 1944 the 56th FG achieved its 200th victory – the first group to reach that total.

Success of the big Thunderbolt in the hands of pilots of the 56th FG was achieved because in Col. "Hub" Zemke, the unit had one of the finest Group Commanders in the entire AAF to lead it from its start in combat until very late in the war.

Jack Jenkins led the 3 February 1944 mission and saw "...where 720 bombers knocked hell out of the ship docks" at Wilhelmshaven. Maj. Tom H. Welch, Jr., 55th FG Historian, wrote: "...there were only seven early returns, which was a good batting average for our temperamental '38s." [4] Seventy-four P-38s from the two groups flew but reported no losses or victories. In total, 508 P-47s accounted for eight kills but lost eight aircraft. The 50 P-51Bs operational that day scored none and lost one. Four of 609 bombers reaching targets were lost and bomber gunners reported no victories.

'Big Week'

From December 1943 onwards bad weather halted the bombing campaign. On 8 February 1944, General Spaatz ordered that "Argument" be completed by 1 March.[5] The Eighth AF needed one full week of clear weather to attack "...about a dozen factories producing fighter components or fighters" and "...at last on 19 February, such a period was predicted." [6] If successful, that week, named after the event as 'Big Week', would put the air plan back on schedule and the planned invasion date would not be delayed.

With the exception of 23 February, hundreds of bombers raided German cities every day starting on the 20th and ceasing after the 25th, when weather closed in over targets or AAF air bases. "Big Week" was to have been primarily a bombing effort directed at German factories supplying the *Luftwaffe*. However, German fighters were the threat which long-range fighters had to defeat and it was during "Big Week" that AAF fighters achieved air superiority and never lost it.

The turning point came because AAF fighters had new internal and external tanks giving them long range. The air war became fighter against fighter because bomber gunners had been unable to win air superiority alone. The necessary long-range fighter appeared at just the saving moment.

Statistics of "Big Week's" fighter victories indicate that the P-51B was superior. The P-38 suffered problems and the P-47 had short range. The Mustang, which had been nearly the costliest mistake, took over the lead in blunting and overcoming the threat against the bombers. These are the fighter aircraft statistics of "Big Week":

20 February
Targets: Tutow, Rostock, Oschersleben, Leipzig, and others
Total escorts: 835
94 P-38s achieved 7 kills

668 P-47s achieved 38 kills
73 P-51s achieved 16 kills
Fighter losses = 4
P-51s = 8.7 percent of the escort force downed 26 percent of the total victories

21 February
Targets: Diepholz, Braunschweig, Hanover, Achmer, Hesepe
Total escorts: 679
69 P-38s achieved zero kills
542 P-47s achieved 19 kills
68 P-51s achieved 14 kills
Fighter losses = 5
P-51s = 10 percent of the escort force downed 42 percent of the total victories

22 February
Targets: Oschersleben, Halberstadt, Enschede, Arnhem
Total escorts: 659
67 P-38s achieved 1 kill
535 P-47s achieved 39 kills
57 P-51s achieved 19 kills
Fighter losses = 11
P-51s = 9 percent of the escort force downed 32 percent of the total victories

23 February
(light operations)

24 February
Targets: Rostock, Schweinfurt, Gotha, Eisenach
Total escorts: 767
70 P-38s achieved 1 kill
609 P-47s achieved 31 kills
88 P-51s achieved 6 kills
Fighter losses = 10
P-51 = 11 percent of the escort force downed 16 percent of the total victories

25 February
Targets: Regensburg, Augsburg, Stuttgart, Furth
Total escorts: 899
73 P-38s achieved 1 kill
687 P-47s achieved 13 kills
139 P-51s achieved 12 kills
Fighter losses = 3
P-51: 15 percent of the escort force downed 46 percent of the total victories

"Big Week" accomplished air superiority and the P-51 made a name for itself. The official history states: "*Never after*

Above: A formation of Mustangs of the 355th Fighter Group. The group was based at Steeple Morden, Cambridgeshire and originally flew P-47s until April 1944 when they were replaced by Mustangs.

Right: P-51B "Little Brown Jug II", s/n 43-691?, of the 355th Fighter Group with only one drop tank during this flight.

Left: Capt. Walter J. Koraleski Jr., posing for the cameraman on his P-51B "Miss Thunder," coded WR⊙L, s/n 43-6968, served with the 354th Fighter Squadron, 355th Fighter Group. Koraleski scored all his victories during March and April 1944 before being taken PoW on 14 April 1944. Of Koraleski's eight kills, four were shared, so his actual total was 5 1/3. Note the non-standard rear-view mirror mounted on the canopy.

Above The Duchess of Kent visits the Americans at Debden. On the far right is Lt.Col. Don Blakeslee.

February was the Luftwaffe to be the menace it had been; though it would inflict heavy losses. Goering's force had lost control of the skies of Europe." [7] The month of February 1944 was only four months past the date in October when Eaker, probably on the advice of desk officers in the US, agreed that the P-51B was only a tactical weapon and gave them to a tactical air force. General Spaatz freed the Mustang and put it in a strategic air force where it belonged.

Fourth But First

The first three P-51B groups in combat during "Big Week" had come from the US and received Mustangs after arrival in England. All of the pilots in these groups had to be indoctrinated into new and foreign conditions and to acquire their first taste of combat. Policy required using experienced leaders to take incoming groups on their first few missions. Fighter groups already in the ETO were expected to carry on with the fighter aircraft in their possession. However, the time would come when the Mustang would re-equip most groups in the theater. Re-equipment meant time-consuming training and temporary removal of a group from combat. Lt. Col. Blakeslee had other ideas about this.

Blakeslee, who had been elevated to command of the 4th FG on 1 January, lobbied to obtain Mustangs for his group. Originally made up of the three Eagle Squadrons of the RAF, the 4th FG was the most experienced unit in the entire VIII FC since some of its pilots had entered combat as early as 1940. In January 1944, Blakeslee began to persuade Gen. Kepner to replace P-47s with P-51Bs. The motto of the 4th FG was "Fourth But First" and under demands of excellence from Chesley Peterson, and Don Blakeslee, the unit eventually became the highest-scoring fighter group in the entire AAF. Both Peterson and Blakeslee had been made aware, prior to induction into the AAF in September 1942, that some of the Eagles were viewed as prima donnas which AAF hierarchy despised. [8] Both officers labored to make the 4th FG the best in the AAF.

Blakeslee became a legend in his own time. All he wanted was to fly fighters and fight the enemy right to the end of a very long war. To accomplish that, he falsified his logbook so that superior officers looked at it, saw that Blakeslee had flown very few missions and had fewer than the number of hours requiring removal from combat. In fact, when his tour was ended by Griswold on 30 October 1944, he had over 1,000 hours of combat time and between 400 and 500 missions. Most fighter pilots went home after 200 or 300 hours of combat time.

Blakeslee had joined the Royal Canadian Air Force in July 1940 and in the following year was assigned to No. 401 Squadron before the unit was transferred to England. One day,

after refusing an order to march the men to church, his Commanding Officer removed Blakeslee from the Squadron and he was ordered into the RAF at Biggin Hill where he joined No. 133 Eagle Squadron. His drive and success got him command of the squadron in August 1942. For breaking another petty RAF rule, Blakeslee was absent from the squadron when it was cut to pieces on a mission over Morlaix, France on 26 September. Only days later the three Eagle Squadrons were inducted into the AAF as the 4th FG.

When leading the 354th and 357th FGs on their first missions in the P-51B, he realized the Mustang was the best fighter in the world and wanted his group to have it. Kepner was slow to be convinced. It was after Blakeslee told Kepner, that, if necessary, Blakeslee would have his pilots learn to fly it on their first combat mission, that Kepner relented and acquired Mustangs for the 4th FG.

A few Mustangs were assigned to the 4th FG on February 14th and two weeks later the group had enough to fly a

Above: Seen in discussion outside 4th FG headquarters at Debden are, (left to right): Colonel Chesley Peterson (group CO from 20 August-23 December 1943), Lieutenant Colonel Oscar Coen, Lieutenant Colonel Don Blakeslee (group CO from 1 January-1 November 1944), Lieutenant Colonel Roy Evans, and Major General Ira Eaker. Note the RAF wings on the uniforms of the pilots.

mission. The P-47s were gone. Maj. Jim Clark led the 4th FG on 28 February, just after "Big Week," and some pilots had no more than an hour of familiarization time as they crossed the Channel to climb high above Europe. Capt. James Goodson led a mission on the 29th. Foul weather had returned.

The AAF had scheduled bombing missions to Berlin twice in 1943, but weather canceled the missions. As March 1944 neared, the weather was often good. Another Berlin mission was planned. Blakeslee and his 4th FG were prepared to take Mustangs right to Hitler's doorstep.

"Big B"

Germany's officials were once confident that its air defenses would prevent enemy aircraft from reaching the city and

Right: Pilot Officer Don Blakeslee of No. 401 "Ram" Squadron, RCAF just about to drop into the "office" of his Spitfire VB (BL753) at Gravesend, Kent in 1942. By the spring of that year, he had claimed one Bf 109 destroyed, three damaged, and two Fw 190s probably destroyed. Except on this one aircraft, Blakeslee never allowed his Crew Chiefs to apply names, kill markings, girlie art or personal insignia. However, Leola, his wife, was honoured when her name was applied to this Spitfire.

Above: Lieutenant Colonel James A. Clark, Jr. the 10.5 victory Ace and the "quiet man" of the 4th Fighter Group, sits in his P-51B. Clark, who was Tommy Hitchcock's nephew and a former Eagle Squadron pilot, was deputy commander of the 4th Fighter Group.

Right: This P-51 coded VF✪Z, s/n 43-6840, of the 4th Fighter Group collapsed to a stop inside a sandbag-protected revetment at Debden.

Left: Capt. Willard Millikan, a 4th Fighter Group pilot accredited with 13 kills, gives an immediate debrief to the Intelligence Officer following a mission. The original "bird cage" canopy of the P-51B (s/n 43-6997) hinged outwards.

Below: Captain Millikan uses his hands in the time-honored way of all fighter pilots, to explain a maneuver in the air — in this case, the way he scored and lived to tell the tale. By the date of this photograph the group had applied red paint to the noses of its Mustangs. The frame of the canopy appears unpainted. Note the revetment in the background.

Right: The best "one-two punch" in the AAF; Lieutenant John Godfrey (left) and Captain Don Gentile of the 4th Fighter Group stand on Debden's extensive Marston matting in front of Gentile's P-51B "Shangri-La." Wingman to Don Gentile, Godfrey ended the war with 16.3 confirmed kills.

Above, right, and below: A series of photographs taken at Debden on 1 April 1944 and showing Capt. Don Gentile with his P-51B-5-NA coded VF✪T, s/n 43-6913, "Shangri-La". In the picture to right, Gentile has brought the official Army photographer into the frame whilst above, he poses with a member of his ground crew as a new victory is painted on his score roll. The white cross signified that the aircraft was modified with a fuselage fuel tank.

COLONEL JACK JENKINS

Jack Jenkins was one of very few P-38 Group Commanders in the ETO and one of the finest. He came from Levelland, Texas, graduated from Texas Tech University and joined the Air Corps in March 1938. He won his wings in early 1939 and was assigned to the 20th Pursuit Group where he flew P-36s and P-40s. 1st Lt. Jenkins was assigned to accompany some P-40s that were transported to Hawaii on a Navy aircraft carrier and as a guest, he was given a ride in the back seat of a torpedo bomber while the pilot made practice carrier landings. The P-40s were off-loaded and Jenkins came home. On December 7, 1941 most of the P-40s were destroyed by Japanese naval carrier air forces.

Jenkins was assigned to the 55th FG when it was activated from a cadre of the 20th FG then based at Hamilton Field in California. He became Squadron Commander when it was based at Tumwater, Washington, near to the HQ of the 55th FG at McChord Field near Tacoma, Washington. He flew P-43s until the group was given P-38s in June 1942. Jenkins' luck ran out on 10 April 1944 when flying his P-38J as escort for a Droop Snoot mission. While making a second strafing run on a German installation at Colummiers, France his aircraft was hit by flak and he bellied it in, injuring his back. A German doctor and nurse helped him return to good health and he was interned in a Stalag Luft until repatriation. He stayed in the USAF and in May 1961 returned to Germany as CO of the 50th Fighter Wing flying F-100s.

disturbing its quite peaceful air, but the RAF had bombed Berlin often. German officials now boasted that an Allied fighter had never reached the city.

Berlin had several hundred industrial, military, and governmental targets. There were rumors of resistance to Hitler and the Allies hoped that if the *Führer* were killed the long, genocidal war might be shortened. Only Washington of all the major capitals of the world's largest countries – and some not so large – would survive the war without suffering some form of terror. Berlin, Moscow, Paris, London, Rome, Madrid, Peking, Tokyo, Prague, Warsaw, and others were either occupied by enemy forces, had been bombed, were under siege, or suffered slavery and death.

On 3 March 1944 Col. Jenkins, newly designated as CO of the 55th FG, led his pilots over Berlin – the first Allied fighters to fly that far and appear over the *Reichstag*.

Jenkins had started off with 45 P-38s but half dropped out and only 20 Lightnings reached Berlin. The bombers were supposed to fly to the city as well, but bad weather had caused a recall message to be radioed. Bomber crews received it but Jenkins did not. Jenkins recalled that his unit "...*stooged around Berlin city limits for fifteen minutes*" and then came out. After landing at Nuthampstead, Jenkins was so cold his "...*Crew Chief had to help lift me out of the cockpit. It took only one hour and forty-five minutes to make the trip to Berlin.*" There had been a swift tailwind.

In his diary, Jenkins wrote that "...*it was the long-awaited show to Berlin! Six months ago General Kepner told me that we would go there and today we did it!*" He suffered from a bad cold and sinus problems but "...*I felt better today and would not have missed this show for anything. General Doolittle released the story of our trip to the press and I have been swamped by phone calls. The radio is playing up this story more than somewhat.*"

Bombing the capital was unfinished business and on 4 March the raid was repeated. Jenkins led his P-38s and got as far as Leipzig before "*plane after plane (began to) drop out with engine trouble.*" Jenkins' own aircraft lost oil on one engine and he had to shut it down and come back. Maj. Charles O. Jones led the rest of the way. A group of bombers reached Berlin and were the first AAF bombers to bomb the capital.

Back at base Jenkins was "...*called to go into London and make a broadcast over Columbia's coast-to-coast US network tomorrow. It was announced that I had led the first group of American fighter planes over Berlin. We had a big party tonight at the club. A big poster over the bar read 'ALL OURS, THE BERLIN BUZZ BOYS'.*"

On 4 March, the bombing mission to Berlin was repeated. Only 249 bombers were effectively in action out of 502 dispatched, but because of bad weather, only a single bomb group struck Berlin. A force of 770 escorts tried to make its way through the murky, dangerous sky. Disaster struck the 363rd FG one week after it had flown its first mission, when it lost 11 Mustangs out of 33 despatched due to the adverse weather. The 4th FG sent out two squadrons of P-47s and one of P-51Bs. In total, eight enemy aircraft were shot down by fighters for 24 losses of which most were from the unlucky 363rd FG. Nevertheless, the Eighth AF had bombed Berlin for the first time and it made big news in Britain as well as in America. Maj. John R. Murphy and 2nd Lt. Paul H. Bateman, both of the 359th FG, downed two enemy aircraft each. P-51 pilots 1st Lt. Nicholas Megura and 1st Lt. Woodrow F. Sooman of the 4th FG, each accounted for one enemy aircraft destroyed; Megura's was his first, a Bf 109 near Leipzig and his final total would be 11.83, all achieved in Mustangs. 1st Lt. Frank Q. O'Connor of the 4th FG, flying his P-51B, shared a Bf 109 credit. Flying Officer Charles E. Yeager of the 357th FG claimed his first aerial victory, a Bf 109 near Kassel.

On 5 March the targets were in France.

Weather over Berlin on the 6th was forecast to be good and 672 bombers raided the city but 69 were shot down. It was the AAF's worst disaster. The number lost was the largest the AAF ever experienced on one mission in its history. It was clear to the AAF that German air defenses were not yet overcome.

Eighty-six P-38s downed three enemy aircraft and 615 P-47s accounted for 36. One hundred P-51Bs accounted for 43 of the 81 kills – half of the aerial victories scored which meant that on average, one out of every two Mustang pilots scored a victory. Twelve percent of the escort force achieved 53 percent of the kills.

The 357th FG downed 20 and the freshly trained P-51B-equipped 4th FG got 14. The 363rd FG did not operate on 6 March and the 352nd and 355th Groups were in the process of converting to Mustangs. P-47 pilots Col. Hubert Zemke, CO of the 56th FG, and Capt. Walter J. Koraleski, Jr., of the 355th FG each claimed three enemy aircraft.

Mustang pilots scoring on 6 March 1944 included Capt. Davis T. Perron of the 357th FG, who claimed three, his total for the war in one day. 1st Lt. Leroy A. Ruder of the 357th FG downed a Bf 110 and shared the kill of another near Berlin. His later total was 5.5, enough to be an Ace. 2nd Lt. Thomas L. Harris, Capt. Glendon V. Davis, and 1st Lt. Donald H. Bochkay of the 357th FG were credited with two each. Bochkay shared a victory on the previous day and he went on to gain a total of 13.83, including two Me 262s. 1st Lt. Kenneth E. Hagan of the 357th FG downed two while 354th FG Mustang pilots, 1st Lt. James R. Dalglish and 1st Lt. Lowell K. Brueland, both got

two each. Capt. Walter J. Koraleski, Jr., of the 355th FG flying a P-47, got 2.33. A few days later Koraleski checked out in the P-51B. His total rose to 5.53. Brueland's total was 14.5 including two MiGs in Korea when he flew F-86s. 1st Lt. Nicholas Megura of the 4th FG downed two.

1st Lt. John T. Godfrey scored a single victory on 6 March, 1944 and finished the war with a total of 16.33 air, and 12.66 ground victories. Godfrey's scoring began back in November 1943 when he was credited with a victory flying a P-47. He achieved his first P-51B victory in March 1944. Godfrey was born in Montreal, Quebec but grew up in America. He ran away from home to join the RCAF in August 1941 and while he was being flight trained, he learned that his brother, Reggie, had been killed while serving aboard a ship sunk by a U-boat. Johnny vowed revenge. Commissioned a Pilot Officer, he was ordered to Britain and served in an Operational Training Unit until April 1943 when he was commissioned into the AAF and joined the 4th FG. He had his airplanes painted with the name "Reggie's Reply." On 24 August 1944, while on a strafing mission, his P-51D was accidentally hit by his wingman and Godfrey had to belly in. He became a PoW. Close to victory day in Europe, he escaped captivity and made his way to the American lines.

Fighter pilot victories in the month of March 1944 made for the kind of success wished for during the same month a year earlier, when introduction of the P-47 had brought with it hopes for air superiority. It took a set of circumstances – pressure from high command forcing success of the air plan, good weather, the massive size of the Eighth AF, the mass

1st Lieutenant E.H. Cater of the 359th Fighter Group had an unidentified symbol painted just forward of the canopy of his P-51B, coded CV✪E. The serial number of this aircraft was 43-6491.

Right Pilots of the 4th Fighter Group take a break and catch up on the newspapers. Left to right: 1st Lt Jack T. Simon, 334th Fighter Squadron; Major John T. Godfrey, 336th Fighter Squadron; and 1st Lt Robert F. Nelson, 336th Fighter Squadron. To take the pressure off waiting for a mission, pin-ups, a dog, and a home-town newspaper were better than most other diversions.

Below: In 1943 the 4th Fighter Group, commissioned from the former RAF Eagle Squadrons, had its own Eagle Squadron calendar. Oscar Coen sits to the right while the portrait of General Eisenhower shares wall space with the ubiquitous "Pin Your Lip" and "Loose Talk Costs Lives" posters.

Below: Colonel Don Blakeslee (right) shares a cigarette and a story with Capt. Victor France at a dispersal point. France was killed in action on 18 April 1944.

Above: In a view intended to show 4th Fighter Group pilots "relaxing," the censor has gone to work on the scoreboards. Note the small heating stove on the right and the aircraft identification models hanging from the ceiling.

Left: The original caption on this photograph stated that the 4th Fighter Group pilots seen here were rehearsing a ceremony which bestowed a tongue-in-cheek medal, the "pointing finger," on any new pilot who "... pulled a boner" — a minor mistake. The wartime censor blanked out whatever was on the left side of the photograph.

Right: In September 1942, the three RAF Eagle Squadrons were transferred into the US Army Air Forces in Britain. Following the change, the 4th Fighter Group, made up of former "Eagles," retained its links to its former identities and two reminders of 71 Squadron — the painting above the door to the briefing room and the unit crest — are surrounded by the seemingly reflective trio of Captain Duane W. Beeson, Colonel Don Blakeslee, and Lieutenant Colonel James Clark.

Below (and Chapter Opener on page 199): A pair of carefully staged scenes depicting Colonel Blakeslee (to right) briefing his pilots. At left is Lt. Col. Jim Clark while the man with the moustache in the front row is Major Jim Goodson. In reality, briefings were conducted in a more military-like formation with the men seated in rows of chairs. *Page 199* Jim Clark "... briefs Mustang pilots of the 4th Fighter Group before a fighter sweep." To the right of him holding his hat is Gentile, and to his left is James Goodson.

Above: Major James A. Goodson, a fighter ace with 15 victories and commander of the 336th Fighter Squadron, spins a yarn to both new and veteran pilots in a 4th Fighter Group dispersal hut. Don Gentile leans on a table and smiles as he listens whilst at far right with a cigarette and cap, his wingman, John Godfrey listens attentively.

Right: M/Sgt. Merle Olmsted crouches on the wing of P-51B s/n 42-106829, G4✪P flown by Lt. Robert Wallen of the 362nd Fighter Squadron, 357th Fighter Group. The combination of a dedicated crew chief and pilot was a relationship immensely valued by the pilots.

Left and below: The 363rd Fighter Group, constituted in February 1943, was redesignated the 363rd Tactical Reconnaissance Group in August 1944. It arrived in Britain in December 1943 with IX FC. It received P-51s in January 1944 and flew combat right up to when it re-equipped with F-5s and F-6s. Here, Lt. Marvin N. Thompson poses for an official photograph in his Malcolm-hooded P-51B "Little Chris II" which carried a white cross next to the data stencil signifying the presence of a fuselage fuel tank. Thompson was shot down over enemy territory but evaded capture and returned to fly. He was credited with 2 1/2 kills. When it arrived in Britain, the 363rd Fighter Group was based at Keevil, Rivenhall, and Staplehurst. Lieutenant Colonel John Ulricson was Group CO to March 1943; then Captain Dave Culberson followed by Major Theodore Bunker in April; Colonel Ulricson again to June 1943; Colonel James Tipton to May 1944; Colonel James Smelley to September; and Colonel Seth Mize was CO after May 1945.

Left: Two P-51Bs of the 363rd Fighter Group take off for another mission from either Rivenhall or Staplehurst. Both aircraft carry drop tanks and gear doors are in transition.

Right and below: "Toni Girl"/"The Duchess" was the backdrop for a photograph of Captain Louis Morrison of the 363rd Fighter Group, whilst in a similar picture, Captain John Robertson of the same group smiles for the camera next to "Donna Mae" which sports very bright metal 75-gallon drop tanks.

Above and below: Lt. Gilbert O'Brien of the 362nd Fighter Squadron, 357th FG flew this P-51B "Shanty Irish," coded G4✪J, s/n 43-6787. O'Brien had seven victories. Note how the number and location of mission symbols has changed in the photograph (*below*) which has been taken on a later date. The three-leaf clover emblem also appears to have been repainted.

Above: Colonel Henry Spicer (center) was CO of the 357th Fighter Group from 17 February to 5 March 1944, on which date he was taken PoW. On the left in this picture taken at Bodney, is Sgt. Currie and on the right is Cpl. Hamilton. Note the white cross on the olive drab paint which signified that the aircraft was modified with a fuselage fuel tank. The mud-caked boots of the ground crew are indicative of operating conditions.

Left: P-51B-7, "Pregnant Polecat," coded C5✪J, s/n 43-6878, was assigned to Capt. Glendon V. Davis of the 364th FS, 357th FG, Eighth AF. He is seen here (right) with his groundcrew at the group's base at Leiston, Suffolk. Davis was credited with 7 1/2 victories during March and April 1944. His last was claimed on 19 April; nine days later, he was forced down in enemy territory as a result of engine failure while flying another Mustang (s/n 43-6867). Davis managed to evade capture with help from the French underground and returned to Allied forces during the Invasion of France. The 357th FG was one of the "hot" fighter units of the Eighth AF; as it was one of the first to enter combat (in February 1944), its pilots scored nearly 600 "kills" by VE-Day and more than 40 of them became Aces.

Left: The only revetment at Debden protected two P-51Bs and one of them belonged to Colonel Blakeslee. Here, 335th Fighter Squadron groundcrew await the return of their aircraft on 6 March 1944 while standing on the top of the revetment wall.

Above: Colonel Blakeslee's P-51B inside its revetment at Debden seen shortly after returning from the mission to Berlin on 6 March 1944. All of Blakeslee's USAAF aircraft were coded WD✪C with no other markings.

Left: Groundcrew eagerly welcome Colonel Donald Blakeslee, CO of the 4th Fighter Group, on his return from the first mission to Berlin on 6 March 1944. Note the Malcolm hood.

Right: The team that makes an aircraft fly. A groundcrewman and a pilot talk after a mission. This 4th Fighter Group team fill out the omnipresent post-mission paperwork while the pilot's face begins to regain its shape after pressure from his oxygen mask.

Left: Major Pierce McKennon of the 4th Fighter Group, just returned from the first Mustang escort mission to Berlin on 6 March 1944, tells "... how it was" to a keen-eared "reception committee."

production of drop tanks, and introduction of the P-51B – for success to come so dramatically. Success might not have come at all, if not for the bravery shown by fighter pilots. But bravery was not reserved for them alone. Who can find words to describe the lives of bomber crews over Germany whose aircraft could not be maneuvered when shot at? Or ground crews who went without sleep to keep aircraft flying?

To choose a date after which VIII FC – and later on, IX FC – fighter pilots' successes in the air began to be so numerous is somewhat arbitrary. A listing of day-to-day and individual air victories is not possible in this volume. However, starting in July 1943, and especially following January 1944, AAF fighter pilots in the ETO began to overwhelm the enemy. From February 1944, consecutive mission totals generally equalled or exceeded those of the few and widely separated best days of 1943. High scoring on most missions continued throughout the remainder of the war. From the time in mid-1942 when VIII FC was formed, until July 1943, the record was less than impressive.

The Eighth AF had struck German soil for the first time on 27 January 1943 with 55 bombers flying beyond the radius-of-action of P-47s. It was not until 30 July of that year when VIII FC's P-47s used drop tanks for only the second time, that AAF fighters reached German airspace and surprised *Luftwaffe* fighter pilots concentrating on attacking Eighth AF bombers. The P-47s shot down several enemy fighters. *Luftwaffe* fighter pilots had not had to contend with opposing AAF fighters over their homeland until July 1943. Hitler's ground and air war in Russia did not end until the war ended, and his war in North Africa lasted until May 1943. When Eighth AF bombers reached Berlin in daylight in March, 1944, the fighter air war in the west reached its highest pitch and stayed there. During the early part of the air war the lament among VIII FC pilots was that the Germans would not

come up to fight. After March 1944 the *Luftwaffe* fought for its life over its homeland. AAF fighter pilots had all the opportunity they wished for.

There had not been a single daylight bombing raid on Berlin by the AAF until 4 March 1944. The *Luftwaffe* intercepted AAF fighters as well as bombers – which had not been the case, generally, prior to July 1943. The official *USAF Historical Study No. 85*, the record of credits to fighter pilots during the war, reads, starting in March, 1944, like an almost endless list of names of fighter pilots achieving success against German aircraft in the air. Mission scores filled many single pages in fine print.

The Eighth AF returned to Berlin in force on 8 March, 1944 and afterward. A force of 539 bombers attacked, and 891 fighters escorted, of which six groups were Mustangs. The 4th, 352nd, 355th, 357th in VIII FC; and the 363rd and 354th in IX FC were now Mustang groups. The 4th FG was credited with 16 victories; the 352nd, two; 355th, one; 357th, seven; 363rd, two; and 354th, four. 1st Lt. Leonard K. "Kit" Carson, who was to become the top Ace in the 357th FG and the number four top Mustang Ace overall, began his scoring on 8 March with a half credit over a Bf 109 over Braunschweig. His total of 18.5 was achieved in Mustangs.

Capt. Dominic Salvatore "Don" Gentile and 1st Lt. John T. Godfrey began flying in combat as a two-man team on 8 March, 1944, and Gentile let Godfrey take his turn in shooting down enemy aircraft. Then and afterward, news spread of their unselfish and successful teamed combat flying. On 8 March, Gentile downed 3.5 Bf 109s over Berlin while Godfrey got 2.5 Bf 109s.

In one respect, the impact of the P-51B upon the role of bomber escort, was as dramatic as was the impact of the Me 262 upon aviation technology. The Me 262 came too late while the P-51B appeared in just the nick of time.

Colonel Don Blakeslee heads a parade of officers and men of the 4th Fighter Group at Debden, spring 1944.

Sources

US Army Air Forces Records

The great majority of reference material used in this study originates from within the Modern Military Section, Army Air Forces, World War Two, in the US National Archives in Washington, DC.

Books

Aldrich, Nelson W., Jr. Tommy Hitchcock: An American Hero. Published privately by Mrs. Margaret Mellon Hitchcock, Fleet Street Corporation, 1984.

Angelucci, Enzo, with Peter Bowers. The American Fighter: The Definitive Guide to American Fighter Aircraft from 1917 to the Present. New York, NY: Orion Books, 1985.

Arnold, Major General H.H., and Colonel Ira C. Eaker. Winged Warfare. New York, NY: Harper & Brothers Publishers, 1941.

Arnold, General of the Air Forces H.H. Global Mission, New York, NY: Harper, 1949.

Berg, A. Scott. Lindbergh, The Berkeley Publishing Group, New York, NY, 1998.

Birch, David. Rolls Royce and the Mustang. Derby, England: Rolls Royce Heritage Trust, 1987.

Blake, Steve. Adorimini - Up and at 'Em. Boise, Idaho: 82nd Fighter Group History, Inc., 1992.

Bodie, Warren M. The Lockheed P-38 Lightning. Hiawassee, Georgia: Widewing Publications, 1991.

Bodie, Warren M. Republic's P-47 Thunderbolt. Hiawassee, Georgia: Widewing Publications, 1994.

Brereton, Lt. Gen. Lewis H. The Brereton Diaries. New York, NY: William Morrow and Company, 1946.

Caidin, Martin. Fork-Tailed Devil: The P-38. New York, NY: Ballantine Books, 1971.

Coffey, Thomas M. Hap. New York, NY: The Viking Press, 1982.

Copp, Dewitt S. A Few Great Captains. New York, NY: Doubleday, 1980.

Copp, Dewitt, S. Forged in Fire. New York, NY: Doubleday, 1982.

Craven, Wesley Frank, and James Lea Cate. The Army Air Forces In World War II. Eight Volumes. Chicago, Illinois: The University of Chicago Press, various dates.

Davis, Benjamin O., Jr. Benjamin O. Davis, Jr., an Autobiography. Washington, DC.: Smithsonian Institution Press, 1992.

Davis, Richard G. Carl A. Spaatz and the Air War in Europe. Washington, DC.: Smithsonian Institution Press, 1992.

Deighton, Len. Battle of Britain. New York, NY: Coward, McCann & Geohagen Publishers, 1980.

Doolittle, General James H., with Carroll V. Glines. I Could Never Be So Lucky Again. New York, NY: Bantam Books, 1991.

Dunn, Bill Newton. Big Wing. Shrewsbury, England: Airlife Publishing Ltd., 1992.

Ethell, Jeffrey. Mustang: A Documentary History. New York, NY: Jane's, 1981.

Freeman, Roger A. The Mighty Eighth: A History of the US 8th Army Air Force. New York, NY: Doubleday and Company, 1970.

Freeman, Roger A. Mighty Eighth War Diary. New York, NY: Jane's, 1981.

Freeman, Roger A. Mighty Eighth War Manual. New York, NY: Jane's, 1984.

Freeman, Roger A. The Hub. Shrewsbury, England: Airlife Publishing Ltd., 1988.

Fry, Garry L., and Jeffrey L. Ethell. Escort to Berlin: the 4th Fighter Group in World War II. New York, NY: Arco Publishing, Inc., 1980.

Gray, John M. The 55th Fighter Group. North Branch, Minnesota: Specialty Press, 1998.

Hallion, Richard P. Test Pilots: The Frontiersmen of Flight. Garden City, NY: Doubleday & Company, Inc., 1981.

Hansen, James. R. Engineer in Charge: A History of the Langley Aeronautical Laboratory, 1917- 1958. Washington, DC.: National Air and Space Administration, 1987.

Harker, R.W., O.B.E., A.E. Rolls Royce From the Wings 1925 - 1971, Military Aviation. Oxford, England: Oxford Illustrated Press, 1976.

Haugland, Vern. The Eagle Squadrons: Yanks in the RAF 1940 - 1942. New York, NY: Ziff-Davis, 1979.

Haugland, Vern. The Eagles' War: The Saga of the Eagle Squadron Pilots 1940 - 1945. New York, NY: Jason Aronson, 1982.

Holley, Irving Brinton, Jr. Buying Aircraft: Materiel Procurement For The Army Air Forces. Office of the Chief of Military History, United States Army. Washington, DC.: US Government Printing Office, 1964.

Howard, James H. Roar of the Tiger. New York, NY: Orion Books, 1991.

Isaacson, Walter, and Evan Thomas. The Wise Men: Six Friends and The World They Made. New York, NY: Simon & Schuster, 1986.

Keen, Patricia Fussell. Eyes of the Eighth: A Story of the 7th Photographic Reconnaissance Group 1942 - 1945. Sun City, Arizona: CAVU Publishers, L.L.C., 1996.

Kimes, Beverly Rae, Editor. Packard: A History of the Motor Car and the Company. Automobile Quarterly Publications. Princeton, NJ: Princeton Publishing, 1978.

Kohn, Richard H., and Joseph P. Harahan, General Editors. Air Superiority In World War II and Korea. Washington, DC.: Office of Air Force History, 1983.

Lacey, Robert. Ford: The Men And The Machine. Boston, Massachusetts: Little, Brown and Company, 1986.

Leary, William M., Editor. Aviation's Golden Age: Portraits From the 1920s and 1930s. Iowa City, Iowa: University of Iowa Press, 1989.

Lloyd, Ian. Rolls Royce: The Merlin at War. London: Macmillan, 1978.

Loftin, Laurence K. Quest for Performance: The Evolution of Modern Aircraft. Washington DC.: National Air and Space Administration, 1985.

McFarland, Stephen L., and Wesley Phillips Newton. To Command The Sky: The Battle For Air Superiority Over Germany, 1942-1944. Washington, DC.: Smithsonian Institution Press, 1991.

Mets, David R. Master of Air Power: General Carl A. Spaatz. Novato, California: Presidio, 1988.

Mondey, David. The Schneider Trophy. London: Robert Hale, 1975.

Parton, James. Air Force Spoken Here. Bethesda, Maryland: Adler & Adler, 1986.

Rogers, William Brevard. Outcast Red. William Brevard Rogers, 1987.

Samson, Jack. Chennault. New York, NY: Doubleday, 1987.

Schlaifer, Robert, and S.D. Heron. Development of Aircraft Engines - Development of Aircraft Fuels. Boston, Massachusetts: Division of Research, Graduate School of Business Administration, Harvard University, 1950.

Stanaway, John. The 348th Fighter Group in World War Two. St. Paul, MN: Phalanx Publishing Co., Ltd., 1992.

Steiner, Edward J., Editor. Kings Cliffe. No publisher, no date.

Terraine, John. A Time For Courage: The Royal Air Force in the European War, 1939 - 1945. New York, NY: Macmillan, 1985.

Tillman, Barrett. Corsair. Naval Institute Press, Annapolis, Maryland, 1979.

Turner, Lt. Col. Richard E. Big Friend, Little Friend: Memoirs Of A World War II Fighter Pilot. Mesa, Arizona: Champlin Fighter Museum Press, 1983.

Wagner, Ray. Mustang Designer. New York, NY: Orion Books, 1990.

Who Was Who In American History - The Military. Marquis Who's Who, Inc.

Magazines and Periodicals

Aeroplane. London. May, 1999.

Aerospace Historian. Winter, December, 1987, pages 272 - 277. This article discusses how Air Corps officers regarded the Japanese Zero in 1940.

Aerospace Historian. Fall, September, 1974. Article, Mark E. Bradley.

Aerospace Historian. Fall, September, 1978. Article, Mark E. Bradley.

Air & Space. Washington, DC.: Smithsonian. August/September, 1996, pages 70 - 79.

Air Force. Washington, DC.: Air Force Association. June, 1981.

Popular Science. New York, NY: Popular Science Publishing Co. January 1943; pages 69 - 83. Maj. Alexander P. de Seversky criticized America's military aircraft and many US publications took him to task. The article in this issue of Popular Science reads in the language and hysteria of the day and offers a laughable portrayal of British preference for the Mustang.

The Packard Cormorant. Contoocook, New Hampshire: Dragonwyck Publishing Inc. Autumn, 1987, Number 48, pages 2 - 9.

The Rolls Royce Magazine. London: Rolls Royce Limited. September-November, 1980. See pages 21 - 25.

Reports, Papers, Lectures, Articles, Case Histories, Final Reports

Air-Flow Behavior Over The Wing Of An XP-51 Airplane As Indicated by Wing-Surface Tufts At Subcritical And Supercritical Speeds, by De E. Beeler, Langley Memorial Aeronautical Laboratory, N.A.C.A., April, 24, 1947.

Atwood, J. Leland. Article: Origin of the Mustang. August 8, 1973.

Atwood, J. Leland. Lecture: Yorkshire Air Museum, June 13, 1998.

Born in the USA Raised in New Guinea, by William Brevard Rogers. A Journal.

Case History of Droppable Fuel Tanks.

Case History of Fighter Airplane Range Extension Program.

Case History of Spitfire Airplane Range Extension. 27 September, 1946. This report indicates that the RAF willingly participated in the project. A cable was received from London, and two Spitfire IXs were shipped to Wright Field. On 14 January 1944 the USAAF said: "Engineering was to be initiated to increase both the internal and external fuel capacity to the maximum on these (two) airplanes."

Case History - XP-54.

Case History - XP-58.

Case History - XP-60.

Case History - XP-71.

Case History - XP-75.

Chennault, Capt. Claire. The Role of Defensive Pursuit. Historical Library. Maxwell Air Force Base, Alabama.

Cockpit. The Society of Experimental Test Pilots. July, 1965.

Confidential Memorandum Report for Tests of the XP-46 Airplane in the N.A.C.A. Full-Scale Wind Tunnel, by F.R. Nickle and W.J. Nelson, January 11, 1940.

Final Report Of Inspection, Performance and Acceptance of North American Airplane Model XP-51, Capt. W.G. Logan, A.C.

Final Report on Test To Determine the Effect of an Additional 85 Gallons of Internal Fuel on Performance and Handling of the P-51B Airplane.

Final Report on Test of Operational Suitability of P-51A-1 Airplane, June 3, 1943.

Final Report on Test of the Armament Installation in the P-51A-1 Airplane A.C. No. 43-6014, June 8, 1943.

Final Report on Tactical Suitability of P-51 Type Airplane, Eglin Field, 20 December, 1942.

Final Report - XP-46.

Flader, Fred. Letter From The Chief Engineer. Curtiss Corporation. October 23, 1943

Hoerner, Fluid-Dynamic Drag.

Horkey, Edward. One of a Kind, The P-51, The Real Story.

Jenkins, Col. Jack S. Col. Jenkins loaned to the author a considerably large number of personal and official documents in his possession regarding his tour with the 55th Fighter Group. (1) Informal notes on Combat Range of P-38J Airplane. (2) Tactical Commander's Report, January 10, 1944. (3) Special Fuels for P-38Js.

Jettisonable Tanks For Fighter Aircraft.

Kelsey, Brig. Gen. B.S. There'll Always Be A Fighter. Transcript of his speech, published in The Cockpit, July, 1965. Society of Experimental Test Pilots. Copy furnished by N.L. Avery.

Report of Board of Officers on Pursuit Interceptor Airplanes (Single Engine) Submitted in Response to Request for Data R40-C. (2) Summary of Proposals. (3) Summary of Figure of Merit.

Report on Tactical Employment Trials, North American P-51-A-10, AAFSAT, June 8, 1943.

Report of The Army Air Forces Board, Orlando, Florida, Tactical Employment Trials, North American P-51B-1, 12 February, 1944.

Saville, Maj. Gordon P. Air Defense Doctrine. October 27, 1941.

Summary of the XB-41 Project.

Tactical Trials P-47C at A.F.D.U., Duxford. Headquarters, VIII Fighter Command.

The Fighting Aspect of Tactical Reconnnaissance By Single-Engined Fighter Aircraft. Prepared and circulated by Air Tactics (Air Ministry) December, 1942. S.7338.

Test of the XP-46 Airplane in the NACA Full-Scale Wind Tunnel.

Vincent, Col. Jesse Gurney. Chronological Development of Packard-Built Rolls-Royce Merlin Engines. Detroit, MI, Packard Motor Car Company, Aircraft Engineering Division, April 1, 1945.

von Karman, Theodore. Aerodynamics: Selected Topics in the Light of Their Historical Development. New York, NY: Cornell University Press.

Wartime Report: Flying Qualities and Stalling Characteristics of North American XP-51 Airplane, by Maurice D. White, Herbert H. Hoover and Howard W. Garris, Langley Memorial Aeronautical Laboratory, N.A.C.A., April, 1943.

Wartime Report: Wind Tunnel Investigation of Rear Fuselage Underslung Fuselage Ducts, by K.R. Czarnecki and W.J. Nelson; Langley Memorial Aeronautical Laboratory, N.A.C.A.; September, 1943.

References

Introduction

1 Arnold, Global Mission, pages 376 and 377.
2 Craven and Cate, Volume VI, pages 217 and 218.

Chapter One

1 Mondey, page 187
2 Schlaifer and Heron, page 56
3 Schlaifer and Heron, page 261
4 Schlaifer and Heron, page 288
5 Mets, page 85
6 Craven and Cate, Vol. 1, pages 64 and 65
7 Copp, A Few Great Captains, pages 159 through 161
8 Samson, page 9
9 Chennault, Capt. Claire, "The Role of Defensive Pursuit."
10 Copp, A Few Great Captains, page 323; and Craven and Cate, Vol. 1, page 65
11 Arnold and Eaker, Winged Warfare, page 176
12 Schlaifer and Heron, page 275
13 Kelsey, There Will Always Be a Fighter, page 2
14 Kelsey, There Will Always Be a Fighter, page 2
15 Kelsey, There Will Always Be A Fighter, page 6
16 Schlaifer and Heron, page 279
17 Mitchel Field was named after a former Mayor of New York city.

Chapter Two

1 "Notes On The Aircraft Situation For The Calendar Year 1940", an unsigned memorandum. Maj. Gen. H.H. Arnold in that month was supplying figures to General George Marshall and Assistant Secretary of War for Air, Robert Lovett, regarding aircraft production for the year 1940 to project figures to June, 1941.
2 "Data On Airplanes Released For Export," a War Department Public Relations Branch news release dated at the time the P-40D was entering manufacture in 1940.
3 Final Report of Inspection, Performance and Acceptance of Curtiss-Wright Airplane Model XP-46. Capt. W. G. Logan. H.Z. Bogert, Colonel, AAF, Chief, Technical Staff. This Final Report is undated. Final Reports were written for aircraft no longer needed by the AAF.
4 Letter, Brig. Gen. B.K. Yount to Dr. G.W. Lewis, NACA, November 4, 1939.
5 Geo. H. Brett, Brig. Gen., Chief of Division; to General Arnold. "NACA High Speed Pursuit Design." July 25, 1939.
6 Cross Reference from Contract Files; from the Assistant Technical Executive to Mr. Burdette Wright, Curtiss Aero. Div., Curtiss-Wright Corp., May 14, 1940. In reference to a letter from Curtiss to the Materiel Division dated May 7, 1940.
7 Schlaifer and Heron, page 304.
8 AIR FORCE magazine, June, 1981, pages 82 through 85.
9 Tests of the XP-46 Airplane in the NACA Full-Scale Wind Tunnel, a report, Nickle and Nelson.
10 "Substitution of Modified P-40 Type Airplanes for P-46 Type Airplanes." Letter, Lt. Col. Ira Eaker for the Chief of the Air Corps, June 17, 1940. Eaker, holding the title of Executive, was an exceptional officer and was known for his writing ability. He said "...the Army will get a better airplane and at an earlier date."
11 Loftin, pages 103 through 120.
12 Hansen, page 196.
13 Letter, Maj. Gen. H.H. Arnold to The Assistant Secretary of War, June 9, 1939. Arnold asked for three new types capable of 425 mph and two capable of 525 mph. Arnold listed five engine manufacturers which did not include Packard.
14 Statements by Mr. Edgar Schmued, interview with the author, at Schmued's home, Oceanside, California; July 29, 1982. Letters; Edgar Schmued; to author: March, 21, 1982; July 8, 1982; August 23, 1982; October 20, 1982; April 23, 1983; May 2, 1983. Edgar Schmued died on June 1, 1985. Schmued was in NAA's employ on the date the Air Force ordered the supersonic F-100 but departed soon after. Schmued referred to Mr. Beverley Shenstone, MASc, Hon FRAes, FAIA; a Canadian who was an aerodynamicist with Supermarine in England until 1938. He then worked in the Air Ministry. Shenstone learned by way of a reply to his letter to Ernst Heinkel in Germany before the war about smoothing the metal skin of aircraft by using countersunk rivets. The Mustang had end-butted metal skinning and countersunk rivets. Larry L. Waite headed NAA's Technical Section. James S. Smithson ran production.
15 Statement from Mr. Edward Horkey, interview with the author; Tempe, Arizona; May 13, 1983. A transcript of the taped interview recorded by the author. Also see: "One-Of-A-Kind, The P-51, The Real Story"; a booklet written by Mr. Horkey and mailed to the author from Tempe, Arizona.
16 "Letter From The Chief Engineer", written by Fred Flader and enclosed within the Curtiss in-house news magazine; October 23, 1943.
17 Ethell; "Mustang, A Documentary History"; page 14. A letter from J.L. Atwood to the author in 1981 disclosed that specification 1592 is no longer available.
18 "Aerodynamics"; von Karman; pages 7 through 9. For related information about low drag in aircraft, see "Fluid-Dynamic Drag"; Hoerner; pages 7-4 through 7-6. Hoerner discusses the value of clipped wings and flying surfaces.
19 "One-Of-A-Kind, The P-51, The Real Story" by Horkey.
20 Telegram; Echols to General Brett; April 19, 1940.
21 Letter; M.F. Harmon; Col.; Assistant Commandant, The Air Corps Tactical School, Maxwell Field, Alabama; to Brig. Gen. B.K. Yount, Office, Chief of the Air Corps; Washington, DC; November 25, 1939.
22 Arnold and Eaker; "Winged Warfare"; page 7.
23 Letter; Maj. Gen. H.H. Arnold to The Assistant Secretary of War; Subject: Request for Data R40-C; February 1, 1940. Arnold referred to CP-39-70 noted in his letter to the Assistant Secretary of June 9, 1939 and eight months later he was asking to "conduct a further survey of the single-engine Pursuit airplane field." Therefore the winner of R-40C would replace the XP-46, XP-47, and DS-312A while the DS-312A would elicit similar designs.
24 Routing and Record Sheet; from the Office of the Chief of the Air Corps to the Materiel Division; May 12, 1940.

Chapter Three

1 Memo for Arnold from Geo. H. Brett, Brig. Gen., Chief of Materiel Division, March 27, 1940; "Military Characteristics of Aircraft, Pursuit Fighter Airplane."
2 Memo for Arnold from Carl Spaatz, Colonel; Chief, Plans Division; March 18, 1940; "Study on Pursuit and Fighter Aircraft."
3 Letter to the Adjutant General from Arnold; March 27, 1940; "Military Characteristics of Aircraft." Within this letter Arnold asked for a 2,700 mile range.
4 Routing and Record Sheet; "Military Characteristics of Aircraft, Pursuit Fighter Airplane"; from Spaatz to Materiel. Materiel asked Spaatz on March 26, 1940 and Spaatz replied on April 16, 1940.
5 Memo from General Marshall to the Chief of the Air Corps; June 13, 1940.
6 M.F. Harmon, Col.; Acting Commandant, The Air Corps Tactical School; to General Arnold, May 16, 1940.
7 Case History of XP-58 Airplane; compiled by the Historical Division, Intelligence, T-2, Air Technical Service Command, Wright Field; December, 1945.
8 Hallion, pages 188 through 191. Jack Reeder of the NACA and Brig. Gen. Gustav Lundquist flew dive tests in the XP-51.
9 Horkey, "One-Of-A-Kind, The P-51, The Real Story."
10 Case History of The XP-71 Airplane; Compiled by the Historical Office, Air Technical Service Command, Wright Field; October, 1944.
11 Letter from B.E. Meyers, Lt. Col.; Exec., Mat. Div. to Chief of Ordnance; September 11, 1941. "75 mm. Cannon Fighter Airplane." The XP-71 project commenced in 1941 and the Case History said the experiment with installing a 75 mm cannon on a B-18 led to the XP-71. In April, 1943, OC & R recommended that the XP-67, XP-69, and XP-71 be discontinued.
12 Terraine, page 606.
13 Summary of the XB-41 Project.

Chapter Four

1 CTI-65; A.J. Lyon, Major, Technical Executive; to the Assistant Chief, Materiel Division; June 17, 1940. "Production, Procurement, and Provision for use of Following Engines: Rolls Royce Merlin XX, Allison 1325 hp, Continental 1500 hp, Rolls Royce Griffon.".
2 Letter; H.H. Arnold, Maj. Gen. to The Rt. Hon. J.T.C. Moore-Brabazon, M.P., Ministry of Aircraft Production; October 28, 1941. Arnold extoled a long list of in-line engines and the R-2800 under development in the US Arnold said: "We are very much interested in the two-stage supercharger application you are sending us."
3 Memorandum; Air Marshal Portal from H.H. Arnold, Lt. Gen., Deputy Chief of Staff for Air; January 12, 1942. "Availability of Additional Packard Merlins."
4 Kimes; pages 174 through 191.
5 Lacey; pages 387 to 389.
6 Vincent, J.G.; Vice President of Engineering, Packard Motor Car Company; Aircraft Engineering Department. "Chronological Development of Packard-Built Rolls-Royce Merlin Engines."
7 Angelucci and Bowers; "The American Fighter"; page 167.
8 Lloyd; pages 35 through 56.
9 Birch; "Rolls-Royce and the Mustang."
10 Letter; J.W. Sessums, Jr.; Col.; Asst. Chief of Staff (P) to Gen. Echols; March 17, 1943. "Packard Merlin Engine Production."
11 Memorandum; O.P. Echols, Maj. Gen.; for the Commanding General; June 14, 1943. "Packard Strike."
12 Telegram; Branshaw; Materiel Command; to Maj. Gen. O.P. Echols, Asst. Chief of Air Staff, MM & D; June 14, 1943. Branshaw offered two solutions: (1) "to divert from the British. Nothing can be done to (the) engine schedule to eliminate airplanes on ground for the next six months." (2) Drastically reduce production on P-51B airplanes to bring in line with engine production."
13 Telegram; Technical Executive to the Asst. Chief of Air Staff MM&D; July 7, 1943. It was noted in the contents that "the Allison plant could not produce Rolls Royce engines for at least twelve months."
14 Memorandum; O.P. Echols, Maj. Gen., Asst. Chief of Air Staff MM&D for General Giles; August 5, 1943. Echols said "arrangements can be made to reduce B-25s to permit the manufacture of additional P-51s."
15 Letter; W.M. Packer, Vice President, Packard Motor Car Company; to Brig. Gen. B.W. Chidlaw, the Materiel Command, the Pentagon; August 18, 1943.

Chapter Five

1 Historical Aviation Album 1974; series produced by Paul R. Matt. "Ryan Broughams and Their Builders", by William Wagner; pages 10 and 11.
2 "Who Was Who in American History - The Military"; published by Marquis Who's Who, Inc.
3 Capt. Lee flew the NA-73, registered as a civilian aircraft with the serial number NX-19998 painted under the left wing. The aircraft suffered an accident from fuel starvation when flown by another pilot later on. Doubt exists that NX-19998 was returned to flight status.
4 Letter; Oliver P. Echols, Brig. Gen.; Chief, Materiel Division; to the Chief of the Army Air Forces; Feb. 1, 1942. "Study re Possibility of Keeping the P-40 Series in Production by Switch Over to the Rolls Royce Merlin-61 or Stepped-up Allison."
5 Letters; Lt. Gen. Ralph Swofford to the author; June 15, 1981; Nov. 25, 1981; and March 19, 1982. General Swofford said: "In mid-1939 Experimental Aircraft Development was removed from the Production Division and put under Col. F.O. Carroll in what I think was called the Experimental Engineering Section but on the chart is labeled Experimental Research Section; in any case at that time I was assigned to Col. Carroll's Section. Perhaps the above helps explain why the NA-73X (XP-51) was assigned to Carroll's outfit rather than the Pursuit Unit of the Production Division."
6 Craven and Cate; Volume VI, page 372. Craven and Cate; Volume I, page 130. Holley; page 267. Memorandum; H.A. Craig, Colonel, G.S.C., Assistant Chief of the Air Staff, Plans; for General Arnold; April 22, 1942. Monthly deliveries to be fulfilled as of April 30, 1942 were shown for all customers including the AAF. Contract DA-AC-140 was for "BR" and 72 Mustangs were to be shipped in July and 78 in August, totaling 150. The estimated schedule listed 3,000 Packard Merlin V-1650-1s for the US and 20,000 for the British for Lancaster bombers. Defense Aid was known officially as the Defense Aid Supplemental Appropriation Act and was "generally known as the Lend-Lease Act."
7 Memorandum; H.H. Arnold, Lt. Gen., US Army, Deputy Chief of Staff for Air; for General Spaatz; December 26, 1941. "Gap Between Existing Models and New Models of Airplanes and Engines." "... that there may be no slowing down of production."

8　Letter; J.H. Kindelberger, President of NAA; to Asst. Chief, Materiel Division, Wright Field; Feb. 3, 1942. "Production of P-51 Mustang Fighter Airplane."

9　Teletype message; P.W. Timberlake, Lt. Col.; Production Engineering Branch; to Chief, Production Engineering Section; March 3, 1942.

10　Letter; Alexander T. Burton, NAA; to Chief, Materiel Divison; March 4, 1942.

11　Memorandum; P.W. Timberlake, Lt. Col.; for Col. H.A. Craig, Air War Plans Division; March 5, 1942. "North American P-51 as a Dive Bomber."

12　Memorandum; Ford L. Fair, Lt. Col., Recorder; to Lt. Col. P.W. Timberlake, Prod. Eng. Division; March 9, 1942. "N.A. P-51 Dive Bomber."

13　Memorandum; P.W. Timberlake, Lt. Col.; for Lt. Col. H.A. Craig, Air War Plans Division; March 22, 1942. "Production of North American P-51."

14　Memorandum; T.J. Hanley, Jr., Col., G.S.C., Assistant Chief of the Air Staff, A-4; for the Chief of the Air Staff; April 7, 1942. "Requirement for Light Bombers."

15　Letter; Muir S. Fairchild, Brig. Gen., Director of Military Requirements; to the Commanding General, Materiel Command; April 19, 1942. "Procurement of 500 North American P-51s."

16　Letter; O.P. E.; CG, A.F. Mat'l. Command; to AFDMR; 4-21-1942. "Dive Bomber Production." AFDMR was Requirements (Fairchild).

17　Letter; B.E. Meyers, Brig. Gen., Executive; to the Technical Executive, Wright Field; May 6, 1942. "P-51 Conversion Into an Interim Dive Bomber." See also: teletype message; from "Executive HL" to the Technical Executive; 4-24-42. "Tactical plands (sic) have been made which were dependent upon the use of this airplane."

18　Letter; B.E. Meyers, Major, Executive; to the Adjutant General; October 18, 1940. "Modification in 18,641 Airplane Procurement Program." In the same letter Meyers requested 312 P-40s with the "Rolls Royce engines."

19　Letter; President Franklin D. Roosevelt; to The Honorable The Secretary of War; January 3, 1942. Roosevelt listed requirements for 45,000 aircraft in 1942 and 100,000 in 1943.

20　Letter; B.E. Meyers, Colonel, Exec., Mat. Div.; to The Chief of the Bureau of Aeronautics; Feb. 16, 1942. "Procurement of Curtiss A-25 Airplanes." Known as BuAer, it was the US Navy's counterpart to the Materiel Division.

21　Report; A.L. Schroeder, Lt. Col., Commanding, HQ, 85th Bomb Gp, (D), AAB, Rice, California; to Commanding Officer, IV Air Support Command, Camp Young, California; March 9, 1943. Because of slow speed of the A-24, it was classified "as an excellent target" while the A-36 "is highly recommended."

22　Letter; J.H. Kindelberger; to Chief, Materiel Center, Wright Field; August 4, 1942. "P-51 'A' Development."

23　Letter; Muir S. Fairchild, Brig. Gen.; Director of Military Requirements; to Commanding Officer, Air Forces Proving Ground Command; Eglin Field, Florida; April 6, 1942.

24　Letter; Grandison Gardner, Brig. Gen.; Commanding, Headquarters Army Air Forces Proving Ground Command; to Commanding General, Director of Air Defense, Washington, DC; 16 December, 1942.

25　Routing and Record Sheet; Morris R. Nelson, Col.; Chief, Air Defense Branch, Requirements Division; to Assistant Chief of Air Staff; Operations, Commitments and Requirements; March 30, 1943. "Policy Regarding Test of Light and Dive Bombardment Aircraft."

Chapter Six

1　Birch; page 10.

2　Birch; page 12.

3　Birch; pages 14 and 15.

4　Birch; page 16.

5　Aldrich.

6　Letter: B.E. Meyers, Brig. Gen.; Executive; to Technical Executive, Wright Field; June 12, 1942. Arnold asked Materiel to send a cable to Winant saying: "The British have repeatedly advised me that they require all the Packard production of (the) Merlin 28."

7　Birch; page 18.

8　Birch; pages 20 and 21.

9　Birch; page 21.

10　Letter; Muir S. Fairchild, Major General; Director of Military Requirements; to Commanding General, Materiel Command; August 31, 1942. Fairchild's letter followed eight days after the contract for 1,200 Mustang was signed. On August 23, the contract said all 1,200 would be "P-51A-1-NA" Mustangs.

11　Leary; pages 113 through 126.

12　Inter-Office Memorandum; F.O. Carroll, Colonel; Chief, Experimental Engineering Section; to Assistant Technical Executive, Wright Field; August 14, 1942. "Installation of British Engines in Mustang Airframe."

13　Lecture; Yorkshire Air Museum; June 13, 1998. Article; Aeroplane magazine for May 1999; pages 30 through 37. Mr. Atwood wrote "Origin of the Mustang Fighter Plane", a three-page article dated August 8, 1973. He said: "I evolved a design concept which involved placing coolant radiators back of the wing." Atwood's title in 1940 was Vice President and Assistant General Manager. He said Schmued was Assistant Chief Engineer and chief of the preliminary design group.

14　Aeroplane magazine article; May 1999; page 30.

15　Schlaifer and Heron; page 238; footnote.

16　Booklet; "One-Of-A-Kind, The P-51, The Real Story"; written by Horkey; page 3; mailed to author.

17　Aeroplane magazine article; May 1999; page 34. Atwood calculated 350 lbs. of thrust from the radiator.

18　Letters; Irving L. Ashkenas; to author; June 6, 1983; June 24, 1983; and notes affixed to my letter of July 6 to Ashkenas returned to author in late July. Ashkenas referred to a German paper by Winter in Luftfahrtforschung, 1938, Vol. 15; with the translated title "Contribution to Theory of Heated, Ducted Radiator." The information probably was translated by the N.A.C.A. and issued as TM893.

19　Booklet; "One-Of-A-Kind, The P-51, The Real Story", page 4.

20　Letter; O.P. Echols, Maj. Gen.; MM & D; to Lt. Col. Thomas Hitchcock, Jr.; Asst. Military Air Attache, American Embassy, London; July 8, 1943. No letter written by Echols to a more junior officer was as warm and personal and open as was this one. It read as would a letter to an old friend or family member. Hitchcock's family social associations with President Roosevelt overcame rank. Echols' letter addressed Rolls Royce's "superior" supercharger; Hitchcock's suggestion to allow J.E. Ellor, Rolls Royce's advisor at Packard to assist Allison; and higher octane fuels. Allison refused help and complained about fuels.

21　An unsigned and undated report labled "Most Secret" criticized handling of the USAAF aircraft program. Letter; Chas. E. Branshaw, Brig. Gen.; to Maj. Gen. Oliver P. Echols, Commanding General, Army Air Forces Materiel Command, Washington, DC; August 8, 1942. Branshaw hoped that Echols would "refute many of the statements made, which

obviously have been made by biased individuals and are not in many instances founded on fact." In the critical report the month of July is noted. One statement said: "We have, so far, definitely failed to produce Army fighter planes which are the equal of the best service types of the Germans and Japanese. In the January report." January was the month when the Truman Committee report was published. The writer said "the P-40 and P-51 are inferior "and "the quality of Navy fighters seems to be comparatively better." The Truman Report seriously affected morale within the USAAF and the anonymous report - coming so soon on the heels of the Truman Report - was like that of a whistle blower.

22　Page 9 of an undated, unsigned rebuttal report labeled "Secret."

23　Page 10; same rebuttal report.

Chapter Seven

1　Letter; Carl Spaatz, Maj. Gen.; Commanding General, Eighth Air Force; to "Dear Arnold"; August 24, 1942.

2　Letter; H.H. Arnold, Lieutenant General, Commanding General, Army Air Forces; to Major General Carl Spaatz; August 26, 1942.

Chapter Eight

1　Routing And Record Sheet. D.M. Schlatter, Colonel, AFRAS; to "AFACT thru AFRAD and AFDMR"; October 31, 1942. "Fighter Aircraft for Observation." AFRAD, Morris R. Nelson, Colonel, Acting Director, was first to comment on November 18, 1942. Muir S. Fairchild, Major General, AFDMR, on November 19, 1942 returned the R & R to Schlatter suggesting "you may care to make additional remarks before this goes forward." Schlatter sent it out again on November 21, 1942 to "AFACT thru AFDMR." AFACT - Training - received the R & R and sent it to its destination where Robert W. Harper, Colonel, asked for more information.

2　Memorandum; Gordon P. Saville, Brig. Gen., Director of Air Defense; to Assistant Chief of Air Staff, Operational Plans (General Anderson); February 3, 1943. "P-40 Airplanes Available for French Fighter Group."

3　Routing And Record Sheet; F.W. Evans, Brig. Gen., Director, War Organization & Movement; to Military Requirements; January 5, 1943. The R & R alludes to the December report from the AFPGC. "Tactical Suitability of P-51 Type Aircraft." See #7 below.

4　Routing And Record Sheet; see above. Evans sent the R & R to Requirements who forwarded it to Schlatter. His remarks are dated January 19, 1943.

5　Memorandum; Gordon P. Saville, Brig. Gen., Commanding General, Air Defense; to Requirements; January 14, 1943. "Distribution of Aircraft."

6　Routing And Record Sheet; AFRAD to AFRAS; December 15, 1942.

7　Final Report on Test of Operational Suitability of P-51A-1 Airplane; Proof Department, Army Air Forces Proving Ground Command, Eglin Field, Florida; June 3, 1943. For further information, see the armament installation test dated June 8, 1943. AAFSAT in Florida presented a "Report on Tactical Employment Trials, North American P-51-A-10" dated 8 June, 1943. The AFPGC "test was started April 1, 1943 and terminated on May 10, 1943."

8　Letter; J.H. Kindelberger, President, North American Aviation, Inc.; to Chief, Materiel Center, Wright Field; August 4, 1942. "P-51 'A' Development."

9　Letter; J.L. Atwood, Vice President, North American Aviation, Inc.; to Commanding General, AAF, Materiel Center, Wright Field; September 25, 1942. "Production of 400 P-51-B Airplanes, as Special Project."

10　Letter; K.B. Wolfe, Brig. Gen., Chief, Production Division; to Chief of Staff, Materiel Command. Washington, DC; September 25, 1942. "North American Proposal to Build 400 P-51B Airplanes."

11　Contract; O.P. Echols, Major Gen., Commanding General, Materiel Commmand; to The Under Secretary of War; December 24, 1942. "Contract W535 ac-33923" paid for 400 P-51Bs. Echols said NAA sent its quotes on prices and conditions on "November 14, 1942 and December 1, 1942."

12　Letter; K.B. Wolfe, Brig. Gen., Chief, Production Division; to Chief, Fighter Branch; December 17, 1942. "P-51 Series Airplanes." Wolfe's changes resulted in: 300 P-51A, Inglewood; 400 P-51B, Inglewood; 900 P-51C, Inglewood; 550 P-51C, Inglewood; and 1,000 P-51C, Dallas. Later changes affected these figures and models.

13　Letter; Brig. Gen. L.S. Kuter, Deputy Air Officer Commanding, N.A.T.A.F.; to Commanding General, US Army Air Forces (through channels); 8 March, 1943. "Observation Aviation." Under "Recommendations" Kuter said "Disband all observation groups."

14　Craven and Cate; Volume VI, page 620.

15　Kohn and Harahan.

16　Letter; George E. Stratemeyer, Major General, Chief of the Air Staff; to Air Vice Marshal F. MacNeece-Foster, British Joint Staff Mission, Washington, DC; Feb. 20, 1943.

17　Letter; Carl Spaatz, Lieutenant General, U.S.A. Air Forces, Headquarters, Northwest African Air Forces; to Lieutenant General H.H. Arnold; 18 March, 1943. For a brief time Spaatz and Arnold held the same rank at the same time. Spaatz believed his request "would greatly ease the pressure on photo reconnaissance during the next six month period."

18　Memorandum; R.H. Kelly, Colonel, Actg. Chief, Allocations & Programs Division, AC/AS, Operations, Commitments and Requirements; to Assistant Chief of Air Staff, Operations, Commitments and Requirements; July 15, 1943. "Allocation of Aircraft to Reconnaissance Aviation." Tab A listed "Proposed Allocation of Aircraft for Reconnaissance Aviation" and from August, 1943 to "July and thereafter" in 1944, 945 P-51s were considered for allocation.

Chapter Nine

1　Memorandum; O.P. Echols, Brig. Gen.. Chief, Materiel Division; to Brig. Gen. George C. Kenney, Assistant Chief, Materiel Division, Wright Field; April 7, 1942. Air Vice Marshal G.B.A. Baker had made the request. Echols asked Kenney for "some preliminary studies" of three aircraft in production that would have turbos installed to give "them an altitude rating of 38,000 feet."

2　Inter-Office Memorandum; K.B. Wolfe, Lt. Col., Engineering Section, Materiel Division, Wright Field; to Chief, Materiel Division, Washington, DC; January 12, 1942. "Pilot's Observations, North American P-51 or Mustang."

3　Inter-Office Memorandum; B.S. Kelsey, Lt. Col., Chief, Pursuit Branch; to Chief, Production Engr. Section, Wright Field; March 4, 1942. "Performance Report on North American Mustang Fighter, dated January 2, 1942." Kelsey showed that the P-51 was better than the P-40F as a fighter type aircraft.

4　Haugland; "The Eagles' War"; pages 156 through 158.

5　Letter; Maj. Gen. Chesley Peterson; to the author; 20 Jan. 83.

6　Copy; Memorandum; F.D.R., The White House, Washington; to General Arnold; November 10, 1942.

7   Routing and Record Sheet; General Arnold; to General Echols; November 12, 1942. "To fill in the blanks and make any changes desireable." "H.H.A." Arnold enclosed Roosevelt's memo and a "draft of a memo to the Pres." to Echols.

8   Arnold's suggested memo for the President, sent to Echols, contains this verbatim sentence at the end of the first paragraph: "We think so much of them that we have already given orders for _____ _____ to go to the British and _____ to us." Echols filled in the first two blanks with the words "approximately 2200" and crossed out "to go to the British and _____ to us."

9   Memorandum; Thomas Hitchcock, Major, Asst. Military Air Attache; October 8, 1942. "History of the Mustang P-51 Aircraft." This memo has been published in every serious book about the Mustang. It and Roosevelt's note to Arnold helped convince Echols to put the Merlin Mustang under a production contract in America.

10   A Routing and Record Sheet was initiated by Chidlaw to AFROM on 9-5-1942 and had as its subject "Allocation of P-51 Airplane" but Chidlaw's purpose was to ask for one P-51 for a modification test. AFROM was the new term for the former War, Organization and Movement section, and Brig. Gen. Hume Peabody signed his comment "Dir., WO&M." Peabody returned the R & R to Chidlaw questioning the request, and on September 18 Chidlaw added another two paragraphs and returned it to Peabody. Col. Schlatter convinced Peabody to accede to Chidlaw's request for one P-51. Chidlaw's praise for the P-51 indicates that he vacillated on his opinions.

11   Memorandum; Chidlaw, B.W. Col.; to M.E. Gross, Col; and B.L. Boatner, Col.; at Wright Field; 25 September, 1942. The British wanted more Mustangs after the 500 A-36s were produced but the USAAF was not prepared in September to state what future contracts would include. Chidlaw said: "In view of the fact that the British have, to date, received no allocations of the P-51Cs and this airplane had not been flown with the changed wing and Merlin installation, an attempt to standardize on this airplane is premature."

12   Report No. 1, Case No. 3002, Joint Aircraft Committee, Sub-Committee on Standardization; Washington, DC; November 17, 1942. "Standardization of North American P-51 (Mustang)." Even before the P-51B was produced there was USAAF interest in a lightweight Mustang and also interest on the part of the British to acquire Merlin Mustangs. While Chidlaw's comment is taken out of context, there is no denying that the P-51B had not been put under contract, and interest in the USAAF to use it as a fighter was nearly non-existent. The most senior AAF representative attending from Wright Field as a test pilot was Maj. W.H. Towner and it may have been Towner who criticized the climb characteristics. Towner was subordinate to Kelsey.

13   Letter; O.P. Echols, Major General, Commanding; to Brig. Gen. Franklin O. Carroll, Materiel Center, Wright Field; November 7, 1942. "Memo for Director of Air Defense - Recommendations Pertaining to the P-60 and P-75 Airplanes." The memo from Saville was enclosed and dated October 29, 1942.

14   Letter; H.H. Arnold, Lieutenant General, Commanding General, Army Air Forces; to Mr. Donald Nelson, War Production Board, Washington, DC; no date.

15   Memorandum; B.W. Chidlaw, Brig. Gen., Assistant Chief of Air Staff, Materiel, Maintnance and Distribution; for General Echols (through Gen. Meyers); June 8, 1943. "Comparison of Fighter Types."

16   See 15 above. Chidlaw's comment was particularly obtuse. He had received a summary of reports of "various fighters" from Col. Bunker in the ETO who condensed his remarks from reports from Duxford, 8th Air Force and AAFSAT and Chidlaw told Echols that: "compared to the British airplanes (this report) makes our own equipment look mighty good." It is worth noting that the date of Chidlaw's memo was just prior to the crisis moment when Lovett cried out for escorts for 8th AF bombers. The P-38 was still the most desired fighter type but in June, none was in 8th AF.

17   Letter; Maj. Gen. Homer L. Sanders, USAF (Retired); to the author; 3 December, 1983. In August, 1942, Sanders sent one letter dated August 17 to his friend, Col. Mark E. Bradley at Wright Field to criticize the P-40 he and his men were flying and to ask "Where are the P-51s?" On August 26, 1942 Sanders wrote to his Commanding General, USAAF, India and China (through Commanding General, Karachi Air Defense Area, India). He reminded the General that he and pilots in his group had "tested (the P-51) before the end of 1941" and requested "that this group be equipped with P-51 airplanes."

18   Routing and Record Sheet; Mervin E. Gross, Colonel, Assistant Chief of Air Staff, OC&R, Requirements Division; to Asst. C/AS, MM&D (Attention: Materiel Division; July 6, 1943. Col. Griswold is listed as having made "Comment No. 1." The subject was "P-51B Aircraft." The R & R was returned to Gross without a name from the sender, saying "Subsequent to receipt of this R & R, the following was received from Colonel Gross." Gross was told to say the P-60 "had been definitely cancelled."

Chapter Ten

1   Davis; page 114.
2   Letter; Frank O'D. Hunter, Brig. Gen., Commanding, VIII Fighter Command; to Commanding General, Eighth Air Force; 17 April, 1943.
3   Freeman; "Mighty Eighth War Diary."
4   Freeman; "Mighty Eighth War Diary."
5   Memorandum; Emmett O'Donnell, Colonel, Advisory Committee; to General Arnold; June 12, 1943. "Ineffective Fighter Support to Bombardment in U.K."
6   Memorandum; Robert A. Lovett, Assistant Secretary of War for Air, War Department, Washington,DC; for the Commanding General, Army Air Forces; June 18, 1943. "P-47 Operations in England."
7   Isaacson and Thomas.
8   War Department Official Business - Outgoing Classified Message; CG AAF (Advisory Council). The message did not specify to whom it was sent. O'Donnell sent the message on Arnold's approval.
9   Fry and Ethell; "Escort to Berlin."
10   Bodie; "The Lockheed P-38 Lightning"; page 185.

Chapter Eleven

1   Freeman; "Mighty Eighth War Diary."
2   Letter; General Arnold; to General Giles; 6/22/43.
3   Routing and Record Sheet; General Giles; to Colonel Gross; 7/1/43. "Fighter to Accompany Bombardment Aircraft."
4   Case History of The XP-75 and P-75 Airplane Project; Compiled by Historical Office, Air Technical Service Command; Wright Field; November, 1944.
5   Routing and Record Sheet; Asst. C/AS, OC&R, Requirements Division; to Asst. C/AS, MM&D, Materiel Division; July 3, 1943. "Fighter to Accompany Bombardment Aircraft."
6   Case History of the XP-75 and P-75 Airplane Project.
7   Case History of the XP-75 and P-75 Airplane Project.

8   Case History of the XP-75 and P-75 Airplane Project.
9   Memorandum; Giles to Arnold; July 1, 1943. "Fighter Requirements in U.K."
10   Letter; George E. Stratemeyer, Major General, Chief of the Air Staff; to Assistant Chief of Air Staff; Operations, Commitments and Requirements; July 4, 1943. "Destroyer Type Aircraft."
11   Case History of The XP-75 and P-75 Airplane Project.
12   Memorandum; R.C. Wilson, Col., ACAS, MM&D; to Echols; July 9, 1943. "Fisher Body XP-75."
13   Letter; George E. Stratemeyer, Major General, Chief of the Air Staff; to Ass't Ch. of Air Staff, OC&R (Attention: General Giles); July 7, 1943. "Fighter Airplane."
14   Routing and Record Sheet; Barney M. Giles, Major General; to Chief of Air Staff; July 12, 1943. "Fighter Airplane."
15   Routing and Record Sheet; Millard A. Libby, Colonel, Secretary of the Air Staff; to AC/AS; Operations, Commitments and Requirements; July 14, 1943.
16   Memorandum; B.W. Chidlaw, Brig. Gen., Chief, Materiel Division, ACAS, MM&D; to Commanding General, Materiel Command, General Branshaw; 26 November, 1943. Chidlaw enclosed a statement from Echols, Major General, Asst. C/AS, MM&D. Chidlaw said "It is requested that the immediate and aggressive action be taken to carry out Gen. Echols' directive."
17   Case History of the XP-75 and P-75 Airplane Project. The second XP-75 made its first flight on January 27, 1944.
18   Case History of the XP-75 and P-75 Airplane Project. On 31 May, 1944 Engel asked a number of questions, including the "number of planes produced annually to date."
19   Case History of the XP-75 and P-75 Airplane Project. A production P-75 made its first flight on 15 September.
20   Telephone conversation between Major General O.P. Echols, Materiel Division, Washington, DC, and Colonel Orval R. Cook and Colonel Mark Bradley, Materiel Command, Wright Field, Dayton, Ohio. July 10, 1943, 4:50 PM. The transcript was given to the author by General Mark E. Bradley, USAF (Retired).
     There is no explanation regarding Echols' reference to the Navy.
21   Interview; General Mark E. Bradley; with the author. Letters; General Mark E. Bradley, to the author.
22   Letter; S.R. Brentnall, Colonel, Chief, Production Engineering Section, Materiel Command, Wright Field; to Engineering Section; July 14, 1943. "Information on P-51-B and P-75 Airplanes."
23   Letter; Paul W. Kemmer, Colonel, Chief, Aircraft Laboratory, Engineering Division; to Chief, Production Engineering Section; July 22, 1943.
24   Letter; S.R. Brentnall, Colonel, Chief, Production Engineering Section; to Commanding General, Army Air Forces; August 18, 1943. This letter was addressed to the "Attn; Major General Echols, ACAS, MM&D." It was to be another full year before the XP-75 was canceled.
25   Letter; R.C. Chilton; to the author; 9 November, 1982; July 23, 1983; October 3, 1984; October 18, 1984; November 8 and 9, 1984; November 14, 1984; December 16, 1985.
26   Memorandum; Major Hill originated this memo and it was routed through his superior at AFRAD, then it went in succession through AFMMD, AFREQ and AFOCR.
27   Freeman; "The Hub", pages 103 and 104.

Chapter Twelve

1   Craven and Cate; Volume II, page 681. The authors refer to "paper tanks" only half full made in America.
2   Memorandum; O.P. Echols, Maj. Gen., ACAS, MM&D; for the Chairman, J.A.C. Subcommittee on Preference Lists. "Change in Preference Rating of P-51 and P-47."
3   Letters; Col. Hubert Zemke, USAF (Retired); to the author; July 15, 1991; August 4, 1991.
4   Letter; Ira Eaker, Maj. Gen., Commanding General, Eighth Air Force; to Major General Barney M. Giles, Chief of the Air Staff, Washington, DC; August 7, 1943.
5   Letter; Col. Hubert Zemke, USAF (Retired); to the author.
6   Letter; W.E. Kepner, Major General, Commanding, Eighth Fighter Command; to Major General Barney M. Giles, Chief of Staff, Washington DC; 7 September, 1943.
7   Letter; Ira Eaker, Maj. Gen., Commanding, Eighth Air Force; to General Arnold; October 22, 1943. Freeman was in charge of the Ministry of Aircraft Production.
8   Craven and Cate; Volume II, page 705.
9   Craven and Cate; Volume III, page 9.
10   Memorandum; from the Commanding General, Army Air Forces; for the Combined Chiefs of Staff; 3 November, 1943. "Air Plan For The Defeat of Germany."
11   Craven and Cate; Volume III, page 8.
12   Craven and Cate; Volume III, page 8.

Chapter Thirteen

1   Stanaway; page 9.
2   Memorandum; General Arnold; to Staff; August 8, 1943.
3   Case History of Droppable Fuel Tanks; compiled by the Historical Office, Materiel Command, Wright Field; 22 February, 1945. On 9 February, 1939 Curtiss-Wright proposed to offer a drop tank for the P-36C but "The Chief of the Air Corps raised the question as to whether the fuel tank would be a serious fire hazard. On May 16, 1939, the Chief of the Air Corps directed that no tactical airplane should be equipped with a droppable fuel tank."
4   Memorandum; B.W. Chidlaw, Brig. Gen., Chief, Materiel Division, Office, Asst. Chief of Air Staff, MM&D; for the Chief of the Air Staff (Through General Perrin); October 19, 1943. "Fighter Airplane Range Extension. (Report No. 4.)"
5   Memorandum; L.T. Bradbury, Lt. Col., Acting Chief, Production Branch, ACAS, MM&D, Materiel Division; to ACAS, OC&R, Requirements Division; 17 September, 1943. "Test of P-51B With Extended Range Tank."
6   Memorandum; W.D. Eckert, Colonel, Comptroller; to Col. T.A. Sims, Deputy Chief of Staff; 26 November, 1943. "P-51 Airplanes, Long Range 85 Gallon Fuselage Tank Project."
7   See #6 above. The Modification Center Branch submitted its schedule and Eckert stated that "It is not believed - it will be met."
8   Craven and Cate; Volume II, page 654.
9   Letter; Ira C. Eaker, Major General, Commanding, Eighth Air Force; to Major General Oliver P. Echols, Commanding General, Materiel Command, Washington, DC; May 13, 1943.
10   Memorandum; Deputy Assistant Chief of Air Staff, MM&D; to Deputy Chief of Air Staff, General Hall; August 16,1943.
11   Craven and Cate; Volume II, page 655.

12 Memorandum; B.W. Chidlaw, Brig. Gen., Chief, Materiel Division, Office, Asst. Chief of Air Staff, MM&D; for the Chief of the Air Staff (Through General Perrin); October 19, 1943. "Fighter Airplane Range Extension (Report No. 4)."
13 See # 12 above. Chidlaw reported on the following types of drop tanks: 75-gallon metal; 75-gallon leakproof; 108-gallon paper; 115-gallon metal; 150-gallon paper; 150-gallon leakproof; 150-gallon metal flat-top; 150-gallon metal Lockheed.
14 Cross Reference; Hqs. AAF Airc. Distributing Office, Patterson Field, Fairfield, Ohio; to Com. Gen. AAF Mat. Comd., W.F., Attn: Airc. Mod. Br.; November 23, 1943. One day later, Branshaw sent a teletype message to the Western Procurement District in Los Angeles notifying NAA to put the plus sign on its P-51s.

Chapter Fourteen

1 Routing and Record Sheet; General Arnold; to General Kuter; July 6, 1943. Kuter replied immediately.
2 Letter; H.H. Arnold, General, Commanding, Army Air Forces; to Lieut. General Carl Spaatz; August 20, 1943
3 In June,1943, priority was raised.
4 Letter; H.H. Arnold, General, Commanding, Army Air Foces; to Air Chief Marshal Sir Charles F.A. Portal, G.C.B., D.S.O., M.C., Chief of Air Staff, Air Ministry; September 29, 1943.
5 Letter; C. Portal; to General Henry H. Arnold; October 24, 1943.
6 Arnold; "Global Mission"; pages 495 and 496.
7 Letter; H.H. Arnold, General, Commanding, Army Air Forces; to Air Chief Marshal Sir Charles Portal, Chief of Air Staff; October 31, 1943.

Chapter Fifteen

1 Brereton; pages 215 and 216.
2 McFarland and Newton; page 146.
3 Letter; Barney M. Giles, Major General, Chief of the Air Staff; to Brigadier General A.B. McDaniel, Commanding General, III Reconnaissance Command; November 30, 1943.
4 Memorandum; Barney M. Giles, Major General, Chief of the Air Staff; for The Assistant Secretary of War (Air); December 30, 1943. "Fighter Aircraft for the 8th and 9th Air Forces."
5 McFarland and Newton; page 146.

Chapter Sixteen

1 Diary; was on temporary loan from Col. Jack S. Jenkins, USAF (Retired); to the author. Returned uncopied.
2 Letter; W.E. Kepner, Major General, Commanding, Eighth Fighter Command; to Commanding General, IV Fighter Command. This letter belonged to Col. Jenkins, was used for quotation and was returned uncopied to Col. Jenkins without the date being noted.
3 Keen; page 53.
4 Caidin; page 161.
5 Report; loaned by Col. Jenkins; to the author. Returned uncopied.
6 Report; Lt. Col. J.S. Jenkins; to Commanding Office, 67th Fighter Wing. Report returned to Col. Jenkins uncopied after use.
7 Report; Lt. Col. Jack S. Jenkins; to Brig. Gen. Edward Anderson, Commanding, 67th Fighter Wing; January 6, 1944.
8 Craven and Cate; Volume II, page 705.
9 "Kings Cliffe"; pages 112 and 126.
10 Blake; pages 114 and 122.
11 Letter; J.H. Doolittle, Major General, Commanding, Eighth Air Force; to The Commanding General, United States Strategic Air Force, Attention: Deputy Commanding General in Charge of Administration; 1 March, 1944. "Special Fuels for P-38Js."
12 Memorandum; H.J. Knerr, Brig. Gen., Commanding General, ASC; to General H.H. Arnold. Commanding General, Army Air Forces; January 25, 1944.
13 LeVier's courage was exceptional. The author believes Mr. LeVier was the world's greatest pilot.
14 Letter; Tony LeVier, President, Safe Action in Flight Emergency, Inc.; to the author; September 6, 1992.

Chapter Seventeen

1 Turner.
2 The author was privileged to pay a visit to the home of Col. Blakeslee and his lovely wife Lee. After dinner at an Air Force Base, 35 years after the end of the war, Col. Don answered my question about making head-on intercepts. He left me with the unmistakeable impression — delivered with the same intensity he used with the 354th FG — of what he and his pilots did when attacked head-on.
3 Memorandum of Agreement Between General Arnold and Air Chief Marshal Courtney; (January 1, 1944); Aircraft Allocation - 1944. General Giles signed the agreement on behalf of General Arnold on January 17, 1944. The agreement also involved C-47 and B-24 production, and continued the British supply of Spitfires for the two USAAF Spitfire Groups until those groups were re-equipped with Mustangs.
4 Dunn; in particular, see pages 97 through 101. As late as in December, 1943 L-M stated that of the Americans, "none of them had any direct war experience."
5 Craven and Cate; Volume III: page 123.
6 McFarland and Newton; page 279, note 44. See also: Craven and Cate; Volume II, page 738; Volume III, pages 5 and 72.
7 McFarland and Newton; pages 170 and 171.
8 Deighton; pages 214 through 216.
9 Craven and Cate; Volume III, pages 109 and 110.
10 Craven and Cate; Volume III, page 112.
11 Craven and Cate; Volume III, pages 134 and 135.
12 Craven and Cate; Volume III, page 149.
13 Craven and Cate; Volume II, page 715.
14 Craven and Cate; Volume II, page 715.
15 Craven and Cate; Volume III, page 6.
16 Craven and Cate; Volume III, page 12.
17 Final Report On Test to Determine the Effect of an Additional 85 Gallons of Internal Fuel on Performance and Handling of the P-51B Airplane; Proof Department, Army Air Forces Proving Ground Command, Eglin Field, Florida; December 22, 1943.
18 Harker; pages 51 and 52.

Chapter Eighteen

1 55th Fighter Group; Report of the Tactical Commander; for the mission of January 5, 1944; January 10, 1944. This report was quoted and then returned to Col. Jenkins.
2 55th Fighter Group; Report of the Tactical Commander; for the mission of January 7, 1944; date not recorded. This report was quoted and then returned to Col. Jenkins.
3 55th Fighter Group; Mission Report; for the mission of February 3, 1944.
4 Craven and Cate; Volume III, page 31.
5 Craven and Cate; Volume III, pages XI and XII.
6 Craven and Cate; Volume III, page XII. See also, pages 63 through 66.
7 Arnold; "Global Mission"; page 219. On February 6, 1941 Robert Lovett sent a memo to General Arnold saying: "I can not see that the problem [with the Eagle Squadrons] is any direct concern of the Air Corps." However, Lovett added that "There will always be a certain number of wild men and grandstanders in any such group of so-called soldiers of fortune." Brig. Gen. Michael J. Scanlon, a member of the US Embassy in London, had criticized the Eagles in a report of January 30, 1941. Scanlon said: "It seems to be a fair presumption that certain elements of the squadron are of the publicity seeking, promoter type, which makes the effort incompatible with the interests and dignity of the United States." Scanlon hoped for the unit to rise in stature to a level comparable to that of the famed "Lafayette Escadrille."
8 Interview with, and letters from, Col. Jack S. Jenkins, USAF, (Retired); to the author.

Glossary

AAF	Army Air Forces	FAREP	Fighter Airplane Range Extension Program	RAF	Royal Air Force
AAFSAT	Army Air Forces School of Applied Tactics			R&R	Routing and Record Sheet
AC	Air Corps	FC	Fighter Command	TacR	Tactical Reconnaissance
ACTS	Air Corps Tactical School	FG	Fighter Group	USAAF	United States Army Air Force
AEAF	Allied Expeditionary Air Force	FY	Fiscal Year	USAFUK	United States Army Air Forces in the United Kingdom
AF	Air Force	ETO	European Theater of Operations		
AFACT	Directorate of Air Force Air Crew Training	GFE	Government Furnished Equipment	USSTAF	United States Strategic Air Forces in Europe
AFGRS	Directorate of Ground Support	GHQ AF	General Headquarters Air Force		
AFPGC	Air Force Proving Ground Command	JAC	Joint Aircraft Committee	WO&R	War, Organization and Movement Division
AMC	Air Materiel Command	MAP	Ministry of Aircraft Production		
"Argument"	Codename for bombing offensive against German fighter production centers	MTO	Mediterranean Theater of Operations	WPB	War Production Board
		NAA	North American Aviation		
BG	Bomber Group	NACA	National Advisory Committee for Aeronautics		
BPC	British Purchasing Commission				
BW	Bomb Wing	OPM	Office of Production Management		
CCS	Combined Chiefs of Staff	"Overlord"	Codename for Allied Invasion of Europe, June 6, 1944		
CMN	Critical Mach Number				
CO	Commanding Officer	"Pointblank"	Directive for strategic air campaign against Germany		
CTI	Confidential Technical Instruction				

Index